Gender, Poverty and Access to Justice

Access to justice is a fundamental right guaranteed under a wide body of international, regional and domestic law. It is also an essential component of development policies which seek to adequately respond to the multidimensional deprivations faced by the poor in order to improve socio-economic well-being and advance the progress of the Sustainable Development Goals. Women and children make up most of Africa's poorest and most marginalized population, and as such are often prevented from enforcing rights or seeking other recourse.

This book explores and analyzes the issue of gendered access to justice, poverty and disempowerment across Sub-Saharan Africa (SSA), and provides policy discussions on the integration of gender in justice programming. Through individual country case studies, the book focuses on the challenges, obstacles and successes of developing and implementing gender focused access to justice policies and programming in the region.

This multidisciplinary volume will be of interest to policy makers as well as scholars and researchers focusing on poverty and gender policy across law, economics and global development in Sub-Saharan Africa. Additionally, the volume provides policy discussion applicable in other geographical areas where access to justice is elusive for the poor and marginalized.

David Lawson is Senior Researcher at The Nordic Africa Institute, Uppsala, Visiting Professor at The University of Helsinki and Associate Professor of Development Economics and Public Policy at the University of Manchester. He has 25 years of developing country public policy experience, particularly in relation to policy implementation and research on extreme poverty and gender, in SSA. He has published in leading development journals and consulted and advised extensively for the UNECA and World Bank.

Adam Dubin is an Assistant Professor of Law in the International Public Law Department of Universidad Pontificia Comillas in Madrid, Spain, an Adjunct Professor of Politics at New York University's Madrid Campus and a Senior Research Associate at the Faculty of Law at the University of Johannesburg, South Africa. Dr Dubin's research and publications focus on the intersection between development and human rights in Sub-Saharan Africa, with a particular interest on access to justice, urbanization and disability rights. He has served as consultant for UNICEF in Angola on projects concerning the implementation of the Convention on the Rights of the Child.

Lea Mwambene is Professor of Law in the department of Private Law, and currently the Deputy Dean: Teaching and Learning of the Faculty of Law, University of the Western Cape, South Africa. Her teaching and research interests are in the general fields of African customary law and human rights. Driven by the genuine concern about the interaction between law, ideology and social practice, her recent research (with Ms Helen Kruuse from Rhodes University, South Africa) has included fieldwork in the Eastern Cape, South Africa, interviewing rural people about the impact of the reformed customary marriage laws in South Africa on the enjoyment of human rights by women and children.

Routledge Studies in Development Economics

148 Full and Productive Employment in Developing Economies
Towards the Sustainable Development Goals
Rizwanul Islam

149 Information and Communication Technologies for Development Evaluation
Edited by Oscar A. García and Prashanth Kotturi

150 Rent Seeking and Development
The Political Economy of Industrialization in Vietnam
Authored by Christine Ngoc Ngo

151 Capital Mobility and Distributional Conflict in Chile, South Korea, and Turkey
Kurtuluş Gemici

152 Cooperation Networks and Economic Development
Cuba's High-Tech Potential
Andrés Cárdenas O'Farrill

153 Undernutrition, Agriculture and Public Provisioning
The Impact on Women and Children in India
Edited by Swarna Sadasivam Vepa and Brinda Viswanathan

154 Gender, Poverty and Access to Justice
Policy Implementation in Sub-Saharan Africa
Edited by David Lawson, Adam Dubin and Lea Mwambene

For more information about this series, please visit www.routledge.com/series/SE0266

Gender, Poverty and Access to Justice

Policy Implementation in Sub-Saharan Africa

Edited by
David Lawson, Adam Dubin and Lea Mwambene

Routledge
Taylor & Francis Group
LONDON AND NEW YORK

First published 2021
by Routledge
2 Park Square, Milton Park, Abingdon, Oxon OX14 4RN

and by Routledge
52 Vanderbilt Avenue, New York, NY 10017

Routledge is an imprint of the Taylor & Francis Group, an informa business

British Library Cataloguing-in-Publication Data
A catalogue record for this book is available from the British Library

Library of Congress Cataloging-in-Publication Data
Names: Lawson, David, 1971– editor, author. | Dubin, Adam, editor, author. | Mwambene, Lea, editor, author.
Title: Gender, poverty and access to justice: policy implementation in Sub-Saharan Africa / edited by David Lawson, Adam Dubin and Lea Mwambene.
Other titles: Routledge studies in development economics.
Description: New York: Routledge, 2020. |
Series: Routledge studies in development economics |
Includes bibliographical references and index.
Identifiers: LCCN 2020004479 (print) | LCCN 2020004480 (ebook)
Subjects: LCSH: Equality before the law—Africa, Sub-Saharan. | Due process of law—Africa, Sub-Saharan. | Justice, Administration of—Africa, Sub-Saharan. | Poor—Africa, Sub-Saharan—Social conditions. | Children—Africa, Sub-Saharan—Social conditions. | Women—Africa, Sub-Saharan—Social conditions.
Classification: LCC KQC575 .G46 2020 (print) |
LCC KQC575 (ebook) | DDC 323.420967—dc23
LC record available at https://lccn.loc.gov/2020004479
LC ebook record available at https://lccn.loc.gov/2020004480

ISBN: 978-1-138-22275-5 (hbk)
ISBN: 978-1-315-40710-4 (ebk)

Typeset in Bembo
by codeMantra

Contents

Illustrations

Figures

Tables

Boxes

Contributors

Paloma Duran, Head of Division, Global Partnerships and Policies, OECD, France

Ifeoma Pamela Enemo, University of Nigeria

Cristina Fernández-Durán Gortázar, Oxfam Intermon, Spain

Aisha Fofana Ibrahim, University of Sierra Leone

Fatima Khan, Director, Refugee Rights Unit, University of Cape Town, South Africa

Kagiso A. Maphalle, University of Cape Town, South Africa

Blessing Mushohwe, University of Western Cape, South Africa

Robert Doya Nanima, University of the Western Cape, South Africa

Isidore Collins Ngueuleu, OMCT (World Organisation Against Torture), Geneva

Aparna Polavarapu, University of South Carolina

Asieh Yousefnejad Shomali, University of Manchester, UK

Julia Sloth-Nielsen, University of Western Cape, South Africa

Basil Ugochukwu, Centre for International Governance Innovation, Canada

Ncumisa Willie, Research Advisor to the Chairperson – South African Human Rights Commission

Bisrat Woldemichael, Intern, Nordic Africa Institute, Uppsala

Foreword

In the last 30 years, I have had the opportunity to travel throughout Africa and work alongside women's groups, policy makers, government officials and non-government organizations to advance the rights and development of women and girls. Unfortunately, I have witnessed far too many women whose right to development and peace, such as freedom from violence, clean water, sanitation as well as land tenure, was not realized. However, this was not because countries did not have resources or the ability to fulfill these rights but rather because they were not enforced.

As Special Envoy of the Chairperson of the African Union Commission on Women, Peace and Security and Founder and President of Femme Africa Solidarité, I have learnt that we cannot talk of development, Agenda 2063, Sustainable Development Goals (SDGs), empowerment or well-being without first putting in place the infrastructure for access to justice. Goal 16 of the SDGs recognizes the importance of access to justice. This is true of all human rights treaties – both international and regional, including the African Charter on Human and People's Rights. All too often, however, justice ends up being a mere abstraction found on paper and in government discourse but lacking in real implementation and effectiveness to protect the very poorest, powerless and voiceless. Unfortunately, women and girls – particularly those who come from conflict-affected countries and economically disadvantaged backgrounds – suffer the most from not being able to enforce their rights. Access to justice, gender and poverty intersect to form a vicious cycle of deprivation and rights violations. Women and girls often bear the burden.

At the heart of what we must do as public officials working for government and international organizations, such as the African Union, is to protect the basic dignity and integrity of all human beings. All Africans deserve the full realization of their rights and to develop their full potential to continue pushing forward Africa's impressive growth and development. Women and girls must take priority in the advancement of rights, especially on a continent where women lag behind in most development indicators. To move forward with a remedy, access to justice must become a central and transversal element to all our policies, programs and laws aimed at ensuring individual and collective dignity.

Gender, Poverty and Access to Justice: Policy Implementation in SSA provides a comprehensive analysis and understanding of the importance of justice and its role in underpinning gender and poverty issues. It reminds me of the importance of strengthening institutions and justice frameworks if we are to develop Africa and not leave our fellow Africans behind. But beyond this initial analysis, and perhaps more importantly, the book offers 12 case studies written by scholars and practitioners about what works and does not work in bringing access to justice to poor women and girls. All too often we talk about these issues in abstraction, failing to bridge the gap between academia and policy makers. This book offers real solutions for governments and non-governmental organization (NGO) workers to begin developing access to justice programs that work for all.

I take away from this book an important message: Access to justice is attainable. In Africa, we have many excellent examples of how women have achieved justice when states, often in conjunction with NGOs, put in place appropriate infrastructure. Unfortunately, there are many examples where access to justice has remained elusive and not much more than a sentence in a treaty. We as policy makers, government officials and NGO workers in Sub-Saharan Africa must heed the call of this book. If we are truly committed to having a sustainable plan of action on women, peace and security, ending marginalization and ensuring gender equality, we must place a greater priority on justice mechanisms that permit the enforcement and fulfillment of rights for the very poorest and most vulnerable. This is the message I take away from this book; this is the message that should guide the work of all those who endeavor to advance and protect the rights of women for a true transformation of Africa.

Bineta Diop is AU Special Envoy on Women, Peace and Security; Founder and President of Femmes Africa Solidarité (FAS) – an international NGO; formerly co-chair of the World Economic Forum on Africa in 2014; named one of the 100 most influential people in the world by *Time Magazine* in 2011.

Preface

In recent years, the United Nations, World Bank, NGOs, donors and governments around the globe have taken an increased interest in developing new policies and programmes to broaden access to justice as a poverty reduction tool, and to protect the most vulnerable in society. There has been a recognition that justice can play a central role in combatting chronic and extreme poverty and helping countries attain the Sustainable Development Goals (SDGs). In this regard, the international community has invested billions of dollars in Africa with renewed focus and, until very recently, a sense of progress on the continent, and in particular within Sub-Saharan Africa.

However, no publication has specifically focused on engendered poverty and access to justice in Sub-Saharan Africa – a region with nearly one billion people, approximately half of whom live in extreme poverty. Furthermore, as applied policy advisors and researchers, we felt a need to bridge the disciplinary divide and bring together leading experts from law and development, policy and academia. Several of the contributors to this volume have spent their entire careers investigating issues of gender, poverty and access to justice, aiming to understand and raise awareness of the associated challenges and potential policy solutions in Africa, in order to reduce engendered poverty and advance the socio-economic well-being of women and children. This book argues for a development approach that is justice centred, and which can be integrated into national and local planning to enhance access to justice towards advancing the SDGs and protecting human rights for women and children.

This publication was finalized at a time when countries around the world, including in Sub-Saharan Africa, are grappling with containing the COVID-19 pandemic that will undoubtedly have devastating effects on the world's chronic and extreme poor. The pandemic presents a new set of challenges that require, perhaps more than ever, that justice and protection for human rights be the cornerstone of development planning and engendered frameworks.

Women and children in Sub-Saharan Africa will likely be disproportionately affected by the consequences of this pandemic. From limited inheritance rights to quarantining with violent partners, this pandemic presents challenges to gender equality on a global scale arguably never witnessed before in history. Access to justice, therefore, is more important than ever in safeguarding the fundamental rights of women and children, and ensuring that the guarantees of justice are within their reach. Geographic isolation, poor infrastructure, complex socio-cultural problems, conflict and underdeveloped institutions make achieving access to justice difficult, if not elusive for much of Sub-Saharan Africa's poorest. Although the book does not specifically address the justice challenges brought on by this pandemic, we hope that the policies presented provide a roadmap that can be adapted to the uncertain times ahead.

The message of this book is that the Right to Access to Justice must be attainable and accessible for everyone, regardless of socio-economic status or gender. Justice has increasingly been recognized not as a parallel component of development programmes, but as a central element and necessary if we are to release what Nobel Laureate, Amartya Sen, calls the "unfreedoms" that perpetuate extreme deprivation and vulnerability. We hope that this book, the first to be published on justice, gender and poverty in Sub Saharan Africa, provides policy solutions showing that access to justice can be transformative in improving the well-being of women and children if countries dedicate the resources to protect, respect and fulfil the Right to Access to Justice.

David Lawson
University of Manchester/Nordic Africa Institute

Adam Dubin
Universidad Pontificia Comillas

Lea Mwambene
University of the Western Cape

Acknowledgments

Many people have helped us to achieve the publication of this book. First, special thanks to the chapter authors who worked under tight deadlines and were willing to share their wealth of experience and direct knowledge about the access to justice challenges plaguing the poorest and most vulnerable. Your tremendous efforts in highlighting these challenges and suggesting solutions that will help with informing future policy making are appreciated.

Especial thanks are due to Ken Barlow, who helped finalize the editing of the volume and provided fresh impetus for the final push toward publication. His diligence and recommendations were invaluable. Thanks also to Chigozirim Bodart and Ngone Diop, who made it possible for us to present key material at the 52nd Session of the Economic Commission for Africa, Conference of African Ministers of Finance, Planning and Economic Development, 2019, Morocco, with sponsored financial support from the Economic Social Research Council/Impact Acceleration Account Grant.

We would also like to thank the Nordic Africa Institute (NAI), Uppsala, for financial and technical support, and in particular Henrik Alfredsson for his exhaustive efforts in helping to produce a NAI Policy Note to accompany this book.

Finally, we would like to express our profound gratitude to our respective families for the overwhelming support received throughout the course of this study, and our careers, and their endless tolerance of our travel, research and absence from home.

David Lawson
Adam Dubin
Lea Mwambene

Part I

Access to justice in Sub-Saharan Africa

Justice policies on reaching the most vulnerable and extreme poor

1 Engendering access to justice for the poorest and most vulnerable in Sub-Saharan Africa

David Lawson, Adam Dubin, Lea Mwambene and Bisrat Woldemichael

Introduction

Nobel Prize-winning economist Amartya Sen argues that for social and economic development to be effective, the poor must be released from their unfreedoms (Sen, 2001). While the reasons behind such unfreedoms vary from country to country, the relinquishing of them depends, at least in part, on the ability of people to exercise their Right to Access to Justice.

Access to justice has become part of the Sustainable Development Goals (SDG 16), in recognition of its importance in social and economic development, as well as the obligation of states to create a gendered justice element in policies, programmes and justice institutions. Noting the transversal importance of justice, the United Nations (UN), in writing about SDG 16, stated that "the first step to fulfilling any aspect of the global sustainable development agenda for 2030 will begin with restoring security and human rights".[1] Echoing this, James E. Goldston, executive director of the Open Society Initiative, in lobbying for the integration of justice into the post-2015 development agenda, claimed, "In short, we know that justice and governance are no less important to equitable and sustainable development than good schools, functioning health clinics and passable roads."[2]

The Right to Access to Justice is commonly referred to as being different from other rights. What distinguishes it is its transversal and interdependent character in relation to other rights, especially socio-economic rights linked to the reduction and alleviation of poverty, gender inequality and other deprivations. Where, for example, the duty-bearing (local) government has failed to meet its obligations, an individual whose main water source is a dirty standpipe requires access to justice in order to enforce their Right to Access Clean Water. In essence, no right contained under international law can be fully separated from the Right to Access to Justice. If fully implemented, this can mean the difference between clean or dirty water, land or no land, liberty or imprisonment.

It is undeniable that access to justice is an enabling right that has the potential to give voice to those who are sometimes voiceless and provides the opportunity of holding accountable the duty-bearing state in protecting, fulfilling and respecting rights that guarantee basic human dignity. It is a right directly linked to broader goals of gender empowerment and poverty reduction and is at the centre of the global community's commitment to fully achieving the SDGs – reducing deprivation and poverty, and working towards gender parity.

The latter point is, perhaps, of even greater relevance within the Sub-Saharan Africa (SSA) context than other regions. Over the last decade, despite strong economic growth and social advances in several SSA countries, the region continues to be home to the majority of the world's extreme poor. Figures from 2015 suggest that about half of the SSA population live below the poverty line, with the majority being women. The number of extreme poor in Africa has risen from 278 million (1990) to 413 million (2015), with the World Bank (2019) estimating that by 2030 nine out of ten of the extreme poor will live in SSA. Interconnected and dynamic deprivations, combined with complex and often prejudicial gender mores, mean that extreme and chronic poverty are major challenges to the full realisation of access to justice, which is often costly, discriminatory, geographically distant and complex to achieve.

This collection brings together leading academics and practitioners, all with extensive experience in the aforementioned areas, to explore access to justice in an SSA context through analysing the intersecting dimensionalities of justice, gender and poverty. The book is a complementary extension to a series of outputs and events that aim to share experiences of measuring and outlining economic and social deficiencies, as well as the programme and policies of "What Works for the Poorest" (see Lawson et al., 2010, 2017, 2020). In doing so, it extends the "What Works" series by considering the discrimination, prejudicial gender roles and customs that impact an individual's rights to access justice. We hope that such a focus will further raise awareness of access to justice's importance within development.[3]

This volume also builds on the Nordic Africa Institute (NAI) Policy Note entitled "Ensuring Women's Access to Justice: Engendering Rights for Poverty Reduction in SSA" (Lawson et al., 2019), which explores the role of effective budgeting with regard to access to justice at the intersection of justice, gender and poverty. In the 13 chapters of this book, we focus on various forms of justice deprivation, exploring the types of policies, programmes and law reforms that can be used to advance greater access to justice. Furthermore, the range of case studies highlight how different countries have responded in different ways, in some cases creatively addressing the challenge of providing justice to women and girls.

Access to justice defined

"Access to justice" is a broad term, frequently used without clear definition, though commonly regarded as a medium through which human rights can be protected, promoted or enforced. It is often understood as ranging from access to formal justice mechanisms (such as courts) to broader secondary categories of justice (such as ombudsman) when demanding access to health care, education and social services. It can also refer to informal justice mechanisms, such as customary courts and laws, which are common to many parts of SSA and are discussed later in this book. The informal justice system is often the most common route of justice-seeking, as it is affordable and – given that the majority of SSA's population continue to live in rural geographies – more accessible to the poor, marginalised and geographically distant. Ibrahim, for example, (Chapter 7 of this volume) highlights that the vast majority of Sierra Leoneans (over 80%) will seek redress through informal systems. Elsewhere, in Burundi, it is estimated that up to 80% of people take their cases to the *Bashingantahe* institution in the first or sometimes only instance, while in Malawi between 80% and 90% of disputes are processed through customary justice forums (United Nations Development Programme [UNDP], 2006:21).[4]

While access to justice is a broad and amorphous concept, with no single definition fully capturing all conceptualisations of the term, the World Bank's (2007) definition presents a comprehensive starting point for understanding its baseline objectives and significance. This definition presents access to justice as meaning people – particularly the poorest and most disadvantaged – being able to access fair, effective and accountable mechanisms for the protection of rights, control of abuse of power and the resolution of conflicts. The UN defines access to justice in similar terms, highlighting the role of both informal and formal institutions. According to UNDP (2005:5), access to justice is "the ability of people to seek and obtain a remedy through formal and informal instructions of justice".

While there is no accurate estimate of how many people lack justice of some form, it is reasonable to assume that most poor people – either knowingly or unknowingly, and especially in developing countries – are or will be deprived of access to justice in some form or another. Furthermore, though access to justice and legal empowerment deprivations affect the poor generally, they are particularly impactful on women. A UNDP (2008:78) report on legal empowerment and property noted that, "Much of the misery in the developing world is due to statutory and customary property systems which disenfranchise women. From national to village levels, justice for women needs reform." In SSA, women in particular confront a host of obstacles and challenges that men are less likely to face. These include sexual violence, biased and antiquated inheritance and land laws, cultural mores, as well as other discriminatory practices that perpetuate cycles of poverty and marginalisation.

Access to justice under international and African regional law

At the international level, this Right of Access to Justice was first codified in the Universal Declaration of Human Rights (though instruments facilitating access to justice have been around much longer) and is recognised as a *jus cogens* and as forming part of customary law. Furthermore, the right is incorporated into nearly all international and regional human rights treaties, including the Convention on the Rights of the Child and the Convention on the Elimination of Discrimination Against Women, as well as national laws, constitutions and other legislative documents. Obligations and pathways for states to ensure justice for women is outlined in the CEDAW General Recommendations No. 33, published by the Committee on the Elimination of Discrimination Against Women.

Despite the many challenges, highlighted across the chapters in this book, that make accessing justice difficult – if not impossible – in some cases, there is a comprehensive and pro-poor rights framework aimed at guaranteeing justice within national territories. In relation to civil and criminal proceedings, the African Charter on Human and People's Rights (Charter) provides for the right "to an appeal to competent national organs against acts of violating his fundamental rights as recognised and guaranteed by conventions, laws, regulations and customs in force". Both the African Protocol on the Rights of Women (Maputo Protocol) and the Charter on the Rights and Welfare of the Child provide extensive protections concerning justice and its corresponding mechanisms. In 1992, the African Commission on Human and People's Rights passed a Resolution on the "Right to Recourse and Fair Trial", which both affirms the access to justice provisions of the Charter, as well as going on to state that people have the "right to have their cause heard and shall be equal before the courts and tribunals".[5] The Resolution recommends to state parties that they "provide the needy with legal aid".

In 1999, in furtherance of the Right to Access Justice and in recognition of the difficulties faced in Africa, the African Commission adopted the Dakar Declaration and Resolutions for a Fair Trial.[6] The Declaration affirms that the right to a fair trial is fundamental, the non-observance of which "undermines all other human rights"[7] and points out that "it is the duty of governments to provide legal assistance to indigent persons in order to make the right to a fair trial more effective". Although the Declaration does not go as far as explicitly saying that legal aid is a right, it makes clear that the fundamental right to a fair trial can only be achieved if governments meet their duties of access to justice in the form of legal aid.

Another normative framework is the African Commission's Principles and Guidelines on the Right to a Fair Trial and Legal Assistance in Africa.[8] The Principles provide a number of policy initiatives towards implementing and expanding access to justice, which can be grouped into three categories: fairness and independence; procedural safeguards; and access to legal aid.

One of the most relevant justice advances Africa took place in 2004 with the passage of the Lilongwe Declaration on Accessing Legal Aid in the Criminal Justice System in Africa, signed in Lilongwe, Malawi. This Declaration has been particularly important for the continent, and could serve as a model for access to justice frameworks elsewhere due to its recognition of the need to develop more multidimensional service delivery procedures. In particular, Article 5 on Diversifying Legal Aid Delivery Systems urges states to employ a "variety of service delivery options" including law centres, judicare programmes, and partnerships with civil society and faith-based organisations.[9]

Despite a small but growing body of African regional and domestic jurisprudence reinforcing the fundamental nature of access to justice, accessibility to both African and domestic institutions has faced myriad challenges, especially concerning NGO access. In a limited number of cases, questions of access to justice have been taken to the African Commission, which has been receptive to rights violations involved in justice denials. However, most cases have centred around civil and political rights, rather than the justice processes necessary to ensuring the fulfilment of socio-economic rights. In *Avocats San Frontieres (on behalf of Gaëtan Bwampamye)/Burundi*, for example, a case in which a defendant was held without access to a lawyer, the Commission held that it "emphatically recalls that the right to legal assistance is a fundamental element of the right to fair trial".[10] Other cases involving denials of justice and access to counsel have also been found to be incompatible with basic notions of justice.[11] In the case of *Government of the Republic of Namibia and Others v. Mwilima and Others*,[12] the court focused on whether the accused in a criminal tribunal has the right to legal aid, answering broadly that "those applicants who cannot afford legal representation will not have a fair trial as guarantees by the provisions of Article 12 … through a statutory legal aid scheme".[13] In *Ndyanabo v. Attorney General* (Tanzania), the court made clear that a financial inability to pay court fees is incompatible with the fundamental right of access to justice, stating that "the doors of justice must always be left open to the poorest man or woman in the country".[14]

Access to justice, poverty and gender in SSA

In 2012, the United Nations Special Rapporteur for Extreme Poverty and Human Rights stated that access to justice is "crucial for tackling the root causes of poverty, exclusion and vulnerability".[15] His comments highlight the intersecting nature of poverty and justice deprivation, identifying the latter as a key driver of socio-economic deprivation and exclusion. Gendered poverty is inextricably linked to social and economic marginalisation, and requires equitable laws and meaningful justice in order to defend against prejudices, biases and other elements that deepen its root causes.

Lack of access to justice impacts significantly on empowering and protecting the rights of women and children regarding United Nations SDG16, specifically the achievement of targets 3, 7 and 10, which promote the rule of law at national and international levels; ensure equal access to justice for all; ensure responsive, inclusive, participatory and representative decision-making at all levels; ensure public access to information; and protect fundamental freedoms, all in accordance with national legislation and international agreements (UN, 2015). Consequently, it also affects SDG5, "Achieve gender equality and empower all women and girls", particularly in realising the targets 1, 2, 3 and 5, which are aimed at ensuring gender equality and empowering women and girls to eradicate poverty both at the national and global level. Access to justice will be particularly critical in attainment of such goals, considering how the economic and social responses to the COVID-19 pandemic are compounding gender inequalities.

Although indexes exist on topics such as corruption, empowerment and democracy, all of which intersect with access to justice, there is minimal desegregated data either on access to justice generally or for women specifically. However, to address this, the World Justice Project has compiled data that considers a host of factors relevant to access to justice in order to build a composite country-by-country index. These factors range from due process to criminal justice, and help to provide a snapshot of the access to justice deprivation currently faced by women in SSA.

According to the index, SSA has amongst the lowest access to justice in all subsections of the indicators listed (see Tables 1.1 and 1.2). This composite index considers gender equality and non-discrimination as a sub-element of the principle indicator on the protection of fundamental rights. The vast majority of SSA countries are ranked in the bottom tercile within the broader indicator of fundamental rights protection. These indicators tell a complex story of how various forms of discrimination compound to limit justice.

Table 1.1 provides cross-country statistics for rule of law, civic liberties, gender inequality and poverty. The closer the rule of law indicator is to the value of one, the stronger the rule of law. The average SSA rule of law indicator is 0.48, lower than the global average of 0.59. Whereas Namibia (0.62) and Rwanda (0.61) have relatively strong rule-of-law indicators (placing them, respectively, 34th and 40th out of 126 countries globally), Uganda, Ethiopia, Mauritania and the Democratic Republic of Congo and all score 0.4 or less (placing them, respectively, 111th, 118th, 122nd and 124th). SSA countries with a relatively low rule-of-law index score appear to have particularly poor criminal justice and fundamental rights (including rights of privacy). For example, Uganda has an average fundamental rights score of 0.38 compared with Rwanda's 0.49.

According to the UN Gender Development Index, men in SSA have a GNI per capita roughly 25% higher than that of women, and on average have more years of schooling (UNSD, 2015). Furthermore, SSA is ranked on the UN's Gender Equality Index and the OECD's Social Institution and Gender Index (SIGI) as having very high levels of discrimination, with only four countries (Rwanda, Namibia, Ethiopia and Mozambique) designated as having "low" levels of discrimination, out of 76 globally. In practice, this translates into low levels of empowerment, and limited economic and social opportunities. As can be seen in Table 1.1, the average SSA SIGI score is just under 40% (the higher the percentage indicating the higher the level of discrimination). Eleven SSA countries have a score of more than 46%, with Cameroon and Guinea having the highest at 51.8% and 56.7%, respectively. In the case of Guinea, discrimination within the family dominates on a number of levels,

Table 1.1 Rule of law, extreme poverty and gender gap in SSA

Country	*WJP rule of law index*	*WJP Rule of law global rank*	*SIGI value %*	*Civic liberties*	*Extreme poverty rate by economy, 2015, %*	*Gender gap in global level*
Angola	0.41	111	N/A	N/A	27.9	125
Benin	0.50	79	39.8	53.3	49.6	118
Botswana	0.59	44	N/A	52.4	12.8	55
Burkina Faso	0.50	73	32.4	13.8	42.8	129
Cameroon	0.37	120	51.8	45.4	22.8	57
Côte d'Ivoire	0.46	93	42.8	20.4	28.2	131
Democratic Republic of Congo	0.33	124	39.5	20.7	72.3	144
Ethiopia	0.39	118	29.6	17.9	27	117
Ghana	0.58	48	34.5	22.7	10.9	89
Guinea	0.44	105	56.7	44.4	33	116
Kenya	0.45	101	35.5	17.2	37.3	76
Liberia	0.46	97	47.5	52.8	40.2	96
Madagascar	0.43	107	47.5	59.4	77.5	84
Malawi	0.51	67	41.4	61.9	69.6	112
Mali	0.45	103	46.0	28.9	47.8	143
Mauritania	0.35	122	N/A	52.2	6.2	N/A
Mauritius	0.61	37	N/A	40.7	0.4	109
Mozambique	0.43	108	24.3	32.9	62.2	49
Namibia	0.62	34	27.1	35.1	13.4	10
Nigeria	0.43	106	46.0	53.9	47.8	133
Rwanda	0.61	40	27.6	23.5	51.5	6
Senegal	0.55	52	37.0	3.6	35.7	84
Sierra Leone	0.45	98	47.6	40.9	48.4	114
South Africa	0.58	47	22.4	21	18.9	19
Tanzania	0.47	91	46.1	35.2	40.7	71
Togo	0.45	100	49.5	62.0	49.2	134
Uganda	0.40	113	45.1	26.6	39.2	43
Zambia	0.47	92	34.8	41.8	57.5	N/A
Zimbabwe	0.40	116	32.4	30.9	16.0	47
SSA Average	0.48	N/A	39.6	32.8	41	N/A
Europe Average	0.70	N/A	17.6	18.4	1.5	N/A
Latin America Average	0.50	N/A	27.5	32.7	4.1	N/A
World Average	0.59	N/A	36.1	39.7	10	N/A

Source: Data sources from: World Justice project (2019) Global rule of Law Index, 1025 Vermont Avenue, NW, Suite 1200, Washington, DC 20005 USA, available at https://worldjusticeproject.org/our-work/research-and-data/wjp-rule-law-index-2019.
OECD (2019) Social Institutions and Gender Index [Online], accessed 1 March 2019, available at https://www.genderindex.org/ranking/?region.
World Bank Group (2018) Poverty and Shared Prosperity, International Bank for Reconstruction and Development/The World Bank 1818 H Street NW, Washington DC 20433, [Online], accessed 1 March 2019, available at https://openknowledge.worldbank.org/bitstream/handle/10986/30418/9781464813306.pdf.
World Economic Forum (2018) The Global Gender Gap Report, Accessed 1 March 2019, available at https://www.weforum.org/reports/the-global-gender-gap-report-2018.
Extreme poverty estimates are from the above documents, and based on $1.90p day ppp, where data permits.

Table 1.2 Access to justice, violence and hardship (%)

	Incidence of legal problems/access to justice index (incidence of legal problems/experienced legal problems) (%)		*Violence (physical violence) (%)*	*Hardship (experienced as a result of their legal problems) (%)*		*Access to justice score (have fully resolved or are done with problems) (%)*
	Female	*Male*		*Female*	*Male*	
Burkina Faso	66	73	6	24	23	48
Côte d'Ivoire	39	45	9	38	42	62
Ethiopia	75	74	26	65	67	39
Madagascar	34	37	24	58	63	67
Malawi	74	72	10	50	57	46
Senegal	70	71	4	28	28	44
SSA Average	59.7	62	13.2	43.8	46.7	51
Latin and Central America Average	39.3	38	7.3	41.2	35	70.7
SSA Countries Average	58.7	57.9	4.1	40.5	40.3	64.5
World Average	52.7	52.2	6.9	39	38.9	63.9

Source: World Justice Project (2018) Global Insights on Access to Justice, [Online], accessed 1 March 2019, available at https://worldjusticeproject.org/sites/default/files/documents/WJP_Access-Justice_April_2018_Online.pdf.

Note: SSA data are taken from six countries. Latin & Central America data taken from six countries.
Europe data are taken from 17 countries. The world data are taken from 45 countries.

as the law does not provide women with the same rights as men to be recognised as the head of a household, nor does it provide women with the same rights as men to initiate divorce.

Table 1.2 shows access to justice, violence and hardship statistics for the few SSA countries where data is available. The high percentages that can be seen regarding incidences of legal problems and physical violence appear to indicate that access-to-justice processes are relatively weak. For example, the incidence of legal problems for women is 58.7% and for men 57.9%, compared with the world average of, respectively, 52.7% and 52.2%. Individuals living in SSA also appear to have "experienced hardship" as a result of their legal problems at higher levels – the incidence being 43.8% for women and 46.7% for men, compared with global averages of, respectively, 39% and 38.9%. Regarding the access to justice score – whereby the percentage score indicates the proportion of people who have fully resolved or are done with their legal problems – across SSA countries the score is 51%, compared with the global average of 63.9%.

Overview of the book

The book is structured into three parts, with 13 chapters. This first part addresses the question of how justice policies reach the most vulnerable and the extreme poor, with a particular focus on children. We open with these issues as evidence suggests that children are particularly vulnerable and commonly face access-to-justice issues connected not only with the judiciary process but also gender equality, political participation and economic alleviation. Specifically, the following questions are posed: "What are the specific policies we can adapt quickly to protect children?" and "How might these policies be implemented?" This first part builds on and complements several chapters from the *What Works For Africa's Poorest Children: From Measurement to Practice* (2020) volume – an output partly aimed at marking the 30th Anniversary (in 2019) of the UN Convention on the Rights of the Child (see, Lawson et al. 2019) that highlights child policy actions for the most vulnerable.[16]

In Chapter 2, Sloth-Nielsen and Mushohwe provide an overview of the formal justice system in Zimbabwe, highlighting the entry points for children. The 2013 Constitution has, for example, brought new opportunities for children to access justice. In this regard, the judiciary has been encouraging in some of its recent rulings on children's rights, particularly regarding child marriages and corporal punishment. In Chapter 3, Shomali and Lawson, consider forced and early marriage in Uganda. More than half of Ugandan women marry below the legal age of marriage, with drivers of child marriage including socio-cultural gender discriminatory norms and religious beliefs; poverty; poor institutional structures and service provision; and a lack of enforcement of laws supporting children's and women's rights. Planning and implementing policies that tackle the discriminatory socio-cultural norms upholding child marriage is key to solving these issues, with civil society organisations playing a major role. In Chapter 4, Maphalle explores how the intricate relationships of woman-to-woman customary marriages in South Africa impact on the rights of children born of such marriages, and suggests that explicit recognition of such marriages as being valid under the Recognition of Customary Marriages Act (RCMA) is required. The chapter also recommends that the duty of supporting children born of woman-to-woman marriages be dealt with as a matter of urgency through reforms to laws relating to the maintenance of children.

The second part of the book focuses on the violence and vulnerability faced by women. In Chapter 5, Duran outlines the background to African Union policies that support access to justice and gender equality through women's empowerment models and social protection schemes, with a particular focus on post-conflict countries (Côte d'Ivoire, Ethiopia, Mozambique and Tanzania). In Chapter 6, Mwambene and Nanima contextualise poverty in Malawi, critically analysing the legal strategies currently being used to promote equal access to justice processes for rural women governed by customary marriage laws. In doing so, they find that enforcement of the constitutional right to equality requires that rural women in customary marriages have meaningful access to justice and gender equality processes. This suggests the emphasis should shift towards taking stock of the impact of legal strategies on women affected by patriarchal customary practices. In Chapter 7, Ibrahim, in focusing on traditional courts in Sierra Leone and how the poor access formal legal systems, highlights the ways in which judgement is gendered, being commonly based in customary practices and laws that discriminate against women. In Chapter 8, Ugochukwa extends such findings to Nigeria, while in Chapter 9 Polavarapu similarly highlights how lack of land rights impede access to justice across SSR.

The third and final part of the book consists of three chapters that explore advocacy and vulnerability, focusing specifically on sexual and domestic violence and refugees. In Chapter 10, Ngueuleu and Fernández-Durán explore issues of justice for victims of conflict-related sexual violence (CRSV) in Central African Republic. Echoing the findings of Chapters 3, 6 and 7, socio-economic factors are highlighted as being of major importance. To address these, multi-dimensional efforts – including legal, military, judicial, political, psychosocial, economic, education and gender measures – are required. In particular, it is essential that non-judicial mechanisms such as a Truth and Reconciliation Commission be mandated to facilitate disclosure of CRSV cases. In Chapter 11, Enemo considers domestic violence in Nigeria, particularly at the rural level, where for poorer women it is undoubtedly a significant problem. Amongst other recommendations, the chapter suggests community media awareness, as well as police and judge training. In Chapter 12, Khan and Willie consider the empowerment of refugees in South Africa, before the final chapter concludes by highlighting the need to cut across government and civil society agencies in order to ensure coordinated and multifaceted approaches to access to justice provision for Africa's extreme poor.

Notes

1 SDG16, un.org.
2 Speech to United Nations General Assembly, June 2014.
3 See, for example, 2019 International Conference "Engendering Access to Justice for Development in Sub-Saharan Africa" (NAI/University of Western Cape) accessed at https://nai.uu.se/news-and-events/events/2019-10-28-engendering-access-to-justice-for-development-in-sub-saharan-africa.html, 28–29 October 2019.
4 We recognise, in line with Dexter and Ntahombaye (2005:5), that the term "informal" is commonly used in contrast to "formal"; however, the *bashingantahe* institution is not informal as such, but rather a veritable institution, and may by strict definition be determined as "traditional".
5 African Commission for Human and People's Rights, Res.4(XI)92: Resolution on the Right to Recourse and Fair Trial (1992), University of Minnesota, Human Rights Library.
6 Recent Developments: The Right to a Fair Trial: The Dakar Declaration, Pages 140–142, African Law Journal, Volume 45 (2001).
7 African Commission on Human and People's Rights, Resolution 41 on the Right to Fair Trial and Legal Aid in Africa (1999).
8 African Commission on Human and People's Rights, Principles and Guidelines on the Right to a Fair Trial and Legal Assistance in Africa (2001).

9 The Lilongwe Declaration on Accessing Legal Aid in the Criminal Justice System in Africa, adopted 2004.

10 *Avocats San Frontieres (on behalf of Gaëtan Bwampamye)*, 231/99, Paragraph 30, African Commission on Human and People's Rights (1999).

11 See, for example, *Media Rights Agenda v. Nigeria, 224/98*, Paragraph 55, African Commission on Human and People's Rights (2000), in which the Commission said that a right to a fair trial includes the ability to communicate in confidence with counsel of choice, and that each individual shall have the right to defence. In *Civil Liberties Organisation v. Nigeria,* 129/94 African Commission on Human and Peoples' Rights (1995), the Commission finds that even where a state nullifies the Charter's incorporation in domestic law, the rights contained in the Charter, including the right to be heard, remain in effect and the state is still obliged to meet its obligations.

12 *Government of the Republic of Namibia and Others v. Mwilima and Others*, Paragraph 127, African Commission on Human and People's Rights (2002).

13 Ibid., Paragraph 94.

14 *Ndyanabo v. Attorney General* [243], Paragraph 44, African Commission on Human and People's Rights (2002).

15 United Nations General Assembly, "Report of the Special Rapporteur: Note on Extreme Poverty and Human Rights", A/67/278 (2012).

16 International Conference (2019), Nordic Africa Institute/University of Western Cape "Engendering Access to Justice for Development in Sub-Saharan Africa" https://nai.uu.se/news-and-events/events/2019-10-28-engendering-access-to-justice-for-development-in-sub-saharan-africa.html

References

Dexter, T. and P. Ntahombaye (2005), *The Role of Informal Justice Systems in Fostering the Rule of Law in Post-Conflict Situations: The Case of Burundi*, Centre for Humanitarian Dialogue. Geneva, Switzerland.

Lawson, D., L. Ado-Kofie and D. Hulme (2017), *What Works for Africa's Poorest: Programmes and Policies for the Extreme Poor*, Practical Action. Rugby, UK.

Lawson, D., D. Angemi and I. Kasirye (2020), *What Works for Africa's Poorest Children: From Measurement to Action*, Practical Action. Rugby, UK.

Lawson, D., A. Dubin and L. Mwambene with B. Woldemichael (2019), "Ensuring African Women's Access to Justice Engendering Rights for Poverty Reduction in Sub-Saharan Africa", Nordic Africa Institute, Policy Note 2, accessed March 20, 2019, available at http://nai.diva-portal.org/smash/get/diva2:1298068/FULLTEXT01.pdf.

Lawson, D., D. Hulme. I. Matin and K. Moore (2010), *What Works for the Poorest: Poverty Reduction Programmes for the World's Extreme Poor*, Practical Action. Rugby, UK.

OECD (2019), Social Institutions and Gender Index [Online], accessed March 1, 2019, available at https://www.genderindex.org/ranking/?region.

Sen, A. (2001), *Development as a Freedom*, Oxford University Press. Oxford, UK.

UN (2015), "Sustainable Development Goals: Peace, Justice and Strong Institutions", accessed March 20, 2019, available at https://www.un.org/sustainabledevelopment/peace-justice/.

UNDP (2005), "Programming for Justice: Access for All. A Practitioner's Guide to a Human Rights Based Approach to Access to Justice", available at https://www.unssc.org/sites/unssc.org/files/UNWomenFactSheet.pdf.

UNDP (2006), "Doing Justice: How Informal Justice Systems Can Contribute", Oslo Governance Centre, The Democratic Governance Fellowship Programme, Ewa Wojkowska.

UNDP (2008), "Making the Law Work for Everyone", Volume II Working Group Reports.

UNSD (2015), "The World's Women 2015: Statistics and Trends", accessed June 1, 2019, available at https://unstats.un.org/unsd/gender/downloads/Ch8_Poverty_info.pdf.

World Bank (2007), "Justice for the Poor: A Framework for Strengthening Access to Justice in Indonesia". January 1, World Bank Briefing Note, World Bank.

World Bank (2018), "Poverty and Shared Prosperity: Piecing Together the Poverty Puzzle", accessed March 1, 2019, available at https://openknowledge.worldbank.org/bitstream/handle/10986/30418/9781464813306.pdf.

World Bank (2019), "Accelerating Poverty Reduction in Africa", accessed June 1, 2019, available at https://openknowledge.worldbank.org/handle/10986/32354.

World Economic Forum (2018), "The Global Gender Gap Report", accessed March 1, 2019, available at https://www.weforum.org/reports/the-global-gender-gap-report-2018.

World Justice Project (2018), "Global Insights on Access to Justice", accessed March 1, 2019, available at https://worldjusticeproject.org/sites/default/files/documents/WJP_Access-Justice_April_2018_Online.pdf.

World Justice Project (2019), "Global Rule of Law Index", available at https://worldjusticeproject.org/sites/default/files/documents/WJP_RuleofLawIndex_2019_Website_reduced.pdf.

2 Access to justice for children in Zimbabwe

Julia Sloth-Nielsen and Blessing Mushohwe

Introduction

This chapter explores and interrogates the various issues affecting children's access to justice in Zimbabwe. After providing context to the situation in which children in Zimbabwe are growing up, the chapter goes on to look more narrowly at the potential of children's constitutional rights to further access justice, examining two concrete issues that have been brought to court in constitutional adjudication: child marriage and corporal punishment of children. Following this, the chapter provides an overall description of the formal justice system and the entry points for children to exercise their rights, as well as the coexistence of traditional justice dispute resolution mechanisms under customary law. Next, the various methods for children to vindicate their rights – from State-funded legal aid to non-governmental organisations (NGOs) active in the justice sector – are explored, as well as victim-friendly courts and child-friendly justice. Finally, the chapter suggests what the future of children's access to justice in Zimbabwe might look like.

Demographic and social context of children growing up in Zimbabwe

According to recent data, children constitute 48% out of Zimbabwe's total population of just over 13 million people (UNICEF/Zimbabwe National Statistics Agency, 2015:8). 67% of the population live in rural areas, the rest in urban areas (Zimbabwe National Statistics Agency, 2012:13). Zimbabwe's fast-track land reform programme, which targeted commercial farms for dispossession and redistribution, triggered sanctions from the international community, leading to investor flight, a shortage of basic commodities, a range of inflationary pressures, and sustained diplomatic isolation, particularly between the years 2000 and 2008 (Government of Zimbabwe, n.p.). This seriously impacted Zimbabwe's social and economic well-being, as well as children's rights. The net enrolment rate in primary school is 91%, but there is a huge drop-off in enrolment – down to 49% of children – in secondary school. Although a government scholarship programme for secondary school fees exists, is it inadequate to meet the needs of the impoverished population. Meanwhile, literacy rates are comparatively high (92%), and enrolment in tertiary education is also quite commendable (40%) (Government of Zimbabwe, n.p.).

Zimbabwe is a constitutional democracy which operates in a multi-party system. The country has ratified the United Nations International Convention on the Rights of the Child (hereafter referred to as the CRC) and two of its optional protocols, as well as the African Charter on Human and Peoples' Rights, the African Charter on the Rights and Welfare of the Child (hereafter referred to as the ACRWC), as well as various other international and African human rights treaties.

The latest National Action Plan (NAP) for Orphaned and Vulnerable Children (2016–2020) records that despite some efforts and advances made under previous NAPs, the situation of children in Zimbabwe remains serious in several areas. Explicitly identified are child protection issues (including child marriage, especially amongst girls), water, sanitation and hygiene, and child mortality. The NAP identifies child protection risks as acute, noting that these range from abuse to exploitation and violence. Hence, one pillar identified is that orphaned and vulnerable children should be able to access justice through a child- and victim-friendly justice system.

Meanwhile, Zimbabwe has developed a National Case Management System Framework for Child Protection to make sure that children are able to access all the social welfare, justice and specialised health care systems that they need within a properly coordinated statutory mechanism.

Zimbabwe has one of the largest human immunodeficiency virus (HIV) incidences in the world: the estimated HIV adult prevalence is 14.3%, with 1.3 million citizens living with HIV/acquired immune deficiency syndrome (AIDS) (National AIDS Council, 2015:4). Although the rate of new infections appears to have dropped in recent times, the number of deaths amongst adolescents aged 10–19 years had increased between 2011 and 2014. As of 2013, the HIV/AIDS prevalence among the youth population (15–24 years) was estimated at 5.31%, while the total number of adults and children living with HIV was estimated at 1.3 million (National AIDS Council, 2014:6). The HIV/AIDS infection rate of persons 15–19 years was 3.8% in 2010/2011, and amongst young adults 20–24 years it was 7.5%. As in the subregion generally, this figure is high.

Impact on access to justice

As the Zimbabwe Human Rights NGO Forum points out (Human Rights Forum, 2013), accessing justice remains out of reach for many Zimbabweans (including children). Barriers identified include the limited access poor and marginalised communities enjoy *vis-a-vis* the legal system, with the costs involved prohibitive in the current climate of economic shortage. In addition, delays and adjournments further increase costs, such as transport costs to get to courts. As a result, the Forum asserts that many people end up dropping their claims or fail to access justice even when they have a valid case.

Another identified factor is a shortage of courts, as "the number of district magistrates' courts countrywide is inadequate to deliver justice to complainants" (Human Rights Forum, 2013:3) who are then forced to travel to courts that are far away. Only Bulawayo and Harare have a permanent sitting High Court, whereas the other provinces are forced to rely on circuit courts. Aside from alleged selective application of the law and some legislative impediments to accessing justice (claims against the police must be brought within eight months), lack of knowledge about the law amongst the general populace, as well as how to access legal assistance, is a further identified impediment (Human Rights Forum, 2013:4).

Since 2009, a key aspect of the economic decline has been an exodus of the social workforce to other countries in search of better working conditions. This impacts children's access to justice, as there is a shortage of social workers to assist with background investigations, statement-taking and provision of reports to courts. Plans are underway to address this in the NAP for Orphans and Vulnerable Children 2016–2020.

The constitutional provisions enabling access to justice

In 2013, Zimbabwe adopted a new Constitution,[1] with a strong bent towards human rights. This is a very progressive Constitution in many respects, and makes provision for children's rights through Section 81, domesticating child rights as provided for by the CRC and the ACRWC. With regards to access to justice for children, Section 81(1)(a) states that every child has a right "to equal treatment before the law, including the right to be heard". While equality before the law is a broad concept, it importantly gives children the right to access justice and be treated in the same manner as any other person before the law. Children are therefore given the opportunity to approach the courts and not be discriminated against or dismissed by virtue of being children.[2]

In addition to being treated equally before the law, the same clause further provides for the right to be heard. While this does not provide much clarity on the right being given, it essentially sets out the right of children to participate in matters that affect them, be they criminal, civil or administrative, and is the domestication of children's right to be heard as provided for by the CRC in Article 12 and the ACRWC in Articles 4(2) and 7. As far as access to justice is concerned, this means that children involved in judicial proceedings should be afforded an opportunity to air their views and have those views given due weight in accordance with their age and maturity. This is profound in that it creates an opportunity for children to speak out directly in court processes and to be heard through representatives such as legal practitioners and probation officers. Decisions that are then reached by judicial officers can therefore be reflective of children's views, opinions and wishes.[3]

Locus standi *in constitutional litigation*

Locus standi refers to the right to approach a court directly to seek appropriate relief in cases arising from an alleged infringement of a fundamental human right or freedom enshrined in Chapter 4 of the Constitution. The *locus standi* provision of the Zimbabwean Constitution is contained in Section 85(1). It provides that any person acting in their own interests; acting on behalf of another person who cannot act for themselves; acting as a member, or in the interests, of a group or class of persons; acting in the public interest; or any association acting in the interests of its members is entitled to approach a court alleging that a fundamental right or freedom enshrined in Chapter 4 has been, is being or is likely to be infringed. The court may grant appropriate relief, including a declaration of rights and an award of compensation.

The provision clearly entails that actions can be brought by persons acting in the interests of a child or a group of children. Whether it provides a child or children with direct access to the Constitutional Court, independent of parental or other assistance, remains to be definitively established, but on the face of it seems possible.[4] The *Mudzuru* case[5] is instructive regarding *locus standi.* In it, the complainants sought a declaration of constitutional invalidity regarding the Marriage Act[6] on the grounds that it did not specify a minimum age of marriage of 18 years and that it differentiated between the minimum age of marriage for girls and boys, which was in conflict with the constitutional requirement of Section 78.[7] Both applicants in the *Mudzuru* fell pregnant before the age of 18. Having fallen pregnant, they proceeded to live with the families of their respective partners, but neither of their pregnancies led to the applicants entering into either a formal or customary marriage. In other words, neither of the two applicants was a victim of child marriage (strictly construed), which was why they could not prove a direct relationship to the cause of action. Moreover, when they approached the court, they were no longer under 18 years of age and therefore were no longer children (as constitutionally defined in Section 81(1)).[8] The applicants' papers further did not refer to any particular girl or girls whose rights had been, were being or were likely to be infringed by being subjected to child marriage, whether such marriage was concluded in terms of Section 22(1) of the Marriage Act or any other law.[9]

Under the previous Constitution, it was not ordinarily possible to seek judicial redress for legal injury suffered by another person, the only exception being when a person was unable to seek relief because they were in detention. However, the 2013 Zimbabwean Constitution gave the *locus standi* principle a much more flexible interpretation. Indeed, the Constitutional Court accepted the challenge posed by the interpretation of Section 85, with the then-Deputy Chief Justice (DCJ) Malaba in the *Mudzuru* case arguing that Section 85(1) in its entirety must be accorded a liberal, broad and generous interpretation rather than the narrow traditional conception of *locus standi.* In this regard, he aptly stated that: "The object is to overcome the formal defects in the legal system so as to guarantee real and substantial justice to the masses, particularly the poor, marginalised and deprived sections of society." This is particularly important with regards to child rights law and access to justice for children, given the disempowered and vulnerable status of children in society who, for various reasons, cannot ordinarily stand up for their rights. In this regard, the then-DCJ rightfully describes children as falling "into the category of weak and vulnerable persons in society".[10]

The court held that even though the complainants could not benefit personally, as they were now aged over 18 years, they were nevertheless representing the public interest on behalf of children, who were a vulnerable group in society. According to the Court, while the Section 85(1)(d) procedure should never be used to protect private, personal or parochial interests, the public interest is, by definition, none of these things.[11] It is therefore imperative that applicants are able to demonstrate that proceedings are in the public interest. However, it does not need to be shown that a significant section of the community is affected.[12] In the past, persons could only seek redress for injuries they themselves had suffered, so this liberalisation of the grounds on which an approach to Court can be made constitutes an important advance in the quest for access to justice on behalf of children.

The Court was clear that it is not necessary for a person challenging the constitutional validity of legislation to give particulars of a person or persons who had suffered legal injury as a result of the alleged unconstitutionality of the legislation.[13]

Regarding children as beneficiaries of constitutional litigation, the Court had the following to say:

> … the applicants acted altruistically to protect public interest in the enforcement of the constitutional obligation on the State to protect the fundamental rights of girl children enshrined in Section 81(1) as read with Section 78(1) of the Constitution. Children fall into the category of weak and vulnerable persons in society and are usually persons who have no capacity to approach a court on their own seeking appropriate relief for the redress of legal injury they would have suffered. The reasons for their incapacity usually arise from minority, poverty, and socially and economically disadvantaged positions. The law recognises the interests of such vulnerable persons in society as constituting public interest.[14]

The Court declared, ultimately, that Section 78(1) of the Constitution sets 18 as the minimum age of marriage in Zimbabwe, and, with effect from the date of judgment (20 January 2016), that no person, male or female, may enter into any form of marriage before attaining that age. Matyszak therefore aptly sums up the commendable elaboration on *locus standi* and public interest litigation by the then-DCJ by stating that

> It is also to be celebrated that the judgment eschews its erstwhile, stifling and restrictive approach to 'locus standi' and now allows an individual to

> approach the court to enforce the rights of the public at large, even where the individual has no self-interest in the matter.
>
> (Matyszak, 2016)[15]

Corporal punishment of children has also been the subject of constitutional litigation. The judgment in *S v C (a minor)*[16] came before the Harare High Court on review in December 2014. The accused had been sentenced to a moderate whipping of three strokes with a rattan cane, which was a lawful punishment for juvenile offenders under an exception to the prohibition on torture or cruel, inhuman and degrading treatment or punishment under the previous Zimbabwean Constitution. However, under the 2013 Constitution, the right to freedom from torture or cruel, inhuman or degrading treatment or punishment is provided for under Section 53, and Section 86(3)(c) lists this right as non-derogable, that is, no law may permit such treatment to occur, and in respect of which no person may be permitted to violate this right. The Court viewed this as leading to the conclusion that corporal punishment was unconstitutional, a conclusion strengthened if regard is given to further provisions in the new Constitution which protect the right to personal security, equality and non-discrimination.[17] The Court relied heavily on international instruments which had been ratified by Zimbabwe, including the key children's rights texts, with particular detail accorded by the ACRWC. Since Section 2(1) of the 2013 Constitution states that it "is the supreme law of Zimbabwe and any law, practice custom or conduct inconsistent with it is invalid to the extent of the inconsistency", it ergo means Section 353 (1) of the Criminal Procedure and Evidence Act, [18] whilst technically remaining in force, is now an invalid law.

The Court opined that although it was not an issue before the Court, it seemed that Section 53 of the new Constitution outlawed the infliction of corporal punishment on children by their parents, guardians or by persons acting in *loco parentis*. This is because, in the view of the Court, the right not to be tortured or subjected to cruel, inhuman or degrading treatment or punishment is an absolute right. Declining to certify that the sentence was in accordance with "real and substantive justice" due to its constitutional invalidity, the Court directed the prosecutor-general to apply to the Constitutional court to have the declaration of constitutional invalidity confirmed.[19]

Most recently, in *Pfungwa and Justice for Children Trust v Headmistress Belvedere Junior Primary School, Minister of Education, Sport and Culture and Minister for Justice Legal and Parliamentary Affairs*[20] the applicants filed for a constitutional declaratory order based on Sections 51 and 53 of the Constitution, alleging that corporal punishment in schools and in the home was constitutionally impermissible. They claimed *locus standi* on the basis of Section 85(1)(d), that is, on the grounds of the public interest. The application centred on a teacher employed by the first respondent's school, who had used a thick rubber pipe to assault the child (who was in the first grade) because the child's mother had failed to sign her reading homework. The child suffered deep red bruises on her back, and was so traumatised that she refused to go to school the following day. According to the Court, her plight came to the public domain via a WhatsApp group on which her mother posted pictures of the injuries, resulting in other children revealing that they too had been assaulted. The mother sought corrective action, which the first respondent evidently undertook to instigate. The second applicant joined the proceedings as,

> a corporate body registered according to the laws of Zimbabwe, [with the] function, it said, [...] to fight for the protection of children. Its main objective, according to it, was to ensure that international standards which protect children were realised and actualised in Zimbabwe.[21]

The applicants averred that

> no one, whether a school, a teacher or a parent at home should inflict corporal punishment on children. They submitted that corporal punishment was physical abuse of children. They averred that the punishment more often than not resulted in physical trauma or injury to children. They insisted that corporal punishment in school was dangerous in that it was administered indiscriminately without any measure or control over the teachers.[22]

They supported their application by reference to the Constitution, domestic and regional case law, expert evidence and international treaties to which Zimbabwe is a party.[23]

The attorney general had applied to be admitted as a friend of the Court but filed only opposing heads of argument without underlying affidavits. However, the Court said his heads of argument "stood on nothing", which was ultimately conceded by his representative. Thus, the order sought was essentially unopposed in the event the Court was satisfied with the merits of the application. The declaratory order was therefore granted and the matter remitted to the Constitutional Court for confirmation of the constitutional invalidity of corporal punishment in schools and by parents, or those acting in *loco parentis*.[24]

The above cases indicate an auspicious start to strategic litigation vindicating children's constitutional rights in Zimbabwe, all of which has been bolstered by international treaty law, the intervention of children's rights NGOs as co-applicants, and by the willingness of the judiciary to take bold steps to advance children's rights. Arguably, too, the nature of the remedy sought was an important factor: in *Pfungwa* a formal declaration of unconstitutionality was arguably a less "confrontational" route to pursue than (for instance) a delictual remedy or the insistence on criminal sanctions being pursued.

Children's rights and access to courts

Section 81(2) of the Constitution provides for the primacy of children's best interests, and Section 81(3) notes specifically that "Children are entitled to adequate protection by the courts, in particular by the High Court as their upper guardian". However, in Section 69(2) and (3) of the Constitution there is already an overarching provision to the effect that "In the determination of civil rights and obligations, every person has a right to a fair, speedy and public hearing within a reasonable time before an independent and impartial court, tribunal, or other forum established by law" and "Every person has the right of access to the courts or to some other tribunal or forum established by law for the resolution of any dispute …" Given this, the question as to what potential value lies in a dedicated provision for children arises. We argue that this provision specifically requires courts to be "on the lookout" for children who may be in need of the court's protection in and outside litigation. It provides an opportunity for children to access justice through their upper guardian, the High Court, even in situations where their natural guardians have denied them access to justice or are the perpetrators of the injustice. If used adequately, this provision has the potential of having judicial officers be proactive in ensuring legal recourse for children already or potentially affected by a matter they may be dealing with, even if the children are not party to such proceedings. Children may thus begin to access justice even in cases where they had not envisaged it or where they had not approached the courts. This is especially important for civil matters such as divorce or evictions, and for inheritance matters where children may not be party to the case but are inevitably adversely affected by decisions reached.

Constitutional provisions relevant to legal representation

The right for children to be heard as provided for by the Constitution is supposed to be realised in practice through the provision of legal representatives for children in matters that affect them. According to Section 31 of the Constitution,

> The State must take all practical measures, within the limits of the resources available to it, to provide legal representation in civil and criminal cases for people who need it and are unable to afford legal practitioners of their choice.

For criminal matters, the Constitution further provides in Section 70(1)(e) for the right of every accused person (including children) to have legal representation by a state-assigned legal practitioner at the expense of the state "if substantial injustice would otherwise result".[25] While the determination of "substantial injustice", without any guidelines, is open to interpretation, especially when it involves children, the provision is commendable.

Constitutional provisions pertinent to juvenile justice

In further domesticating provisions of the CRC and the ACRWC on children's access to justice, the Constitution of Zimbabwe provides for children in conflict with the law. According to Section 81(1)(i), a child has the right not to be detained except as a measure of last resort and, if they are detained, for it to the shortest appropriate period; to be kept separately from detained persons over the age of 18 years; and to be treated in a manner, and kept in conditions, that take account of their age.

This mirrors Article 37 of the CRC and Article 17 of the ACRWC on juvenile justice. The above constitutional provisions are important in that, while acknowledging that children may sometimes be in conflict with the law, such involvement with the justice system should be sensitive to the fact that it is a child, and detrimental practices such as long detention and being detained with adult prisoners should be avoided. Children are further protected by the rights covering accused, arrested and detained persons as provided by Sections 50 and 70 of the Constitution. These include, among others, *Miranda* rights, *habeas corpus*, presumption of innocence until proven guilty, the right to judicial review, the right to be informed promptly of the charges on arrest, the right to be visited by family and friends while in detention, and the right to food and shelter (Vergesai, n.p.:26). This is complemented by rights to a fair hearing for both civil and criminal matters, as provided for by Section 69 of the Constitution.

Overall context of the justice system pertaining to children

Access to justice for children requires more than just a legal framework; it has to work within a framework of functional institutions sympathetic to children accessing justice. This refers to Children's Courts, as provided for by Article 40(3) of the CRC. The CRC Committee has recommended that States establish juvenile courts either as separate units or as part of existing courts, or where that is not immediately feasible, to ensure the appointment of specialised judges or magistrates when dealing with cases of juvenile justice. While this is specific to children in conflict with the law, access to justice for both civil and criminal matters affecting children may also require such specialised courts.

With regards to civil matters affecting children in Zimbabwe, this is provided for by the Children's Act. For cases such as custody, adoption and guardianship, Sections 3–6 of the Children's Act establish Children's Courts by designating every Magistrate's Court a Children's Court, and requiring a Magistrate be designated for the Children's Court where a case involving a child is concerned. To safeguard the best interests of the child while accessing justice, a Probation Officer is provided for the child. Section 5 of the Act further requires adoption of a "child sensitive" environment for the court process, where formality of procedure may be done away with in order to make the child feel comfortable enough to contribute. This is in addition to such processes being done in camera so that the identity of the child is not made public.

The Domestic Violence Act recognises children as potential victims of domestic violence and includes violence committed in the presence of children as emotional abuse. In defining a potential complainant, Section 2 of the Act includes "a child of the respondent, whether born in or out of wedlock, and includes an adopted child and a step-child." Thus, a child may make a complaint directly to the authorities via a number of individuals outlined in the Act. These include a police officer, a social welfare officer, an employer of the complainant, a person representing a church or religious organisation or a private voluntary organisation concerned with the welfare of victims of domestic violence, a relative, neighbour or fellow employee of the complainant, or a counsellor.[26]

While the above applies for civil cases, there are no direct provisions of similar import for children in conflict with the law. Zimbabwe does not have a Child Justice Act as yet. As such, children in conflict with the law are dealt with in terms of the general criminal law of the country, in the form of the Criminal Procedure and Evidence Act (CPEA) and the Criminal Law (Codification and Reform) Act.[27] Protection clauses enhancing access to justice for children under the CPEA include prohibitions against publishing the identity of the juvenile accused, and concealment of the identity of a juvenile complainant or witness. The CPEA cements its protections through Section 319A-H, which comprehensively deals with protection of vulnerable witnesses, protecting children through requirements for in camera proceedings and the use of intermediaries and support persons, amongst other measures.

While these are critical for children's access to justice in criminal matters, there is now an urgent need for a comprehensive Child Justice Act which integrates the child justice provisions in various Acts into one document for ease of reference, as well as removing any ambiguity or confusion that may be caused by having various pieces of law about a single issue. Also, diversion (discussed below) needs to be concretised in formal legal provisions, and with the ruling of constitutional invalidity on corporal punishment as a sentence, new sentencing provisions will need to be adopted.[28]

Methods for vindications of rights

State legal aid

The Legal Aid Act[29] is meant to provide the means through which children can access justice using legal aid. The Act, which set up the Legal Aid Directorate, is meant to provide for state-assisted legal aid in civil and criminal courts for indigent persons, children included, thus giving effect to the Constitutional provisions for legal representation of children. According to Section 7 of the Act, any person may apply for state-assisted legal aid. The legal aid system in Zimbabwe is, however, seriously underdeveloped, lacking the necessary resources and personnel. According to Chiware (n.p.:2), between 1996, when the Legal Aid Directorate became a stand-alone department, and 2011, when it opened its doors to the people of Zimbabwe's second-largest city Bulawayo, it was operating only in the capital Harare. Chiware further states that the Harare office is currently manned by 12 lawyers, while the Bulawayo office has four. This means that a total of just 16 lawyers are supposed to meet the needs of all indigent Zimbabweans, which is highly impractical. Apart from this, the lawyers only operate in Harare and Bulawayo, meaning eight provinces with equally indigent children are left out.

The legal aid system in Zimbabwe does not have a separate legal representation framework for children, whose representation generally requires specialised competence in children's issues. Furthermore, in the legal aid framework mentioned above, there is no mandatory requirement for legal representation of children in matters that affect them, be it in criminal or civil matters. Coupled with the highly under-resourced and underdeveloped nature of the system, access to justice by children using state-provided legal aid is almost non-existent.

Non-state actors and access to justice

While the state system for children's access to justice through legal aid has been described as lacking, *ad hoc* efforts by non-state actors such as NGOs have been used to afford children legal representation in matters affecting them. NGOs have thus been central to legal representation of children in courts. Of note are NGOs such as Justice for Children Trust, Legal Resources Foundation (LRF) and Care at the Centre of Humanity (CATCH) (see Box 2.1).

Box 2.1 NGOS involved in matters relating to legal aid and legal representation for children in Zimbabwe

Justice for Children Trust

Justice for Children Trust claims its vision is "A Zimbabwe in which all children have access to justice and enjoy their human rights" and lists the provision of legal aid to children in difficult circumstances as part of its Mission.[30] Established in 2002, the Trust has enhanced access to justice for children in communities through legal aid mobile clinics, community focal persons (CFPs) and volunteer lawyers.

Legal Resources Foundation (LRF)

While the LRF has always been involved in legal aid, its work on access to justice for children has recently become more pronounced through the development of the National Strategy for Legal Assistance for Children 2012–2015 by the Ministry of Justice, Legal and Parliamentary Affairs in partnership with United Nations Children's Fund (UNICEF). The strategy sets up partnerships for the referral of children for legal representation conducted by child-rights NGOs, among them the LRF, and is funded by UNICEF. Through this programme, LRF reports that

> A total of 8,749 children were reached within this first year of the project. 180 cases involving children were taken to court by LRF lawyers and 122 of these were successfully closed. It is important to note that of these 122 cases represented in court and successfully closed, 47 such cases were criminal juvenile cases.[31]

According to the LRF's Annual Report 2015–2016, 34% of cases that it handled were on children's rights.

Care at the Centre of Humanity (CATCH)

CATCH's main objective is protecting the welfare and human rights of children, including their right to a fair trial. Activities under its Legal Aid Department include legal representation, legal advice sessions, court accompaniment, bail application, payment of fines, and weekly visits to detention facilities housing child offenders in order to identify new cases needing services and to monitor their conditions of detention.[32]

Aside from the above, there are other NGOs such as Zimbabwe Lawyers for Human Rights(ZLHR) and Women and Law in Southern Africa (WILSA) which, while not necessarily focussing on children, have a broader human rights thrust within which they sometimes litigate for children.

Zimbabwe Human Rights Commission

Complaints regarding abuses and violations of rights and freedoms enshrined in the Constitution of Zimbabwe and in any international human rights agreements that the country has signed can be submitted to the Zimbabwe Human Rights Commission (ZHRC), [33] as well as any complaints arising from abuse of power or maladministration by the State and public institutions. The Commission may also initiate an investigation under its own initiative.[34] While the ZHRC has a Children's pillar, which could receive complaints from children, it must be pointed out that the work of the ZHRC is in its infancy, and there is not yet information available to determine whether children have availed themselves of its services.

Non-legal means of accessing justice

Pre-trial diversion

International instruments have long been advocating for a move away from the formal justice system for children involved in crime and towards the use of rehabilitative, reform-oriented and education-focused alternatives. Of note is Article 37 of the CRC which prohibits children being treated in a cruel, inhuman or degrading manner, while Article 40 requires state parties to treat children who have committed crimes with dignity and self-worth, with a view to reintegrating them back into society. Article 40(3)(b) specifically advocates measures for dealing with children outside formal court systems, provided that human rights and legal safeguards are respected. Similar provisions are found in the ACRWC in Articles 16 and 17.

Furthermore, there are a number of other international rules and guidelines which are non-binding but, taken together, constitute a comprehensive framework for the care, protection and reform-oriented treatment of child offenders. These include the United Nations Standard Minimum Rules for the Administration of Juvenile Justice, the United Nations Guidelines for the Prevention of Juvenile Delinquency and the United Nations Rules for the Protection of Juveniles Deprived of their Liberty. Of note in this regard is the diversion of children in conflict with the law from the formal justice system. According to UNICEF,

> Diversion means the conditional channelling of children in conflict with the law away from formal judicial proceedings towards a different way of resolving the issue that enables many – possibly most – to be dealt with by non-judicial bodies, thereby avoiding the negative effects of formal judicial proceedings and a criminal record, provided that human rights and legal safeguards are fully respected.
>
> (UNICEF, 2009)

Box 2.2 Zimbabwe's pre-trial diversion pilot programme

In 2009, Zimbabwe's Ministry of Justice, Legal and Parliamentary Affairs began piloting a Pre-Trial Diversion (PTD) programme for child offenders in Harare, Bulawayo, Chitungwiza, Murehwa and Gweru. This effectively introduced an alternative for children accessing justice that is rehabilitative, educative and restorative rather than being on punitive practices such as incarceration, detention and formal criminal trials in courts. Diversion thus allows the system to hold young people accountable for their actions while at the same time providing them an opportunity to re-think their lives without getting a criminal record or going through the stigmatising criminal justice system.

This framework has since been cemented by the Constitution of Zimbabwe, which reflects international standards and has a solid legal framework outlining the rights of accused persons, including children. Read with Section 81(2) of the Constitution, this effectively domesticates the international guidelines alluded to earlier, and together with the PTD Pilot Programmes that have been running since 2009 provides a firm foundation for widespread expansion of the PTD framework throughout the country.

The diversion programme in Zimbabwe has, however, faced teething problems, mainly as a result of lack of resources. This has meant the establishment of proper structures and institutions to coordinate the programme has been delayed. According to the (unofficial) Draft Report of the PTD Programme in Zimbabwe: End of Pilot Programme Evaluation, the programme had no diversion officers in post to coordinate and carry out diversion services between inception and 2012, at which point UNICEF and Save the Children provided budgetary support for the programme (Penal Reform International, 2016:3). As of 2016, the Ministry of Justice, Legal and Parliamentary Affairs has taken over the employment of diversion officers, with 16 officers now fully employed by the Ministry in the five pilot programme areas.

As a result of the above developments and the injection of budgetary support by UNICEF and Save the Children, it is reported that 1,728 children in conflict with the law were diverted from the formal criminal justice system in Zimbabwe between 1 January 2013 and 28 September 2016 (Penal Reform International, 2016:8). During that time, only 429 children were referred to the formal criminal justice system, meaning that 80% of children in conflict with the law were diverted. This points to the programme's commendable success in enhancing access to justice for children but more particularly in increasing the use of alternatives to the formal justice system when children are in conflict with the law.

With the End of Pilot Programme Evaluation concluded, Zimbabwe's diversion programme is now due for revision and possible expansion to the rest of the country. Such an expansion must, however, be grounded on comprehensive guidelines that allow for consistency and uniformity of application across the country. While the PTD National Steering Committee established at the commencement of the pilot programme did draft some guidelines that were being used in the Pilot programme, these guidelines have not yet been finalised. With the Pilot programme having supposedly ended in May 2016 and the possibility of a new programme being introduced, there is a compelling need for finalised, comprehensive guidelines that may be used for any future activities in relation to PTD. This should be anchored by a Child Justice Act, as discussed earlier, wherein diversion is properly provided for.

Access to justice for victims

The Victim-Friendly System (VFS) is a set of measures designed to ensure the protection and active participation of survivors in the criminal justice system.[35] The system was initiated by the Zimbabwean Government and women and children's rights activists in the early 1990s. The result is a multisectoral approach to offering welfare and judicial services to survivors of sexual violence and abuse (Government of Zimbabwe, n.p.:15).[36]

In 1997 the amendment to Section 319 of the Criminal Procedure & Evidence Act addressed the needs of witnesses deemed vulnerable during criminal proceedings in the victim-friendly court. The specific provisions of the amendment include (Government of Zimbabwe, n.p.:16) the following:

- Having a support person during Court proceedings;
- Availability of closed-circuit television (CCTV) in all specialised courts;
- Use of an intermediary or specialist interpreter to work with vulnerable witnesses;
- Establishment of the multisectoral victim-friendly system court sub-committees, referred to in the Protocol as the National Victim Friendly System Committee (NVFSC) and Sub-committees;
- Use of anatomically correct dolls for child survivors and witnesses;
- Provision of witness expenses by Government;
- In camera trials;
- Allowing judicial staff to behave less formally before and during trial;
- Awareness-raising campaigns.

The provisions also enabled the development of the Protocol on the Multi-Sectoral Management of Children's Sexual Abuse in Zimbabwe. The original Protocol described stakeholders' roles and responsibilities regarding the delivery of medical care, support and judicial services to survivors of sexual violence and abuse. The second edition of the Protocol was issued in June 2003, and strengthened the focus of the Protocol on the rights of child survivors of sexual violence and abuse. A revised version was developed by the Judicial Services Commission in 2012.[37]

Government has, through the Ministry of Women Affairs, Gender and Community Development, established Gender Clubs in most schools, according to the Zimbabwe initial report to the African Committee of Experts on the Rights and Welfare of the Child (Government of Zimbabwe, n.p.:22). These clubs are reportedly guided safe platforms, created to allow the girl/young woman and boy/young man to openly learn, share and discuss the issues they face in achieving their individual child rights. These empower the girl/young woman to speak up for their rights, challenging peers, schools, communities and systems that limit their empowerment socially, politically and economically. Access to justice for children can be increased through such initiatives and platforms. However, as lawyer Tinomuda Shoko points out,

> Zimbabwe as a nation has not fully recovered from the economic meltdown that hit the country during the past decade thus making it difficult for the State to be able to meet the socio-economic needs of girl children

> in the justice system. Victims of sexual abuse have to travel long distances to go and report sexual abuse or get medical care after an abuse resulting in many unwanted pregnancies and sexually transmitted infections that may never be treated or cured. The Multi-Sectoral Approach Protocol to the Management of Sexual Offences provides guidelines to the management of sexual offences but without the adequate resources the Protocol can remain a fantasy.[38]

The other worrying aspect is the absence of safe houses for victims of sexual abuse in the family setup. Most child victims are abused by people close to them and so need to be removed from the environment in question until the matter is finalised or proper counselling or rehabilitation is done. Furthermore, if girls have to go back to the same homes they come from there will be greater interference by the public with State witnesses. Appropriate measures need to be put in place requiring the reporting of such safety risks to appropriate authorities, and to thereby protect the child from risk before, during and after the justice process.

Conclusions

While Zimbabwe's child justice system is still lagging behind compared to other countries in the Southern African region, such as South Africa and Namibia, it is at a critical juncture. The 2013 Constitution has brought with it the potential for new opportunities in accessing justice for children. The expansive provisions on children's rights set out in Section 81 are commendable as far as access to justice for children is concerned. Coupled with other general provisions in the Constitution for accused persons, which are likewise applicable to children, the outlook for access to justice for children is encouraging, provided it can be supported by the necessary political and judicial will. The judiciary has already been encouraging in this regard if consideration is given to its recent rulings on children's rights, specifically on child marriages and corporal punishment. Further encouragement can be drawn from the judiciary's broad interpretation of *locus standi*, and the possibilities it brings for increased vindication of children's rights generally and access to justice for children specifically, through other actors acting on their behalf. It remains to be seen if and how the Constitutional Court proceeds with this momentum towards vindicating children's rights. We suggest that the pending confirmation of the ban on corporal punishment by the High Court affords the Constitutional Court a perfect opportunity to continue on this path.

Furthermore, the use of diversion as an alternative to the formal justice system for children has provided additional encouragement with regard to access to justice for children. While the programme has had teething problems due to lack of resources, funding from development partners and buy-in by government through the employment of full-time diversion officers again point to increased access to justice for children, more so as the diversion programme expands beyond the initial five pilot areas to the rest of the country. However, in all these developments, the icing on the cake would be the enactment of a new Child Justice Act for Zimbabwe. This will put to rest such problems as lack of uniformity and consistency, fragmented access to justice, and a lack of a guiding law and policy regarding child justice. Overall, though, the future of access to justice for Zimbabwean children looks bright.

Notes

1 Constitution of Zimbabwe Amendment Act 20 of 2013.
2 This is significant in view of the usual incapacity of children to litigate in their own names without parental assistance.
3 Interestingly, there is no "clawback" provision related to the exercise of this right being dependent on their age or maturity.
4 See 167(6) of the Constitution of Zimbabwe, which states that

> National legislation or the rules of the Constitutional Court must allow a person, when it is in the interests of justice and with leave of the Constitutional Court: (a) to bring a matter directly to the Constitutional Court; or (b) to appeal directly to the Constitutional Court from any other court.

See further Chidzura and Makiwane (2016).
5 *Loveness Mudzuru & Ruvimbo Tsopodzi vs Minister of Justice, Legal & Parliamentary Affairs N.O; Minister of Women's Affairs, Gender & Community Development & Attorney General of Zimbabwe* Case CCZ 12/2015.
6 Marriage Act [Chapter 5:11].
7 Section 78 is titled "Marriage Rights", with 78(1) providing that "Every person who has attained the age of eighteen years has the right to found a family."
8 See also Sloth-Nielsen and Hove (2016).
9 Such as the Customary Marriages Act [Chapter 5:07].
10 *Loveness Mudzuru & Ruvimbo Tsopodzi vs Minister of Justice, Legal & Parliamentary Affairs N.O; Minister of Women's Affairs, Gender & Community Development & Attorney General of Zimbabwe* Case CCZ 12/2015. p. 24.
11 Ibid., p. 15.
12 Ibid., p. 16.
13 Ibid., p. 22.
14 Ibid., pp. 24–25.
15 See also Sloth-Nielsen and Hove (2016).
16 *S v C (a minor)* 2014 ZWHHC 718.
17 See Section 53(a) and Section 56 of the Constitution of Zimbabwe.
18 Criminal Procedure and Evidence Act [Chapter 9:07].
19 The application was brought before the Constitutional Court and submissions received. At the time of writing there has been no judgement.
20 *Pfungwa and Justice for Children Trust v Headmistress Belvedere Junior Primary School, Minister of Education, Sport and Culture and Minister for Justice Legal and Parliamentary Affairs* HH 148-17 of 28 February 2017.
21 Ibid., p. 2.
22 Ibid., p. 2.
23 In particular, the ACRWC (1990).
24 In neighbouring South Africa, with similar constitutional provisions protecting children "from all forms of abuse neglect maltreatment and degradation", repeated attempts to outlaw corporal punishment in the home via legislation have failed. Hence the Children's Act 38 of 2005 does not contain an express provision

relating to corporal punishment, despite the inclusion of a lengthy clause in the Bill that was introduced in Parliament in 2003 and again in the regulations tabled for Parliamentary approval in 2007. Both were ultimately omitted at the behest of Parliament.

25 Both the CRC (Article 40(2)(b)(ii)) and the ACRWC (Article 17(2)(c)(iii)) provide that a child must be afforded legal or other appropriate assistance in the preparation of their defence.

26 Domestic Violence Act (Act 5 of 2006) Section 2. see Government of Zimbabwe (n.p.:29).

27 Criminal Law (Codification and Reform) Act [Chapter 9:23].

28 As of March 2019, Government has accepted a policy document outlining the principles to be included in a stand-alone Child Justice Act. Drafting is to commence shortly, with the first author of this chapter (Julia Sloth-Nielsen) having been contracted to assist with this process.

29 Legal Aid Act [Chapter 7:16].

30 see www.justiceforchildren.org.zw/index.php/about/background (accessed 7 March 2019).

31 see www.lrfzim.com/legal-services (accessed 7 March 2019).

32 see www.catch.org.zw (accessed 7 March 2019).

33 Zimbabwe Human Rights Commission Act [Chapter 10:30], available www.zhrc.org.zw/legal-framework. In 2016, the ZHRC was awarded "A" status for compliance with the Paris Principles (principles relating to the Status of National Institutions) adopted by General Assembly resolution 48/134 of 20 December 1993.

34 Section 4 of Zimbabwe Human Rights Commission Act 2 of 2012.

35 Victim-friendly courts have been established at 17 out of 30 Regional Courts in the country in order to create a confidential and conducive criminal justice delivery system. The increase and countrywide distribution of the establishments has significantly reduced the distance children have to travel to access justice while also easing the case backlog in the courts. See Government of Zimbabwe (n.p.:33).

36 See further in Government of Zimbabwe (n.p:33):

> Additional structures in place include health institutions and victim friendly units in the police stations. All health institutions have the capacity to provide survivors of sexual abuse services which include counseling, forensic examination, administration of post-exposure prophylaxis, prophylactic treatment for sexually transmitted infections and treatment for prevention of pregnancy. Government is in the process of establishing 'child sensitive' survivor friendly clinics within the institutions. To date four survivor friendly clinics have been established. There are 269 police stations with victim support units manned by 817 police officers.

37 Protocol on the Multi-Sectoral Management of Children's Sexual Abuse in Zimbabwe, 2012, available www.togetherforgirls.org/wp-content/uploads/2017/10/Multi_Sectoral_Protocol_2012-Zimbabwe.pdf (accessed 29 March 2019).

38 "Environment affects Children's Access to Justice." Blogpost, available www.lrfzim.com/environment-affects-childrens-access-to-justice (accessed 7 March 2019).

Bibliography

Chidzura, L and PN Makiwane (2016). Strengthening Locus Standi in Human Rights Litigation in Zimbabwe: An Analysis of the Provisions in the New Zimbabwean Constitution. *PER/PELJ* 2016(19). doi: 10.17159/1727-3781/2016/v19i0a742

Chiware, F (n.p.). Towards a Holistic Approach to the Legal Aid System in Zimbabwe: Challenges Indigent Women Face in Instituting Proceedings and Enforcing Judgments in Civil Matters. Unpublished Thesis for Masters in Women's Law, University of Zimbabwe, 2014.

Government of Zimbabwe (n.p.). Zimbabwe Initial Country Report to the African Committee of Experts on the Rights and Welfare of the Child. Submitted 2015. (Copy on file with the authors).

Human Rights Forum (2013). Access to Justice. *Human Rights Bulletin.* April 2013. Available www.hrforumzim.org/wp-content/uploads/2013/06/Bulletin-83-Access-to-justice.pdf (accessed 24 April 2017).

Matyszak, D (2016). A Note on the Child Marriage Judgement. Research and Advocacy Unit, January 2016.

National AIDS Council (2014). Zimbabwe National HIV and AIDS Estimates 2013. June 2014. Available www.medbox.org/zimbabwe-national-hiv-and-aids-estimates/download.pdf (accessed 29 March 2019).

National AIDS Council (2015). Smart Investment to End HIV/AIDS in ZIMBABWE Based on Hotspot Analysis. Available https://documents.wfp.org/stellent/groups/public/documents/ena/wfp281708.pdf?_ga=2.148552439.1573146412.1553592202-1625333101.1553592202 (accessed 29 March 2019).

Penal Reform International (2016). Pre-trial Diversion Programme in Zimbabwe: End of Pilot Programme Evaluation Report. (Copy on file with the authors).

Sloth-Nielsen, J and K Hove (2016). Mudzuru & Another v The Minister of Justice, Legal and Parliamentary Affairs & 2 Others: A Review. *African Human Rights Law Journal* 15:554.

UNICEF (2009). Toolkit on Diversion and Alternatives to Detention. Available www.unicef.org/tdad/index_55660.html (accessed 30 April 2017).

UNICEF and Zimbabwe National Statistics Agency (2015). Descriptive Child and Youth Atlas: Zimbabwe: A District and Ward Analysis of Social Determinants. Harare, Zimbabwe: UNICEF Zimbabwe and Zimbabwe National Statistics Agency.

Vengesai, S (n.p.). Juvenile Justice in Zimbabwe: A Contradiction between Theory and Practice: An Analysis of Zimbabwe's Compliance with Article 37and 40 CRC and Article 17 ACRWC. Unpublished LLM Thesis, Tilburg University, 2014.

Zimbabwe National Statistics Agency (2012). Zimbabwe Population Census Report 2012: National Report.

3 Children, forced and early marriage

Preventing and responding to early marriage in Uganda

Asieh Yousefnajad Shomali and David Lawson[1]

Introduction

Child marriage is a global problem affecting millions of girls across the world. According to United Nations Population Fund (UNFPA) (2012), "child marriage" is defined as any marriage carried out before the age of 18 years when the girl is – whether physiologically or psychologically – unready to take on the responsibilities of marriage and childbearing. Child marriage may involve one or both spouses being children, and may be conducted with or without formal registration, and under religious, customary or civil laws.

In addition, child marriage often includes an element of coercion (Otoo-Oyortey and Pobi, 2003), with forced marriage being defined as a marriage taking place without the valid consent of one or both spouse(s). Any child marriage constitutes a forced marriage based on the assumption that anyone under the age of 18 (i.e. the minimum age for marriage) is not able to make a fully informed decision about whether to get married (Joy for Children Uganda). Child marriage, early childbearing, and subsequent low educational attainment for girls have a wide range of adverse impacts, not only on the girls themselves but also on their children, their families and (in the context of this chapter) on Ugandan society at large (World Bank, 2017).

Although there has been a slow decline in child marriage worldwide, the global number of child brides is now estimated at more than 700 million (UNICEF, 2015b), with one in seven girls marrying before the age of 15 in the developing world. According to the UNFPA (2012) more than 142 million girls will become child brides by 2020. Moreover, 50 million of these child brides will marry below the age of 15 years (ibid.). Therefore, in order to address the harmful consequences of child marriage and advance gender equality, the United Nations (UN) Sustainable Development Goals include preventing, responding to and eliminating child marriage by 2030 as a key target (5.3) (World Bank, 2016; UN, 2017).

However, this chapter argues that the practice of child marriage in Uganda is deeply entrenched in social norms and traditional conventions (Kyomuhendo Bantebya et al., 2014; UNICEF, 2015a; Muhanguzi et al., 2017); therefore, in order to address the problem, initiatives and interventions must be geared towards addressing such discriminatory norms.

The prevalence of child marriage in Uganda

According to International Center for Research on Women (ICRW) (2007), the highest rates of child marriage are reported in Sub-Saharan Africa, parts of Latin America and the Caribbean, and South Asia. ICRW, after reviewing the data from 68 developing countries, ranked Uganda ninth in terms of having the highest proportion of child marriage (Jain and Kurz, 2007).

More than 53% of women between the age of 20 and 49 years were first married below the age of 18 years (UBOS and ORC Macro, 2001; UBOS and Macro International, 2007; UDHS surveys, 2001, 2006). It is worth mentioning that while the legal age for marriage is set at 18 years in the Uganda Constitution, and any type of sexual relations with a child under 18 years is criminalized by the Penal Code in Uganda, figures by United Nations Children's Fund (UNICEF) (2011) and World Vision (2013) reveal that 12% of women are married before the age of 15.

In conflict and war situations, as well as camps for refugees and internally displaced people, child marriages are more common (Schlecht et al., 2013).[2] In terms of Uganda, forced marriages were reportedly more prevalent in Northern Uganda where girls were abducted and forced to marry rebel soldiers (Rubimbwa and Komurembe, 2012).

In Uganda, there is a decline in the trend of marrying very early, with only 3% of the women aged 15–19 years marrying by age 15, comparing with 19% of those aged 45–49 years (UBOS, 2011; UDHS, 2006). Despite this, the situation remains worrying, as over the last 50 years there has only been very slight or even no change in the median age of women entering their first marriage, with the average age being 17.9 years. Age at first marriage can be related to various factors including wealth quintile, residence and educational level. It may also vary in different regions of the country. Women living in urban areas aged 25–49 years marry about two years later than women in the same age bracket living in rural areas (20 years vs. 17.6 years). The median age at first marriage is also higher among wealthier and better educated women (UNICEF, 2015a).

Uganda has committed itself to addressing all forms of discrimination and violence against women and children, and as such has passed – with the exception of the Hague Convention on Inter-country adoption (Ssembatya, 2016) – various regional and global conventions and declarations addressing these issues. These include the Convention on the Elimination of All Forms of Discrimination Against Women (CEDAW), the 1994 Cairo International Conference on Population and Development (ICPD) Declaration. the Beijing Declaration and Platform of Action, The Convention on the Rights of the Child, the Declaration on Violence Against Women; the African Charter on the Rights and Welfare of the Child (ACRWC), and the African Charter on Human and Peoples Rights – Women's Rights Protocol (UNICEF, 2015a; World Bank, 2016).

The Ugandan Government has also recently adopted a comprehensive strategy on the elimination of child marriage and teenage pregnancy (Ministry of Gender, Labour and Social Development and UNICEF, 2015). However, at a local level, the implementation of national policies is often weak (Watson et al., 2018). Moreover, as articulated in the National Development Plans (NDPs) (2010, 2015), child protection is and has been a core responsibility of the government, yet when it comes to implementing practical initiatives that protect children from early marriages, little has been done (UNICEF, 2015a).

Negative consequences of child marriage

Child marriage is globally recognized as a human rights issue, as well as a violating children's rights.[3] A significant body of evidence has also related early marriage with negative health, economic and education outcomes (Green et al., 2009, Davis et al., 2013; Harper et al., 2014, World Bank, 2017). Global reviews on child marriage have documented that girls who marry under the age of 18 are more likely – comparing with their peers – to experience earlier and more frequent childbearing; higher maternal mortality (FIDH and FHRI, 2012), higher infant mortality; complications in pregnancy; obstructed labour and obstetric fistula (Kyomuhendo Bantebya et al., 2013; Schlecht et al., 2013); increased risk of human immunodeficiency virus (HIV) infection; low nutrition status (Rubin et al., 2009); early school departure; and lower earning capacity (Singh and Samara, 1996; UNICEF, 2001; Mukuria et al., 2005; UNICEF, 2005; ICRW, 2007).

With regard to human rights, many girls who experience early marriage are deprived of the opportunity to choose for themselves whether and when they want to marry; and, in the majority of cases, this single event will shape their entire adult lives. As a result of premature nuptials, these child brides have little or no role in household decision-making (Rubin et al., 2009) and are exposed to wide age differences in marriage, gender-based violence (Davis et al., 2013; Harper et al., 2014; ODI, 2015; Watson et al., 2015; World Bank, 2016; Muhanguzi et al., 2017; World bank, 2017; Kyomuhendo Bantebya et al., 2018;), polygynous marriages and lack of basic protection and social status (Schlecht et al., 2013; Kyomuhendo Bantebya et al., 2014).

Turning to health-related issues, child marriage is recognized as contributing significantly to the high levels of teenage pregnancies and population growth in Uganda (UBOS, 2011; Rutaremwa, 2013; World Bank, 2017; Watson et al., 2018). The latter, in turn, has negative implications for economic growth (Klasen and Lawson, 2007, DHS, 2006, 2011; World Bank, 2017) According to the Uganda Bureau of Statistics (UBOS, 2012a), 39% of women aged 20–49 years had their first birth before the age of 18 years, while 63% had their first birth before the age of 20 (UDHS, 2011). In the same vein, the likelihood of death in pregnancy or child birth for girls aged 10–14 years is five times that of women aged over 20 years. Additionally, the risk of delivering pre-term or low birth-weight infants is significantly higher in adolescent girls compared with mothers older than 19 years (Davis et al., 2013; World Bank, 2017;). Similarly, the rate of infant mortality is 60% higher among the new-borns of adolescent mothers (Sekiwunga and Whyte, 2009; UWONET, 2010; FIDH and FHRI, 2012). Furthermore, young brides are 2–6 times more likely to be infected by HIV/AIDS than their peers who are not married (Ministry of Health [MOH] and ORC Macro 2006) due to having unprotected sex with their husbands who are much older and at the higher risk of being HIV-positive by the virtue of age.

Regarding education, despite the Government supporting and implementing universal primary education (UPE) and universal secondary education (USE), which has led to more access to education for Ugandans, there is an increasing rate of girls dropping out of school. Both at primary and secondary school level, the completion rates for girls (66% and 34% respectively) continue to lag behind those of boys (68% and 52%), with progression to secondary school more realizable for boys (53.4%) than for girls (46.6%) (MoES, 2012). Child marriage and teenage pregnancies are noted as major causes of school dropout (Tumushabe et al., 2000; Grogan 2008; Muhanguzi, 2011; FIDH and FHRI, 2012; Kyomuhendo Bantebya et al., 2013; Ochan et al., 2013; Schlecht et al., 2013; Warner et al., 2013). The data above implies that a large number of girls leave school prematurely, thus limiting their ability to be productive in the labour market and, consequently, their employment opportunities and economic capabilities (Rubin et al., 2009; UNICEF, 2014; World Bank, 2017).

From an economic perspective, according to ICRW (2010), child marriage perpetuates the intergenerational cycle of poverty, retards economic and human capital progress and functions as a break on development (Rubin et al., 2009; Pereznieto et al., 2011; Schlecht et al., 2013; World Bank, 2017).

Early marriage also has major negative impacts on boys' achievements in a variety of capability domains, yet boys also have significant role in ending child marriage (Santillan, 2013 cited in UNICEF, 2015a). Studies revealed that boys are forced to leave school and take menial jobs to support their families (Kyomuhendo Bantebya et al., 2014) and that, furthermore, child marriage hinders boys from enjoying optimal health, obtaining an education, and bonding with others their own age (Lubaale, 2013).

Overall, child marriage is recognized as both a cause and consequence of gender inequality and poverty (Warner et al., 2013), and is an obstacle to achieving most of the Millennium Development Goals (MDGs) (Davis et al., 2013).

Dialectics of driving factors

In Uganda, child marriage is driven by a variety of factors, including gender discriminatory sociocultural norms (Bicchieri, and Mercier, 2014; UNICEF, 2015), acute poverty and shortage of employment opportunities (Davis et al., 2013), lack of an egalitarian/quality education system (Muhanguzi et al., 2017) and deficient legal and policy actions. These drivers can be seen at individual, interpersonal, community and societal levels.

To gain a better understanding of these contributing factors to child marriage, as well as the sociocultural environment in which child marriage can take place, this study applies a four-level ecological model of development (Krug et al., 2002). This model not only recognizes the complex interrelation of drivers of child marriage – including individual, political, sociocultural and environmental factors – but also identifies the key entry points for intervention and prevention (Powell et al., 1999 cited in UNICEF, 2015a) (Figure 3.1).

Individual-level influences are the micro-level factors, including personal beliefs and practices, as well as household-related issues, that can promote and perpetuate early marriage. For instance, growing up in conflict situations and refugee environments has been found to predispose children to child marriage due to loss and trauma, lack of security, as well as breakdowns in family networks (Rubimbwa and Komurembe, 2012; Schlecht et al., 2013). Having been raised in such a high-risk environment means children develop attitudes that adhere to and consolidate child marriage. Similarly, in rural communities where child marriage is the norm, children will be motivated to get married early (Amin et al., 2013).

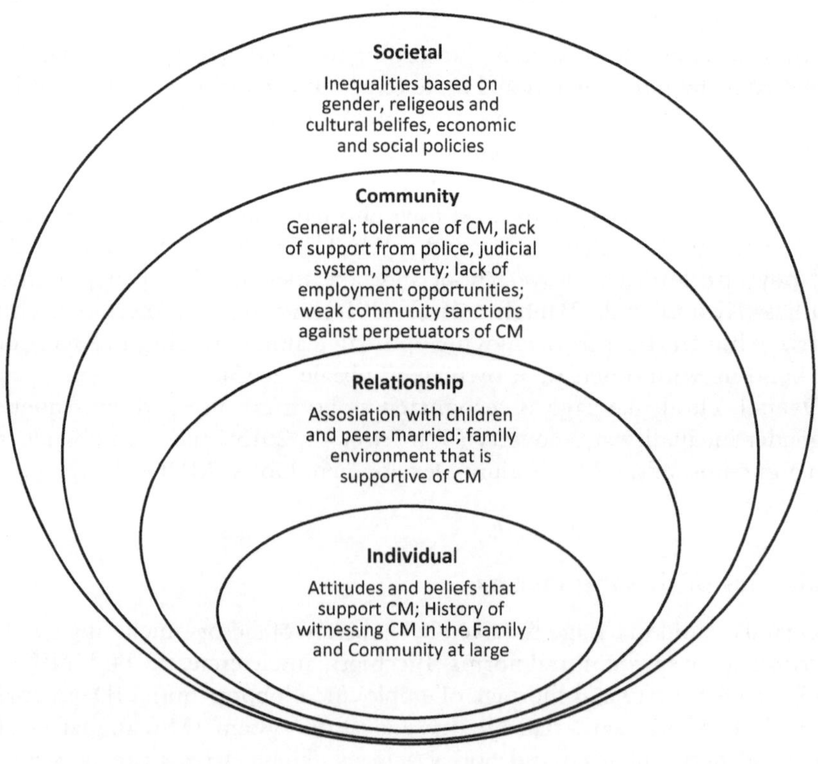

Figure 3.1 The applied ecological model.

Interpersonal-level influences are the contributing factors which escalate the risk of a girl getting married early due to her relationships with her closest social circle, that is, family members, teachers and peers.

Evidence shows a strong correlation between child marriage and the normative beliefs of parents. For instance, in some local communities sexual maturation is conceived of as being readiness for marriage (Kyomuhendo Bantebya et al., 2014). In a study conducted by Sekiwunga and Whyte (2009) in Eastern Uganda, adolescents attributed child marriage and teenage pregnancy to inadequate provision of basic necessities; lack of parental care, concern and guidance; parental negligence about children's mobility and morals; mistreatment of girls at home; children copying the behaviours of a female parent who had married early; and the role of a paternal aunt, who is the source of sexual education (*ssenga*) in encouraging girls to engage in sexual activities (Green. et al., 2009). In the same study, parents attributed child marriage to indiscipline and moral decay, peer pressure and greed for material things.

Poverty is a significant factor driving child marriage in many communities in Uganda, where the girl may be perceived as an economic asset (Rubin et al., 2009; Lubaale, 2013). Some studies have revealed that while parents may conceive of their daughters as a source of wealth due to bride price, and so force or encourage them to marry early – sometimes to old men who are financially capable of paying the bride price (MGLSD, 2007; Rubin et al., 2009; Walker, 2012; Schlecdt et al., 2013; Kyomuhendo Bantebya et al., 2014) – in poor households, girls may, on the other hand, be perceived as an intolerable economic burden, with their parents not able to meet their basic needs (Bell and Aggleton, 2014).

In traditional ethnic communities, many families see child marriage as preserving the family's dignity by protecting their daughters against early sexual initiations and pregnancy (Davis et al., 2013; Kyomuhendo Bantebya et al, 2014; Muhanguzi et al., 2017; UN, 2017;). Child marriage is also perceived as offering lifelong security for the girls (Rubin et al., 2009), with this indicating a low value being placed on girls' education – parents consider educating a girl a waste of time and resources where she is expected to marry (Rubin et al., 2009; Sekiwunga and Whyte, 2009).

However, a Health Policy Initiative analysis of Uganda Demographic and Health Survey (UDHS) data noted some contradictions between assumptions of parents and the overall behaviours of girls. For instance, parents believe that girls attending secondary school are more likely to become sexually active compared with other girls. In reality, UDHS (2006) data reveals that women attending secondary or higher education became sexually active about two years later, compared with those who have no education or only a primary education.

Parents state that girls are engaging in premarital sex at increasingly younger ages, with the problem being even more severe when they attend boarding school. Again, this perception of a worsening issue was contradicted by the survey's data, with UDHS data showing that the median age for first sexual intercourse was 16.7 for women aged 20–49 years in 2001, and a barely changed 16.6 for the women of same age range in 2006.

Furthermore, while parents assume that marriage protects their daughters from HIV infection, the 2004/2005 HIV/AIDS Sero-Behavioural Survey[4] reveals that married women aged 15–24 years were around five times more likely to be HIV-positive compared with those who had never been married.

Community-level influences are the factors which elevate the risk of child marriage in different communities and social environments, including neighbourhoods and schools. For instance, many girls get married early as a consequence of unintended pregnancy. Whether as a result of sexual abuse or adolescent sexual exploration, pregnancy can reduce a girl's options (MGLSD, 2007; Ochan et al., 2013; Kyomuhendo Bantebya et al., 2014). Since premarital pregnancy remains stigmatized and shameful, pregnant girls have to leave school (Davis et al., 2013; Harper et al., 2014; Watson et al., 2015). Without education and skills, they are unable to earn an adequate livelihood, resulting in their parents perceiving marriage as the only available choice (Watson et al., 2015; World Bank, 2017). This is in accordance with the social ecological theory of resilience, which highlights the interaction between the child's social and physical ecologies – from caregivers to neighbourhoods – accounting for distal and proximal factors, as predictors for children's resilience to adversity and their thriving development (Bronfenbrenner, 1979, cited in Ungar et al., 2013). Early exposure to pornography and peer pressure that provokes "experimentation" at adult relationships can be a concrete example of a child's social and physical ecologies (Kyomuhendo Bantebya et al., 2014).

Societal-level influences are the most significant, macro-level factors contributing to child marriage. These include religious or cultural belief systems, gender inequality, social norms, [5] and economic and social policies that can create and/or sustain gaps between different groups of people (Harper et al., 2014; UNICEF, 2015a).

Among the significant sociocultural contributing factors affecting women are low social status of women, the general schema of gender roles and power relations between men and women, lack of control over resources (Abadian, 1996; Perezenieto et al., 2011; Davis et al., 2013), low educational attainment (2006 UDHS data), and lack of available paid jobs.

Therefore, at a macro level, child marriage is a social norm, with parents making the decision to marry off their daughters below the age 18 years in compliance with empirical and normative expectations (Bicchieri, 2013). Furthermore, if they avoid making this choice, they will face a social sanction; that is, they will be seen as bad parents and their daughter's future will be compromised (Bicchieri, 2017). Similarly, girls make the decision to marry below the age of 18, in conformity with the empirical and normative expectations of people from their reference networks, including their peers. Additionally, in cases where girls disobey their parents, they will face a punitive social sanction for disobeying prescribed social rules (Ibid.).

Regarding socio-political factors, social customs are reported to be hindering the implementation of laws and policies (Watson et al., 2018) that aim to support children's rights, which in turn fuels child marriage. The study conducted by Kyomuhendo Bantebya et al. (2014) found that although the legal age of sexual consent and marriage is specified as 18 years by the Ugandan constitution, and despite the fact that the Ugandan Government strives to enforce the law on "defilement" in order to prohibit sexual relations between/with underage children, measures have only driven early marriage underground, where the rights of young married girls and their children are not legally and materially protected (Kyomuhendo Bantebya et al., 2014; World Bank, 2016; Watson et al., 2018).

National strategy on child marriage

The National Strategy on Child Marriage and Teenage Pregnancy (NSCM&TP), spearheaded by the Ministry of Gender, Labour and Social Development (MGLSD), has been developed through a participatory process and includes government ministries, foreign and local civil society organizations (CSOs), and UN agencies (UNICEF, 2015).

The Government of Uganda has striven to improve the social status of girls over the past decade. This is reflected in the measures government has taken to provide opportunities for girls' education; and to create a policy and legal environment in which women and children's rights are protected and promoted. This includes National Adolescent Reproductive Health Policy (Ministry of Health 2004 change and continuity), and a comprehensive strategy on the elimination of child marriage and teenage pregnancy (Ministry of Gender, Labour and Social Development and UNICEF, 2015). The Ugandan Government has introduced policies on universal primary education (1997) and universal secondary education (2007), accompanied by a strategy for girls' education (2015) and programs such as the additional "1.5 Points Scheme", which aims to increase the number of girls entering university. All of the above highlight the national commitment to girls' empowerment (Kyomuhendo Bantebya et al., 2018).

However, despite the Government's efforts to protect and promote the rights of women and girls, gender-specific vulnerabilities persist. This is more conspicuous in remote rural regions, where discriminatory norms and practices combined with constrained service provision and uncertain economic opportunities limit the development of adolescent girls' capabilities.

Legal framework

The Ugandan Government's commitment to improving the welfare and protection of children is reflected in various legal provisions as well as related policies, systems and structures. These include the Children's Act (2006); the Orphans and Other Vulnerable Children Policy (2007); the Universal Primary

Education Act (2008); the Universal Secondary Education Act (2008); and the Domestic Violence Act (2009). The government has also put in place an institutional framework aimed at promoting the rights of children, which includes the National Council for Children; the Uganda Human Rights Commission (Vulnerable Persons' desk); the Ministry of Gender, Labour and Social Development – Department of Youth & Children; secretaries for children's affairs appointed at all levels of local government; and the family and children's courts in the police structure.[6]

Additionally, the Government has been striving to end child marriage through such legal and policy frameworks as the Constitution of Uganda (1995), and the amendment of the Penal Code Act (Cap 120) (UNICEF, 2015a).

According to the Article 31 of the Constitution of Uganda (1995), men and women aged 18 years and above are entitled to marry and have equal rights in/during marriage and at its dissolution (World Bank, 2016). Furthermore, the third part of the same article prohibits forced marriage and demands that man and woman should give free consent to enter into marriage (Ibid.).

Article 33(6) of the Ugandan Constitution proscribes laws, customs, cultures and traditions which are against the dignity, interest and/or welfare of women, as well as those which undermine their status (Constitution of Uganda, 1995). Similarly, the Amendment Act (Cap 120) 2007 of the Penal Code specifies that any sexual relationship with a person below the age of 18 is a criminal offence (defilement), and can be punishable by a life sentence. Given the wide scope of the law, however, prosecutions regarding illegal premarital sexual relations have overwhelmed under-resourced local services (Harper et al., 2014).

The Convention on the Elimination of All Forms of Discrimination Against Women (CEDAW) (1979), which the Ugandan Government has signed up to, states that any marriage or betrothal of a child (below the age of 18) must not have any legal status. In the same vein, according to Article XXI in the Rights and Welfare of the Child (1990), child marriage should be prohibited and effective measures, including legislation, taken in order to specify the minimum age of marriage.

Although these laws provide for the protection of children from child marriage, they operate alongside other Ugandan laws which are lax with regard to the age of marriage. For instance, the Marriage Act of (1904) endorses 21 years as the age of consent but authorizes the marriage of minors if the written consent of their parents or guardians is given (Wodon et al., 2017, cited in World Bank, 2017). The Marriage and Divorce of Mohammedans Act of 1906 is silent on the age of consent (World Bank, 2016), while the Hindu Marriage and Divorce Act of 1961 and the Customary Marriages Act (1973) state that the age of consent is 16 years for girls and 18 years for boys but permit marriage of minors upon the consent of their parents or guardian. These contradictions not only hinder effective enforcement of law but also, in the long term, contribute to perpetuating child and forced marriage in Uganda.

Since 1987, efforts made to amend the old marriage laws have faced severe resistance. The Marriage and Divorce Bill (2009), proposed in Parliament in 2012, met substantial resistance from male legislators. Many saw it as a threat to their gender identities and male power, as the bill challenged the status quo regarding power relations in the family, which overemphasizes male dominance. Therefore, the bill was withdrawn and put on hold (Ministry of Gender, Labour and Social Development and UNICEF 2015; Kyomuhendo Bantebya et al., 2018). This highlights the deeply entrenched social norms related to marriage and male bias.

National development plans/policies

The Ugandan Government has put in place a number of policies and plans to challenge child marriage. The NDP 2010/11–2014/15 recognizes child marriage as a harmful social-cultural practice. Similarly, the National Population Policy (2008) acknowledges the cultural norms, customs and practices related to child marriage as harmful, with negative ramifications for the welfare and status of children and women.

The National Adolescent Reproductive Health Policy (NARH) (2004) commits to reviewing existing medical, legal and social barriers for adolescents in accessing health and information services; and to provide social and legal protection for adolescents against all detrimental traditional practices.

Additionally, the Uganda Adolescent Health Policy (2004) pledges to provide health and information services to sexually active as well as pregnant adolescents; take measures to delay sexual initiation; promote safe sexual relationships; and help postpone first pregnancy until age 20 years or later. In a similar vein, the Reproductive, Maternal, New-born and Child Health plan undertakes to reduce the rate of teenage pregnancy to less than 15% by 2017 (MoH, 2013).

The NDP also pledges to postpone early marriages through promoting access to primary and secondary education. Nonetheless, this can only be achieved through addressing sociocultural barriers to school attendance and through promoting positive cultural norms, values and practices regarding marriage within school curricula (UNICEF, 2015). Furthermore, the Gender in Education Policy (2009), initiated by the Ministry of Education, Science Technology and Sports (MoESTS), commits the government to supporting the re-entry of girls into education who dropped out early due to marriage or teenage pregnancy (UNICEF, 2015a).

The Uganda Gender Policy (2007) prioritizes gender and rights. Consequently, the government pledges to ratify, reform and implement laws that address gender-discriminatory sociocultural norms, values and practices; initiate interventions that tackle gender-based violence; advance reproductive health and sexual rights; and inform communities about women's and children's rights. However, since these commitments remain very broad, they obscure the significance of tackling child marriage as an obstacle to girls' development (Kyomuhendo Bantebya et al., 2014). For instance, while the NDP makes strong pronouncements against child marriage, there is no explicit strategic intervention for tackling the practice. Additionally, ratification of domestic relations law, which consolidates the age of marriage/consent, has been a significant challenge. Furthermore, the enforcement of current laws on defilement is documented as being weak (Development Alternatives, 2011). Access to justice is also reported as a challenge due to gender-biased laws relating to defilement (Uganda Gender Policy, 2007).

Ongoing programmes and interventions

Currently, there are various programmes by government, national and international development partners, civil society and other stakeholders, all aiming to address child marriage in Uganda. The majority of these programmes and interventions address the drivers of child marriage, which can be roughly categorized into four main themes, namely, acute household poverty, negative social-cultural and religious beliefs, inefficient mediating institutions and poor service provision (such as health and education) and lack of enforcement of laws supporting children/women (UNICEF, 2015, Green et al., 2009).

A summary of ongoing programmes and interventions addressing child marriage by Ugandan Government, international agencies and CSOs is presented in Tables 3.1, 3.2 and 3.3 below.[7]

Assessing what works and what doesn't

Although there are a growing number of interventions initiated by international agencies, the Ugandan Government and CSOs that aim to address the negative impacts of child marriage, noticeable gaps in existing interventions have been identified. For example, UNICEF, MoESTS and MGLSD initiated programmes targeting child mothers, with the aim of providing them with health and psychological care. However, none of these organizations have direct interventions that aim at either preventing or mitigating the negative consequences of child marriage.

The UNICEF supported assessment also found that although there are multiple programmes focussing on child marriage, they only cover a limited number of issues, with most interventions addressing single issues, such as sexual and reproductive health, education or economic empowerment (See for example Lawson et al., 2020). Therefore, taking a more holistic perspective on tackling child marriage, their outcomes will be limited (UNICEF, 2015a). Among the various factors contributing to deficient programming in tackling child marriage, the following are worth mentioning: poor or non-functional partnerships, weak collaborations between stakeholders, unnecessary replication of interventions, overdependence on donors, funding constraints, a poor or non-existent monitoring and evaluation system, lack of sustainability due to the absence of practical exit strategies, insufficient

Table 3.1 Ugandan Government interventions addressing child marriage

Stakeholder	*Beneficiaries*	*Issues/objectives*	*Interventions*
Ministry of Gender, Labour and Social Development	Community members; local government; medical workers; police officers; other concerned bodies.	Children's, girls' and women's rights	Medical, legal and counselling services; capacity building
Ministry of Education, Science, Technology and Sports: Gender and Equity Program	Community members; local government; religious leaders; police officers	Children's, girls' and women's rights: early marriage	Advocacy; capacity building
Ministry of Health	Students; local community leaders; parents; health workers	Girls' and women's rights: reproductive health and early marriage; gender equality	Advocacy; capacity building
National Council for Children	Parents; teachers; local government; local community leaders	Children's and girls' rights: early marriage	Material support; advocacy; capacity building

Notes: Financial support: school fees, medical, legal and counselling services fees, and so on.
Material support: office furniture, books, women's health and sanitary materials, and so on.
Advocacy: campaigning and promoting for policy intervention and empowerment through media, arts, flyers, billboards, and so on.
Capacity building: short-term training, dialogue, workshops, counselling, education; formal (school, university, vocational), and non-formal (group discussion, meeting, dancing, theatre, music, etc.).

national geographical coverage (UBOS, 2011) and poor public services (UNICEF, 2015a).

As observed in the interventions mentioned above, there is poor or even non-existent coordination between the different stakeholders – with the exception of some CSOs – regarding interventions and communications initiatives. In particular, a gap between those providing social services (e.g. public access to education), and those providing a quality and girl-friendly school environment, has been observed. Given the drivers of this harmful practice are intertwined, a balanced and integrative long-term strategy should be applied. This approach should be composed of "top-down" measures (strengthening laws and enforcement around child marriage and obligatory education), together with "bottom-up" initiatives (community-led activities, youth clubs/associations and communications dialogues) (e.g. African Network for the Prevention the Protection Against Child Abuse and Neglect [ANPPCAN]).

Closer inspection of the above interventions shows that only a limited number of interventions (e.g. ANPPCAN, Gender Roles, Equality and

Table 3.2 Selected international programmes addressing child marriage and teenage pregnancy in Uganda

Stakeholder	*Beneficiaries*	*Issues/objectives*	*Interventions*
UNICEF; RMNCH collaboration with MoH; HIV/AIDS (treatment and testing) collaboration with Baylor; APR collaboration with World Vision; Nutrition, teenage mothers, collaboration with MoH; gender and peace-building programme with FAWE and DRT	Children; teenaged mothers; local government institutions; local community and religious leaders	Children's rights; gender equality	Financial support; material and technical support; proving legal and counselling services; advocacy; capacity building; research
United Nations Fund for Population Activities (UNFPA)	Young people (aged 10–19 years); community members and health workers	Girls and women's rights: early marriage and reproductive health	Advocacy; capacity building; research
World Health Organization	Young people (aged 10–24 years)	Girls' and women's rights: reproductive health	Material support; advocacy; capacity building

Financial support: school fees, medical, legal and counselling services fees, etc.
Material support: office furniture, books, women's health and sanitary materials, etc.
Advocacy: campaigning and promoting for policy intervention and empowerment through media, arts, flyers, billboards, etc.
Capacity building: short-term training, dialogue, workshops, counselling, education; formal (school, university, vocational), and non-formal (group discussion, meeting, dancing, theatre, music, etc.).

Transformations [GREAT], Church of Uganda) are comprehensive, interactive, well-coordinated and inter-sectoral. However, according to Bicchieri (2013), the key driver of change is tackling the normative and empirical expectations of the reference networks sustaining child marriage. This entails well-coordinated, collective actions incorporating all members of the relevant reference networks and, consequently, more initiatives and communications efforts that are community-led.

Interventions taking this approach aim to raise awareness about the negative consequences of child marriage as a means of changing people's empirical and normative expectations about the practice. In so doing, families, influencers and communities are sensitized through a variety of communication channels, including community dialogues and debates; use of mass media

Table 3.3 Selected CSO programmes addressing child marriage and teenage pregnancy in Uganda

Stakeholder/Programme	*Beneficiaries*	*Issues/objectives*	*Interventions*
Action for Development (ACFODE)	Women; Service providers	Women's and children's rights; gender equality	Advocacy; capacity building
World Vision	Local communities and local government	Children's rights	Advocacy; capacity building
Empowerment and Livelihood for Adolescents (ELA) by BRAC	Girls and women (aged 12–22 years)	Women's rights: reproductive health	Financial support; capacity building through formal and non-formal education
CEDOVIP/Raising Voices	Girls; parents and any of bodies concerned about girls	Children's and women's rights	Advocacy; capacity building
Concern for the Girl Child Uganda	Girls and women; local communities	Children's and girls' rights	Financial and material support; advocacy; capacity building through formal and non-formal education
FAWE Uganda	Students; parents; teachers; community leaders	Girls' rights	Policy intervention empowering girls; capacity building
Joy for Children Uganda (Girls Not Brides)	Girls and boys (aged under 18 years); married girls; schools; local communities	Children's and girls' rights	Economic incentives for disadvantaged families; advocacy; capacity building through formal and non-formal education
Wakisa Ministries	Abandoned teenage mothers	Girls' rights: focused on victims	Material support; counselling; capacity building
MIFUMI	Adolescent girls in schools	Children's and girl's rights: child marriage	Capacity building through formal and non-formal education
TPO Uganda	Girls (aged under 18 years); Parents; Community leaders	Girls' and women's rights: female genital mutilation, early marriage and education	Advocacy; capacity building
Stromme Foundation (BONGA/ Dialogue programme)	Out-of-school adolescent girls (aged 13–18 years)	Children's and girl's rights	Capacity building through formal and non-formal education
Straight Talk Foundation	Girls and women; boys and men; teachers	Women's rights: reproductive health	Material support; advocacy; capacity building

(*Continued*)

Stakeholder/Programme	*Beneficiaries*	*Issues/objectives*	*Interventions*
Reproductive Health Uganda (RHU)	Girls and women; boys; government officials; local communities	Girls' and women's rights	Material support; advocacy; capacity building
Restless Development: Keep It Real Project	Girls and women (aged 10–24 years)	Girls' and women's rights	Advocacy; capacity building
Marie Stopes Uganda	Girls and women (aged 10–25 years)	Girls' and Women's rights: reproductive health	Material support; advocacy; capacity building
Uganda Women's Network (UWONET)	Community members	Women's rights and gender equality	Material support; capacity building
Church of Uganda Provincial Secretariat	Children, women and men (aged 12–35 years)	Children's and women's rights; gender equality	Capacity building
Uganda Catholic Secretariat Uganda Episcopal Conference (UEC)	Children; youth; church's community members	Girls' and women's rights	Financial support; material support; capacity building
BRAC Empowerment and Livelihood for Adolescents (ELA)	Urban and rural girls (aged 14–20 years)	Girls' and women's rights	Capacity building
Save the Children: Responsible, Engaged, and Loving (REAL) Fathers Initiative	Children (aged 1–3 years); married fathers (aged 16–25 years)	Children's rights; gender equality	Capacity building
Choices Voices Promises	Girls (aged 10–14 years); boys; parents; community members	Girls' rights; gender equality	Capacity building
Straight Talk Foundation (STF) and Youth Efforts (part of the SRHR Alliance): Unite for Body Rights	Students; teachers; curriculum designers and educational policy makers	Girls' and women's rights; gender equality	Advocacy; capacity building
African Network for the Prevention the Protection Against Child Abuse and Neglect (ANPPCAN)	Children, including orphans; mothers; lawyers; teachers	Children's and women's rights; gender equality	Legal and psychological services support; advocacy; capacity building
Gender Roles, Equality and Transformations (GREAT), with partners	Young people (aged 10–19 years), both married and unmarried	Gender equality	Advocacy; capacity building

Financial support: school fees, medical, legal and counselling services fees, etc.
Material support: office furniture, books, women's health and sanitary materials, etc.
Advocacy: campaigning and promoting for policy intervention and empowerment through media, arts, flyers, billboards, etc.
Capacity building: short-term training, dialogue, workshops, counselling, education; formal (school, university, vocational), and non-formal (group discussion, meeting, dancing, theatre, music, etc.).

(including printed and electronic media); production and use of information; providing formal and informal education to girls (including life skills); and promotion of peer education. Other commonly used initiatives include strengthening livelihood and vocational skills; capacity-building in financial literacy and increased access to microfinance; mentoring; and social empowerment of women, including young wives and mothers, through social media (Facebook and Twitter), print media (newspapers, newsletters, reports) and school talks, music, dance and drama (Green et al., 2009, Watson et al., 2015, Watson and Harper, 2016).

Other programmes (GREAT, ANPPCAN) have aimed at strengthening weak mediating institutions including health, education, and Police Child Protection Unit through a range of interventions such as capacity building for local governments, legal administrators, local leaders, cultural and religious institutions, and teachers in order to promote and protect children and women's rights.

While most local governments and some CSOs facilitate workshops for policy making, they do not promote the implementation processes. However, the social actors in the communications initiatives are operating as the moderator between community and the elites. In that ANPPCAN, create a hotline for reporting sexual and gender-based violence (SGBV) and violence against children (VAC), refer the victims of SGBV to the related legal agents, and follow up the prosecution process. These can be translated as bottom-up approach to promotion of access to justice for children and women.

Last but not the least, unlike some government-led programs and international agencies' interventions, the CSOs-initiated interventions – especially ones with communications approach – have applied a rather robust internal monitoring and evaluation system and presented a brief account of the outcome and impact of their interventions. However, different types of communications-based initiatives are effective strategies to address the social norms upholding child marriage provided that they are backed with social service strengthening and support for institutional development at local level, enforcement of gender-responsive laws, and consistent implementation of national policies (Watson et al., 2015; Kyomuhendo Bantebya et al., 2018).

Conclusions

Child marriage remains an ongoing issue, with more than half of Ugandan women marrying below the legal age of marriage. As outlined in this chapter, the drivers of child marriage in Uganda include sociocultural gender discriminatory norms and religious beliefs, poverty, poor institutional structures and service provision, and the lack of enforcement of laws that support children's and women's rights.

For these reasons, programmes advocating against child marriage should be focussed on keeping girls in school, improving their families' economic circumstances, confronting negative social norms and practices and promoting enforcement of laws and implementation of policies aimed at delaying marriage to later ages (Green et al., 2009). Moreover, since many contributing drivers to child marriage are interrelated, this study argues that specific interventions geared towards tackling the discriminatory sociocultural norms upholding child marriage should be planned and implemented.

Based on a critical analysis of the interventions listed in Tables 3.1, 3.2 and 3.3, and an extensive literature review, a number of gaps and constraints can be identified. Reviewing the scope, focus and impact of these interventions indicates that those implemented by CSOs, and that take a communications approach, are potentially the most effective strategies for challenging the gender-discriminatory social norms sustaining child marriage. However, for such initiatives to be truly successful, significant investment in coordination and infrastructure is required. As such, the following measures are recommended: ongoing investment in initial situation analysis, capacity development; economic strengthening initiatives; monitoring and evaluation; coordination with local government; combining communications with other interventions; and monitoring enforcement of child rights-related laws.

In a country with about half of its population (48.5%) under the age of 15 (Republic of Uganda, 2017), delaying marriage and child pregnancy can benefit girls by: providing them with the time and opportunity to make autonomous decisions, acquire vocational skills, and gain more education; reducing the risk of experiencing spousal violence and contracting HIV; and increasing the possibility of gaining more control over decision-making and household resources. Consequently, these benefits may also lead to wider social benefits, including improvements in child health and economic growth.

Notes

1 The authors wish to thank several anonymous sources for comments and suggestions from Maithili Pai, Law Clerk, Supreme Court of India.
2 As a result of rape or premarital sex between young people, at least one of whom is a minor (Uganda child marriage), families may resort to marriage as a coping mechanism in order to support the survival or protection of girls or/and their family.
3 Universal Declaration of Human Rights (1948) Article 16.2: Marriage shall be entered into only with the free and full consent of the intending spouses; therefore, early and forced marriage is a violation of human rights.
4 https://dhsprogram.com/pubs/pdf/AIS2/AIS2.pdf
5 Thus a social norm is a rule of behaviour whereby individuals prefer to conform to it on condition that the majority of people in their relevant network also conform to it (empirical expectation); and most people in their relevant network believe they ought to conform to it (normative expectations) (Bicchieri, 2013).
6 World Vision Uganda, https://www.wvi.org/uganda/article/marry-or-not-marry-18-years-age
7 Developed by the author based on UNICEF 2015, Joy for Uganda, Green et al. (2009) and Watson et al. (2015).

Bibliography

Abadian, S. (1996) 'Women's Autonomy and Its Impact on Fertility', *World Development,* vol. 24, no.12, pp. 1793–1809.

Amin, S., Austrian, A., Chau, M., Glazer, K., Green, E., Stewart, D. and Stoner, M. (2013) *The Adolescent Girls Vulnerability Index: Guiding Strategic Investment in Uganda*, The Ministry of Gender, Labour and Social Development of the Government of Uganda, Population Council, and UNICEF, Kampala, Uganda and New York.

Bell, S. A. and Aggleton, P. (2014) 'Economic Vulnerability and Young People's Sexual Relationships in Rural Uganda', *Journal of Youth Studies*, vol. 17, no. 6, pp. 814–828.

Bicchieri, C. (2013) *Social Inferences: Gender and Roles*, Penn-UNICEF Programme Advances in Social Norms and Social Change.

Bicchieri, C. (2017) *Norms in the Wild: How to Diagnose, Measure, and Change Social Norms*, Oxford University Press, Corby, UK.

Bicchieri, C. and Mercier, H. (2014) 'Norms and Beliefs: How Change Occurs', in *The Dynamic View of Norms*, Edmonds, B. (eds), Cambridge University Press, Cambridge, UK, pp. 37–54.

Davis, A., Postles, C. and Rosa, G. (2013) *A Girl's Right to Say No to Marriage: Working to End Child Marriage and Keep Girls in School*, Plan International, Woking, UK.

DELTA (2011) *Corruption and Gender Based Violence in Uganda: A Case Study of Defilement in Soroti and Hoima Districts*, Development Alternatives, Uganda.

FIDH (International Federation for Human Rights) and FHRI (Foundation for Human Rights Initiative) (2012) *Women's Rights in Uganda: Gaps between Policy and Practice*, FIDH and FHRI, Uganda.

Green, C., Mukuria, A. and Rubin, D. (2009) *Addressing Early Marriage in Uganda*, Futures Group, Health Policy Initiative, Washington, DC.

Grogan, I. (2008) 'Universal Primary Education and School Entry in Uganda', *Journal of African Economics*, vol. 18, no. 2, pp. 183–211.

Harper, C., Jones, N., Presler-Marshall, E. and Walker, D. (2014) *Unhappily Ever After: The Fight against Early Marriage*, Overseas Development Institute, London, UK.

Harper, C., Jones, N., Ghimire, A., Marcus, M. and Kyomuhendo Bantebya, G. (eds) (2018) *Empowering Adolescent Girls in Developing Countries: Gender Justice and Norm*, Routledge, New York.

International Centre for Research on Women (ICRW) (2007) *Child Marriage and Domestic Violence*, ICRW, Washington, DC.

Jain, S. and Kurz, K. (2007) *New Insights on Preventing Child Marriage: A Global Analysis of Factors and Programmes*, ICRW, Washington, DC,

Joy for Children Uganda (n.d.) *Child, Early, and Forced Marriage in Uganda*, Joy for Uganda, Uganda.

Klasen, S. and Lawson, D. (2007) The Impact of Population Growth on Poverty Reduction and Economic Growth in Uganda, Diskussionsbeiträge 133, University of Gottingen, Germany.

Krug, E., Dahlberg, L., Mercy, J., Zwi, A. and Lozano, R. (2002) World Report on Violence and Health. World Health Organization, Geneva, Switzerland.

Kyomuhendo Bantebya, G., Kyoheirwe Muhanguzi, F. and Watson, C. (2013) *Adolescent Girls and Gender Justice: Understanding Key Capability Domains in Uganda*, Overseas Development Institute, London, UK.

Kyomuhendo Bantebya, G., Kyoheirwe Muhanguzi, F. and Watson, C. (2014) *Adolescent Girls in the Balance: Changes and Continuity in Social Norms and Practices Around Marriage and Education in Uganda*, Overseas Development Institute, London, UK.

Kyoheirwe Muhanguzi, F., Bantebya-Kyomuhendo, F. and Watson, C. (2017) Social Institutions as Mediating Sites for Changing Gender Norms: Nurturing Girl's Resilience to Child Marriage in Uganda, *Agenda*, vol. 31, no. 2, pp. 109–119.

Kyomuhendo Bantebya, G., Kyoheirwe Muhanguzi, F. and Watson, C. (2018) 'From National Laws and Policies to Local Programmes: Obstacles and Opportunities in Communications for Adolescent Girls' Empowerment in Uganda' in *Empowering Adolescent Girls in Developing Countries: Gender Justice and Norm*, Harper, C., Jones, N., Ghimire, A., Marcus, M. and Kyomuhendo Bantebya, G. (eds), Routledge, New York, pp. 102–119.

Lawson, D. (2018) "Can Uganda Use High Fertility Rates to Tackle Extreme Poverty?", Nordic Africa Institute, Newsletter 11/2018 https://mailchi.mp/nai/newsletter-november-2018, Accessed 12/2018.

Lawson, D., Angemi, D. and Kasirye, I. (2020), *What Works for Africa's Poorest Children: From Measurement to Action.* Practical Action, UK.

Lubaale, Y. M. A. (2013). 'Child Marriages in Uganda After Enacting the Death Penalty for Defilement', *Psychology and Mehavioural Sciences*, vol. 2, no. 3, pp. 138–147.

Marcus, R. and Harper, C. (2014) *Gender Justice and Social Norms – Processes of Change for Adolescent Girls*, ODI, London, UK.

Marcus, R. and Harper, C. (2015) *Social Norms, Gender Norms and Adolescent Girls: A Brief Guide. Knowledge to Action Resource Series*, Overseas Development Institute, London, UK.

Marcus, R. and Page, E. (2014) *Changing Discriminatory Norms Affecting Adolescent Girls Through Communication Activities: A Review of Evidence*, Overseas Development Institute, London, UK.

MGLSD (Ministry of Gender Labour and Social Development) (2007) 'National Gender Policy', Kampala, Uganda.

Ministry of Finance, Planning and Economic Development. (2008) *For Social Transformation and Sustainable Development*, Kampala, Uganda.

Ministry of Gender, Labour and Social Development. (2007) The Uganda Gender Policy, Ministry of Gender, Labour and Social Development Kampala.

Ministry of Gender, Labour and Social Development and United Nations Children's Fund (UNICEF). (2015) *The National Strategy to End Child Marriage and Teenage Pregnancy (2014/15–2019/20)*, Ministry of Gender, Labour and Social Development and United Nations Children's Fund, Kampala, Uganda.

Ministry of Health. (2004) *The National Adolescent Reproductive Health Policy*, Ministry of Health Kampala.

MOH (2004) *Adolescent Sexual and Reproductive Health in Uganda: Results from the 2004 National Survey of Adolescents*, MOH, Kampala, Uganda.

MOH (2013) *Plan for Reproductive Maternal New Born and Child Health in Uganda (RMNCH)*, Kampala, Uganda.

Muhanguzi, F. K. (2011) 'Gender and Sexual Vulnerability of Young Women in Africa: Experiences of Young Girls in Secondary Schools in Uganda', *Culture, Health and Sexuality*, vol. 13, no. 6, pp. 713–725.

Mukuria, A., Casey, A. and Themme, A. (2005) 'The Context of Women's Health: Results from the Demographic and Health Surveys, 1994–2001', *DHS Comparative Studies*, no. 11. MD: Macro International Inc, Calverton.

Ochan, W., Nalugwa, C. and Apuuri, F. A. (2013). 'Too Young for Motherhood: Profile, Consequences and Drivers of Teenage Pregnancy in Uganda,' in The

Republic of Uganda and UNFPA Uganda (2013) *The State of Uganda Population 2013 Report*, pp. 118–130.

Otoo-Oyortey, N. and Pobi, S. (2003) *Early Marriage and Poverty: Exploring Links for Policy and Programme Development*, Forum on Marriage and the Rights of Women and Girls, London, UK.

Pereznieto, P., Walker, D., Villar, E. and Alder, H. (2011) *Situation Analysis of Children and Poverty in Uganda*, ODI, London, UK.

Republic of Uganda. (2015) Second National Development Plan (NDPII) 2015/16–2019/20, Kampala, Republic of Uganda.

Rubin, D, Green, C. and Mukuria, A. (2009) *Addressing Early Marriage in Uganda*, U.S. Agency for International Development (USAID), Washington, DC.

Rutaremwa, G. (2013) 'Factors Associated with Adolescent Pregnancy and Fertility in Uganda: Analysis of the 2011 Demographic and Health Survey Data', *American Journal of Sociological Research*, vol. 3, no. 2, pp. 30–35.

Saranga, J. and Kurz, K. (2007) *New Insights on Preventing Child Marriage: A Global Analysis of Factors and Programs*, ICRW, Washington, DC.

Schlecht, J., Rowley, E. and Babirye, J. (2013) 'Early Relationships and Marriage in Conflict and Post Conflict Settings: Vulnerability of Youth in Uganda', *Reproductive Health Matters*, vol. 21, no. 41, pp. 234–242.

Sekiwunga, R. and Whyte, S. R. (2009) 'Poor Parenting: Teenagers' Views on Adolescent Pregnancies in Eastern Uganda,' *African Journal of Reproductive Health*, vol. 13, no. 4, pp. 113–127.

Singh, S. and Samara, R. (1996) 'Early Marriage Among Women in Developing Countries', *International Family Planning Perspectives*, vol. 22, pp. 148–157.

Ssembatya, K. (2016) Uganda Child Protection Systems & The Role of Community Presentation to Learning Workshop on Community Driven Approaches http://childprotectionforum.org/wp-content/uploads/2016/08/UGANDA-CHILD-PROTECTION-SYSTEMS-MAPPING-Aug-2016-workshop.pdf, Accessed 1/2/2019

The Republic of Uganda (1904) *The Marriage Act of 1904' CAP 251*, Kampala, Uganda.

The Republic of Uganda (1906) *The Marriage and Divorce of Mohammedans Act of 1906 Cap 252*, Kampala, Uganda.

The Republic of Uganda (1961) *The Hindu Marriage and Divorce Act of 1961' Cap 250*, Kampala, Uganda.

The Republic of Uganda (1973) *The Customary Marriage (Registration) Act CAP 248 (1973*, Kampala, Uganda.

The Republic of Uganda (1995) *The Constitution of the Republic of Uganda*, Kampala, Uganda.

The Republic of Uganda (2007a) *The Penal Code (amendment) Act* (CAP 120), Kampala, Uganda.

The Republic of Uganda (2007b) *Uganda Gender policy*, MGLSD, Kampala, Uganda.

The Republic of Uganda (2010) *The National Development Plan* (NDP) 2010–2014/15, National Planning Authority, Kampala.

The Republic of Uganda (2017) The State of Uganda Population Report 2017, Kampala, Uganda.

Tumushabe, J., Barasa, C. A., Muhanguzi, F. K. and Otim-Nape, F. J. (2000) *Gender and Primary Schooling in Uganda*, IDS, Brighton, UK.

UBOS and Macro International Inc. (2007) *Uganda Demographic and Health Survey 2006*, UBOS and Macro International Inc, Calverton, MD.

Uganda Bureau of Statistics (UBOS). (2011a) *Higher Local Government Statistical Abstract: Mayuge District*, Uganda Bureau of Statistics, Uganda.

Uganda Bureau of Statistics (UBOS). (2011b) *Uganda Demographic and Health Survey*, Uganda Bureau of Statistics, Kampala.

Uganda Bureau of Statistics (UBOS). (2012a) Uganda Demographic and Health Survey (2011), UBOS, Kampala.

Uganda Bureau of Statistics (UBOS). (2012b) Uganda Demographic and Health Survey 2011, Uganda Bureau of Statistics, Kampala.

Uganda Bureau of Statistics (UBOS) and ORC Macro. (2001) *Uganda Demographic and Health Survey 2000/2001*, UBOS and ORC Macro, Calverton, MD.

Uganda Ministry of Health (MOH) (2004) *National Adolescent Health Policy for Uganda*, MOH Reproductive Health Division, Uganda.

Uganda Ministry of Health (MOH) and ORC Macro. (2006) Uganda HIV/AIDS Sero-behavioural Survey 2004–2005, MOH and ORC Macro, Calverton, MD.

Uganda Women's Network (UWONET) (2010) *'Reproductive Rights Survey'*, UWONET, Kampala. UNICEF (2014a) *Ending Child Marriage: Progress and Prospects*, UNICEF, New York.

UNFPA (2012) *Marrying too Young: End Child Marriage*, United Nations Population Fund, New York.

Ungar, M., Liebenberg, L., Dudding, P., Armstrong, M. and van de Vijverd, F. J. (2013) 'Patterns of Service Use, Individual and Contextual Risk Factors, and Resilience Among Adolescents Using Multiple Psychosocial Services', *Child Abuse & Neglect*, vol. 37, no. 2–3, pp. 150–159.

UNICEF (2005) *Early Marriage, a Harmful Traditional Practice: A Statistical Exploration*, UNICEF, New York.

UNICEF (2014) *Analytical Issues Paper on Child Welfare for the National Development Plan 2015/16–2019/20*, UNICEF, Kampala.

UNICEF (2015a) *The National Strategy to End Child Marriage and Teenage Pregnancy: Society Free from Child Marriage and Teenage Pregnancy* ***2014****/2015–2019/2020*, UNICEF, Uganda.

United Nation (2017) *Human Rights Council Thirty-Fifth Session 6–23*, 35/...*Child, Early and Forced Marriage in Humanitarian Settings*, UN.

United Nations Children's Fund (UNICEF) (2001) *Early Marriage, Child Spouses*, Innocenti Digest, No. 7.

United Nations Children's Fund (UNICEF) (2011) *Adolescence: An Age of Opportunity*. United Nations Children's Fund, New York.

United Nations Children's Fund (UNICEF b) (2015b) *A Profile of Child Marriage in Africa*, UNICEF, New York.

Universal Declaration of Human Rights (1948) [Online], http://www.un.org/en/universal-declaration-human-rights/ Accessed 27/12/ 2017

Walker J. A. (2012) 'Early Marriage in Africa: 'Trends, Harmful Effects and Interventions', *African Journal of Reproductive Health*, vol. 16, no. 2, pp. 231–240.

Warner, A., Allison M., Thompson, G. L. and Redner, J. (2013) *Ending Child Marriage: What Will it Take?* Girls Not Brides, USA.

Watson, C. and Harper, C. (2016) *How Communications Can Change Social Norms around Adolescent Girls: Lessons Learned from Year 3 of a Multi-Country Field Study*, Overseas Development Institute, London.

Watson, C., Kyomuhendo Bantebya, G. and Kyoheirwe Muhanguzi, F. (2015) *Communications for Social Norm Change Around Adolescent Girls: Case Studies from Uganda*, Overseas Development Institute, London.

Watson, C., Kyomuhendo Bantebya, G. and Kyoheirwe Muhanguzi, F. (2018) 'The Paradox of Change and Continuity in Social Norms and Practices Affecting Adolescent Girls Capabilities and Transitions to Adulthood in Rural Uganda', in *Empowering Adolescent Girls in Developing Countries: Gender Justice and Norm*, Harper, C., Jones, N., Ghimire, A., Marcus, M., Kyomuhendo Bantebya, G. (eds), Routledge, New York, pp. 102–119.

World Bank (2016) *Compendium of International and National Legal Framework on Child Marriage*, World Bank, Washington, DC.

World Bank (2017) *Accelerating Uganda's Development: Ending Child Marriage, Educating Girls (Uganda Economic Update 10th edition, 2017)*, World Bank, Washington, DC.

World Vision. (2013) *Untying the Knot: Exploring Early Marriage in Fragile States*, London.

4 A child belongs to (s)he who has paid the bride price

Customary law adoption of children in Limpopo, South Africa

Kagiso A. Maphalle

Introduction

The practice of the adoption of children under customary law is widely practised by different cultures in South Africa,[1] and goes by different names under the various traditions. It is known as *o e gapa le namane* in Sepedi/Sesotho/Setswana; *ukuthata inkomo nenkonyana* in isiZulu/isiXhosa/isiSwati; *u tshi kokodza luranga na mafhuri a a tevhela* in TshiVenda, *ku koka rhanga na vana va rona* in Xitsonga; *ikomo iragwa nekonyana* in isiNdebele; *stiefoueraanneming* in Afrikaans; and step-parent adoption in English (Mokotong, 2015:344).[2] For the purposes of this chapter, the term *o e gapa le namane* will be used with reference to customary law adoption in the South African context. This is because the Pedi and Lobedu communities discussed in this chapter generally fall under the Sepedi language, culture and tradition, although with varied dialects. Furthermore, the term *magadi* will be used to refer to the bride price, or what is commonly known and referred to as *lobola*.

Customary law adoption forms an important part of culture and tradition in South Africa and is an existing reality for many black families. It forms part of marriage processes and *magadi* negotiations, and has been put in place to provide for the welfare and maintenance of children.[3] Customary law adoption secures a home and identity for children who are under the age of 18 years; putting in place obligations for their upbringing, and securing inheritance rights (Maphalle, n.p.:99).[4,5] However, there has not been sufficient literature shedding light on the practice of customary law adoption of children in rural communities. This was reflected recently in the case of *ML v KG*[6] and in the empirical research conducted by the author in the Bolobedu and Sekhukhune area of the Limpopo Province of South Africa. Box 4.1 below provides definitions of concepts used in this chapter as they relate to customary law adoption of children.

Marriage under Lobedu and Pedi living customary law

The Recognition of Customary Marriages Act (hereinafter referred to as the RCMA) provides recognition for traditional marriages entered into and

> **Box 4.1 Definitions of legal concepts relating to customary law adoption of children**
>
> **Customary law** is defined as the customs and usages traditionally observed among the indigenous African peoples of South Africa and which form part of the culture of those peoples.[7]
>
> **Customary marriage** is defined as a marriage concluded in accordance with customary law.[8]
>
> ***Lobolo*** is defined as the property in cash or in kind, whether known as *lobolo, bogadi, bohali, xuma, lumalo, thaka, ikhazi, magadi, emabheka* or by any other name, which a prospective husband or the head of his family undertakes to give to the head of the prospective wife's family in consideration of a customary marriage.[9]
>
> An **adopted child** is defined as a child adopted by a person in terms of any law.[10]

concluded in accordance with customary law.[11] It defines customary law as the customs and usages traditionally observed among the indigenous African people of South Africa, and which form part of the culture of those people.[12] In order to understand the changes brought about by the RCMA, one has to understand the nature of customary marriage. A customary marriage can be regarded as a contract or an agreement between two families, which includes the payment of *magadi*,[13] permits polygamy and obligates all parties to perform specific duties.[14] It is more than an agreement between two individuals; rather, it is a union between two family groups, and it therefore endures until the formal dissolution by settlement of the *magadi* (Bennett, 1991:410).[15]

Given this, the death of a spouse does not automatically terminate a customary marriage because, in technical terms, a marriage is a union of two families, not two individuals. As a result, in order to make the bride wealth fully productive, the untimely death of a spouse gives rise to particular types of marriages, such as woman-to-woman marriage.

In terms of a customary marriage, the woman's childbearing potential is thought to be her most important attribute (Bennett, 1991:419).[16] If she dies, or proves to be barren, the loss of this asset can be compensated for instituting a woman-to-woman marriage. Woman-to-woman marriages are customary marriages entered into between two women for the purposes of providing children, preferably a male heir, and is a way of ensuring continuity of a house in the absence of sons. In this case, a childless woman will marry one or more women to bear children for them, or a woman without a son will marry another woman in order to bear an heir to her husband's property. In this case, either the female husband appoints a lover for her wife, or the wife selects a suitor of her own choice. This is the relationship that provides the case study for this chapter (Bennett, 1991:412).[17]

According to Bennett,[18] a woman-to-woman marriage may also be undertaken by a childless widow in order to provide a son for her deceased husband. Among the South Sotho, Pedi, Zulu, and the Lobedu, a widow who has no sons may use the cattle paid to her house from the marriage of a daughter in order to provide a son for her dead husband, and therefore an heir to his property (1991:412).[19] Woman-to-woman marriages appear to be more frequent in the Lobedu, Pedi and Venda than in the other groups mentioned above.[20] For the Lobedu and Venda, a woman who has earned wealth from divining or trade may use the money to marry a wife in her own right. These were the two most prominent occupations in previous times that afforded women economic and political power within their communities. The children of such unions take the surname of the female husband. In both the Lobedu and Pedi, another variant of woman-to-woman marriage occurs, with a woman having the right to a daughter from the house which was established with bride wealth obtained from her own marriage. If the woman has no son, and especially if her husband is deceased, she marries the girl for herself, using the bride wealth received from a daughter's marriage (Bennett, 1991:412).[21]

Woman-to-woman not equivalent to same-sex under customary law

The issue of woman-to-woman marriages was overlooked by legislators in discussions preceding the adoption of the Recognition of Customary Marriages Act (Oomen, 2000:277).[22] This is because, despite questions regarding these marriages and how the proposed legislation would address them coming up during the workshops, it appears no effort was made to ensure they were included in the legislation. The South African Law Commission's report on Customary Marriages, in a discussion about the registration of customary marriages,[23] refers to woman-to-woman marriages as marriages which are "strictly speaking" not common, do not constitute new marriages, and are not accompanied by typical marriage ceremonies and payment of *magadi*.[24] These comments were in response to questions raised at a workshop in the Northern Province,[25] the same province where the empirical research of this chapter was conducted.

The discussion below attempts to show the reasons why the RCMA failed to recognise woman-to-woman marriages explicitly in its provisions, with the ongoing debate about the recognition of homosexual marriages under customary law providing some context and rationale. As Oomen notes, the adoption of the Constitution in 1994 led to debates on the justifiability of excluding homosexuals from marriage (2000:288).[26] This argument is based on the equality clause, which prohibits discrimination on the basis of sexual orientation, as provided for in Section 9(3) of the Constitution.[27]

It is important to note that same-sex marriages and woman-to-woman marriages are not one and the same institution. Same-sex marriages take place between persons who wish to consolidate their love on the basis of their homosexuality, while woman-to-woman marriages are more concerned with procreation, protection and perpetuation of lineage, inheritance and wealth redistribution (Oomen, 2000:288).[28] Admittedly, some level of affection exists between spouses in woman-to-woman marriages, but this affection is not sexual in nature as participants' responses on this matter attest to (Maphalle, n.p.:99).[29]

The parallel that does exist between the two institutions of marriage is that the partners find a degree of security and socio-economic benefit for themselves and their children in the recognition of their marriages (Maphalle, n.p.:99–101).[30] This, however, does not take away the fact that the recognition of the two marriage institutions is based on different legal rationales. The argument for the recognition of same-sex marriages was based on the above-mentioned Section 9(3) of the Constitution, a battle which was ultimately won through the promulgation of the Civil Union Act[31] in 2006. The defence for the recognition of woman-to-woman marriages is based on the right to culture, and the right not to be discriminated against on the basis of culture, which is also provided for in Section 9(3). Woman-to-woman marriages are a cultural practice, and as a result Section 31, combined with Section 211(3), provides the constitutional basis for the recognition of woman-to-woman marriages.[32]

In giving possible reasons why the woman-to-woman marriages issue was not dealt with explicitly, Oomen notes that while the ideals behind the recognition of customary law in post-apartheid South Africa seem to be entrenched in the provisions of the Constitution, the method of ascertaining the validity of such practices remains the same as it was in colonial and apartheid South Africa (2000:281).[33] This is because of the reliance by judges and legal researchers on textbooks about customary law. These are largely based on case law, which reflect only certain aspects of customary law due to the influence of colonialism on customary law institutions.[34]

O e gapa le namane customary adoption practice

O e gapa le namane is one of the legal aspects affecting and regulating children's lives, particularly their rights to inheritance and maintenance, legal status, and the right to care. It is interesting to note that despite a Constitution that places the interests of children as being of paramount importance,[35] the treatment of this practice from a legal perspective and by scholarly works has been very minimal. Put simply, customary law adoption in South Africa has been overlooked. Mokotong notes that literature on the subject reveals very few accounts of the practice from either anthropological or sociological perspectives (2015:344).[36] He further notes that this literature, although limited, does reveal the existence and resilience of the practice in diverse black South African societies.[37] This is unsurprising given the important functions the practice serves in the lives of rural children. The courts' judgements in cases involving the care and maintenance of children under customary law were progressive, given they took place before the enactment of the Recognition of Customary Marriages Act.[38] This shows that the provisions of the Constitution do apply to customary law when they are applicable.[39]

One of the earlier cases dealing with the practice of *o e gapa le namane* was *Thibela v Minister van Wet en Orde*.[40] The plaintiff in this case was suing for damages for loss of support due to the death of her husband, who was killed by the police. The plaintiff also sued on behalf of her son, who was born from a previous relationship with another man. During the court proceedings, expert evidence was given highlighting the relationship between marriage and adoption of children under customary law. This was demonstrated by explaining that the adoption of the son born of a previous relationship was sealed by the successful negotiation and delivery of *magadi*, according to the Pedi customary law applicable to the plaintiff's tribe. The court concluded that the *magadi*, which was paid after the negotiation process between the plaintiff and the deceased's family, made the son born from the previous relationship the deceased's son under customary law.

The recent case of *ML v KG*[41] set out the requirements for the *o e gapa le namane* practice, and the process of its conclusion. It further shed light on the context and meaning of the practice, and its importance with reference to children's rights under customary law. This case is particularly important in South Africa's current constitutional era, where debates are underway on the relationship between human rights and customary law, particularly how this relationship impacts on the rights of vulnerable groups, such as children. In the broader context of the interaction between state law and customary law, this case provides a basis for comparing the provisions of the Children's Act with children's rights under living customary law. It also highlights the challenges of legal pluralism arising from the regulation, or lack thereof, of adoption of children under both official and living customary law. This case, combined with the empirical research undertaken, helps identify the gaps that exist in the Children's Act. It further shows the legislature's neglect in recognising the scope, legal content and enforceability of cultural adoptions. The Children's Act does not take account of the fact that one of the most essential provisions of the Constitution is that the best interests of children are of paramount importance, including those living under the system of customary law (Mokotong, 2015:344).[42]

The applicant in *ML v KG* alleged the existence of a marriage which was entered into and celebrated in terms of customary law. The respondent denied the existence of such a marriage, which led the court to interrogate the processes by which the alleged marriage was concluded, and its validity under customary law as well as the RCMA. This was especially important, as the validity of the marriage impacted on the rights to maintenance of the children, one of whom was the applicant's from a previous relationship. The negotiation of the *magadi* was pivotal to the claim, as it revealed two important factors regarding the validity and enforceability of the child's right to claim maintenance from the respondent. First, it revealed the respondent's knowledge of and acceptance of the child. Second, it revealed the respondent's agreement to assume responsibility of the child as his own, and to be responsible for the care, upkeep and maintenance of all matters concerning the child.

The court held that the respondent was made aware of the child's existence, and the child's move from her maternal home to the respondent's home showed that the respondent assumed responsibility for her shelter, subsistence and travel, educational and medical needs, and general maintenance. This, combined with the acceptance of such children during the *magadi* negotiations, gave effect to the *o e gapa le namane* practice and made the adoption legally valid under customary law. The marriage process was concluded by a transfer of both the applicant and children to the respondent's home. These events met the requirements for the conclusion of a valid customary marriage under the RCMA.[43]

The relationship between *magadi* and children's rights in customary marriages

There is significant literature on the practical applications and limitations of the RCMA in customary marriages. One of the arguments made is that the legislation does not accurately reflect the institution of customary marriage. This argument arises from the lack of explicit inclusion regarding the requirement of *magadi* for the valid conclusion of customary marriages (Himonga & Nhlapo, 2014:91).[44] Implicit inclusion is found in the RCMA's provision stating that marriage must be concluded in accordance with customary law. Himonga and Moore (2015:63–68)[45] discuss the implicit provisions for *magadi* in the RCMA, and state that court decisions have confirmed the payment of *magadi* to be one of the core requirements for the conclusion of customary marriages and therefore for confirming their existence. There was majority consensus among participants of the research conducted in Bolobedu and Sekhukhune that *magadi* was not only a requirement but also essential for securing the legitimacy of the children born in the marriage and their inheritance rights (Maphalle, n.p.:73).[46]

Marriage and adoption are inextricably linked in the *oe gapa le namane* customary adoption practice. Therefore, the payment of *magadi* is deeply embedded within this practice, because the marriage and adoption will not be complete unless the *magadi* is paid. It is also through *magadi* that the parental responsibilities of the adoptive step-parent are established in relation to the bride's child or children from her previous relationship(s). Children become to all intents and purposes the children of their mother's husband (Mokotong, 2015:348).[47] This Sepedi provision is equivalent to the Lobedu provision "*ngwana ke wa dikgomo*", which means a child belongs to he who has paid the bride price. The court established in both the *ML* and *Thibela* cases that *magadi* had been paid, thus giving effect to customary law adoption.

Registration of customary marriages

People in rural communities face a number of possible challenges in proving the conclusion of a customary law adoption. Although the *ML v KG* case involved persons of high social and financial standing,[48] the practice of customary law adoption is mostly concluded by people in rural communities, where challenges relating to access to courts arise for a variety of reasons. Section 4 of the RCMA states that spouses in a customary marriage have a duty to register their union. Section 4(4)(a) provides that a registering officer, if satisfied that the spouses have concluded a valid customary marriage, must register the marriage by recording the identity of the spouses, the date the marriage was concluded, any *magadi* agreed to, and any other particulars prescribed. Himonga and Moore discuss the challenges faced by spouses trying to register their marriages at the Department of Home Affairs (DHA) (2015:111–128).[49] The discussion notes how the processes followed and documents required for registration show that the provisions of the RCMA were not complied with, and civil marriages were registered instead of customary marriages (Himonga & Moore, 2015:113).[50]

There is a contradiction in the Act that, while placing a duty on spouses to register their customary marriage, non-registration does not, in fact, affect the validity of such marriages (Himonga & Nhlapo, 2014:105).[51] This renders the provision ineffective, and as Maithufi and Bekker have noted, this part of the Act will remain paper law for a long time to come (2002:196–197).[52] Himonga's and Moore's discussion on the challenges relating to registering customary marriages under the RCMA confirms this observation (2015:111–128).[53] The fact that the majority of participants in Bolobedu did not know about this provision supports what has been said by the aforementioned authors. This section of the Act is important due to the effect it has on enforcing inheritance rights, with succession often dependent on providing proof of the existence of a marriage (Himonga & Moore, 2015:128).[54]

There are also practical concerns to consider regarding the registering of customary marriages, which largely concern the officers tasked with registration. Section 4(2) states that either spouse may apply to have his or her marriage registered. However, it has been found that, in practice, officers require that both spouses be present (Himonga & Moore, 2015:249–250).[55] The DHA has issued a manual,[56] a circular[57] and the Recognition of Customary Marriages Amendment Bill, 2009[58] that have between them made it significantly more difficult for women in rural communities to register their customary marriages. This is seen particularly in the case of widows who wish to register their customary marriages in order to claim benefits (De Souza, 2013:245–246).[59]

An important and ironic aspect of the registration of customary marriages regards the circumstances in which registration often takes place. It has been shown that registration often takes place when one of the spouses passes away, and where the family has vested interests in denying the existence of a customary marriage of the deceased to someone. This is most especially related to inheritance (Kovacks et al., 2013:278).[60] Furthermore, the registration of a customary marriage may be hindered by circumstances where a party to the marriage denies the existence of such marriage, as seen in the case of *ML v KG*.

Court cases where the existence of a customary marriage was an issue of contention have shown how the registration of a customary marriage, which results in a marriage certificate, was the basis on which the validity of the marriage was sought to be proved by the courts.[61] The failure to produce such proof has led to courts dismissing cases. This was seen in *Road Accident Fund v Mongalonkabinde*,[62] where it was held that a marriage certificate provides "conclusive proof" of a customary marriage (De Souza, 2013:246).[63] The applicant in the case of *ML v KG* was fortunate to have had access to technological ways of capturing and recording the celebration of the marriage.[64] This often requires funds which most people in rural areas cannot afford, thus placing them in a difficult position when trying to prove the existence of a marriage.

The geographic location and socio-economic status of the majority of women and children in woman-to-woman marriages will most often result in this requirement not being fulfilled. This is for the following reasons:

- Lack of knowledge about relevant legislation;
- Lack of education regarding rights relating to customary marriages;
- Lack of access to relevant government institutions;
- Unfamiliarity with the registration for customary marriages;
- The perception that the woman wants to sell or take over the property of the male or female husband;
- The registering officer, owing to lack of knowledge regarding the nature and existence of woman-to-woman marriages, may refuse to register the marriage;
- The registering officer may suggest that the spouses register a civil union in accordance with the provisions of the Civil Union Act,[65] perceiving the woman-to-woman marriage to be a same-sex marriage. A civil union is equivalent to civil marriage between spouses of the same sex, and can thus be understood to exclude polygamy.

The successful implementation of the RCMA in registering customary marriages is important for children's rights in customary marriages, as it will ensure the protection of inheritance rights for spouses and children where proof of a marriage's existence is required. We therefore agree with Himonga and Moore's appeal to the DHA to "open their doors to researchers to explore registration practices" (2015:128).[66] The findings from such explorations will provide evidence-based information that can assist in amending the RCMA in order to ensure successful implementation.

Legal pluralism challenges

This chapter is situated within the theoretical framework of legal pluralism, and specifically adopts the concept of deep legal pluralism. In South Africa, customary law as a legal system has been subordinated to state law. This has led to certain categories of people – specifically women and children in rural communities – and the customary marriage institutions which they conclude, being caught in a legal blind spot. The legal blind spot is a result of the non-recognition of certain customary marriage institutions, an example being woman-to-woman marriage, under legislation such as the RCMA. This leads to women and children in rural communities not being able to enjoy rights supposedly provided for and protected by the Constitution.

In contemporary South Africa, there are two systems of law governing the life and activities of communities and individuals in rural areas. In the context of this chapter, the plurality of laws is even more pronounced due to the interconnected and complex nature of the relationship between traditional and political leadership in Bolobedu. Legal pluralism is defined as the operation of more than one system of law in a given society (Griffiths, 1986:1),[67] with Sally Engle Merry noting that every society is both legally and culturally plural, irrespective of any colonial past (1988:869).[68] This is true for South Africa because, despite its colonial history, it has a diversity of cultures governed by customary legal systems which differ both in content and application. Legal pluralism in a South African context reflects the realities and complexities of a diverse society, and the impact this has on its legal system(s). Legal pluralism here is apparent in the existence of state and non-state law. State law includes the official customary law and living customary law. Himonga and Nhlapo argue that living customary law forms part of state law due to its recognition in Constitutional Court cases such as *Bhe*, *Gumede* and *Shilubana* (2014:46).[69] They further note that living customary law originates from the community under consideration and not from the state.

The concept of legal pluralism has, over the years, become the subject of emotionally loaded debates. The issue most often addressed in these debates, and the one that distinguishes it from more common discussions over concepts of law, is whether one is prepared to admit the theoretical possibility of more than one legal order or mechanism within one socio-political space (von Benda-Beckmann, 2002:37).[70] According to von Benda-Beckmann, legal pluralism was initially introduced as a concept used to sensitise opinion about the existence of more than one system of law operating in parallel, with one system at times mirroring the intentions of the other. Now, though, the discussions relating to legal pluralism are increasingly dominated by debates over its conceptual validity (von Benda-Beckmann, 2002:37).[71]

Deep legal pluralism can be regarded as the factual situation reflecting the realities of a society in which various legal systems are observed; some officially, others unofficially. In South Africa, the common law and customary law comprise "official" legal pluralism, while these two legal systems, together with the various "unofficial" legal systems (e.g. Hindu, Jewish and Muslim law) embody "deep" legal pluralism (Rautenbach, 2010:145).[72] Deep legal pluralism recognises that multiple systems of law can co-exist without being sourced from the same authority. Multiple systems govern people's lives; communities are able to generate systems of law while at the same time being under the government of state laws (Himonga & Nhlapo, 2014:46–47).[73] In the South African context, recognition is given to systems of law other than state law. These take the form of customary, international and religious law, as provided for by the Constitution.[74]

Pluralism is part of the fabric of legal systems in most, if not all, African countries. The traditional institutions and customary laws that regulated past civilisations and societies in African have changed over the years (see Seymour, 1970).[75] Customary rules have had to adapt over time because of the significant changes brought about by colonial rule, then decolonisation. In addition to customary law, most African[76] countries are now bound by the provisions of their Constitutions, statutory law, and common law, as well as international and regional human-rights treaties.

The South African Constitution enshrines the right to culture,[77] and obliges the courts to apply customary law where applicable. This is, though, subject to the provisions of the Bill of Rights. This picture of legal systems based on customary law subordinated to constitutional and formal legal rules does not, however, accurately portray the more complex reality on the ground (Higgins et al., 2007:1662).[78]

Section 15 of the Children's Act[79] regulates the adoption of children in South Africa, effectively giving the impression that customary law adoptions are provided for in this legislation. Mokotong notes that this is unfortunately not the position, as the Children's Act does not enable children adopted under customary law, nor their adoptive parents, to benefit from government welfare or the rights enjoyed by children and parents involved in non-customary law adoptions (2015:345).[80] According to the Children's Act, adopted children are those who are contemplated in Sections 23, 25 and 239(1) (a)–(d), in terms of which a judicial act is required in order to effect the adoption. This is in contrast to customary law, with the majority of adoptions taking place within the context of family negotiations in rural communities, where neither courts nor judicial orders are deemed necessary (Mokotong, 2015:345).[81] From a practical point of view, it can be argued that the legislation's insufficient recognition of the customary law process deems such adoptions to be, in effect, illegal, with the requirement for a judicial order undermining the position of living customary law as provided for by the Constitution.

Best interests of the child under customary law

Children hold a special place in indigenous African cultures. They are important for the continuity of the family name, the succession and inheritance of family property and political positions, conferring the status of womanhood on a married woman and the final conclusion of the marriage upon the birth of the first child. At the centre of customary law marriage institutions such as woman-to-woman marriage, as well as *sororate* and *levirate* unions, is the care and well-being of children. These marriage institutions are concluded to ensure the presence of a parent to care for and provide for children, often through the process of customary law adoptions.

Customary adoption takes place in the best interests of the child, and the child's needs are couched in the context of the interests of the family.[82] The customary law concept of family includes extended family and community, where family members other than the mother and father also perform parenting functions. This is reflected in the idiom: "It takes a village to raise a child." The customary law approach is that the sentiments and support of a family exist even when not all family members necessarily have a close biological link to each other. Those involved in a family group could include a neighbour, church member or even a step-parent. Section 1 of the Children's Act includes the extended family in its provisions, going as far as to incorporate within this description any person with whom the child has developed a significant relationship based on psychological or emotional attachment, which resembles a family relationship.[83] It thus recognising the customary law principle that a child belongs to a family group, and that this is in the best interests of the child.

In addition, the Act provides for a broad definition of "caregiver", including any person who cares for a child with the implied or expressed consent of a parent or guardian. This includes the adoptive step-parent of the child.[84] These broad definitions of family member and caregiver embrace the role that extended families can play in the upbringing of a child and reinforce the fact that children are at the heart of a family and community system in customary law. African tradition honours children as blessings given by God, hence the celebrations that take place when a child is born or adopted into the family (Mönnig, 1967:103).[85] Where there are no children, the homestead is considered to have an "echo" that can only be filled by the laughter of children.

The principle of the best interests of the child is a standard also followed by the courts handling cultural adoptions.[86] The importance of this in customary law adoptions was emphasised in *Metosi v Padongelukfonds*.[87] The case did not involve *oe gapa le namane* adoption but rather an adoption by the brother of the deceased father.

Conclusion

The findings derived from this chapter require legislative intervention in two ways: first, explicit recognition under the RCMA of woman-to-woman marriages as valid customary marriages, and second, amendments to the wording of certain sections in order that they relate to the context of woman-to-woman marriages. This includes replacing "woman-to-woman marriage" with a suitable African term that clearly distinguishes these marriages from same-sex marriages. This will assist in demystifying misconceptions surrounding this marriage institution and prevent it from being used to confirm the existence of same-sex marriages under customary law, the two of which are fundamentally different.

Amendments to the legislation are proposed in order to provide fully for all marriages under customary law, making clear their legal requirements, proprietary consequences, and rights to inheritance and succession. Section 2 of the Recognition of Customary Marriages Act Amendment Bill of 2009 has the potential to perpetuate the misconception that woman-to-woman marriages are same-sex marriages, as provided for by the Civil Union Act. Instead of more efforts being made to include other types of marriages under customary law into the 2009 Act. The bill will magnify the challenges faced by spouses in woman-to-woman marriages by perpetuating the misconception that woman-to-woman marriages and same-sex marriages are one and the same marriage institution. In addition, it is recommended that the duty of supporting children born of woman-to-woman marriages be dealt with as a matter of urgency through reforms in the laws relating to the maintenance of children. This will prevent the children falling into the unfavourable position of there being an absence of obligation on the part of their mother's female husband, and a discretionary duty on the part of their biological father. It is suggested that child support be claimed upon proof of paternity, irrespective of the marriage institution of the mother.

Positive amendments to the Children's Act are also required in order to effectively cater for the needs of persons subject to customary law. This will be in line with the objectives of South Africa's Constitution, which, it is submitted, are geared towards the greater protection of children, including those living under customary law. This will also assist in improving the effectiveness of the maintenance system, as there are a huge number of people regulated by customary law and who find themselves in similar circumstances as those involved in the case of *ML v KG*. Such people should have access to state legal system services in order to enforce their rights to claim maintenance for customarily adopted step-children (Rautenbach, 2010:150–162).[88] The culturally adopted step-children should also be encouraged to approach the DHA in order that their names be changed to the family name of their adoptive step-parents or to approach the office of the Master of the High Court to claim an inheritance from the estates of their adoptive step-parents. The adoptive parents should also be able to exercise their parental rights without hesitation. Should the above change come about, the legislative recognition of cultural adoption will rightly be seen as a progressive and positive contribution to the advancement of cultural adoption.

Notes

1 Mokotong M, "O e Gapa le Namane Customary Law Parenting (Step-Parent Adoption from an African Perspective)" (2015). *THRHR* 78: 344–355 at 344.
2 Ibid.
3 Maphalle K A, Succession in Woman-to-Woman Marriages under Customary Law: A Study of the Lobedu Kingdom (LLM thesis, University of Cape Town, 2017) at 93.
4 Ibid.

5 Ibid., at 99.
6 *ML v KG* Case no 15078/2012 [2013] ZAGPJHC 87.
7 Recognition of Customary Marriages Act 120 of 1998, Section 1.
8 Ibid.
9 Ibid.
10 Children's Act 38 of 2005, Section 1.
11 Recognition of Customary Marriages Act 120 of 1998, Section 2.
12 Ibid., Section 1.
13 Section 1 of the RCMA defines this term as the property, in cash or in kind, which a prospective husband or the head of his family undertakes to give to the head of the prospective wife's family in consideration of a customary marriage. It may also be known as *bohali, xuma, lumalo, thaka, ikhazi, magadi, emabheka* or by other names.
14 Himonga and Nhlapo (2014:92) further note that traditional marriages are more group orientated, encourage polygamy as an ideal, place emphasis on childbearing and are very difficult to terminate.
15 Bennett T W, *A Sourcebook of African Customary Law for Southern Africa* (1991). Cape Town: Juta & Co Ltd at 410.
16 Ibid., at 419.
17 Bennett, note 15 at 412.
18 Ibid.
19 Ibid.
20 Ibid.
21 Ibid.
22 Oomen B, "Traditional Woman-to-Woman Marriages and the Recognition of Customary Marriages Act" (2000). *Tydskrif vir Hedendaagse Romeins-Hollandse Reg* 63(2): 274–282 at 277.
23 South African Law Commission Project 90, "The Harmonisation of the Common Law and the Indigenous Law Report on Customary Marriages", August 1998, p. 30, para 3.1.10. www.justice.gov.za›salrc›reports
24 Ibid.
25 Now renamed Limpopo Province.
26 Oomen, note 22 at 280.
27 Section 9(3) provides that persons may not be discriminated against on the basis of their sexual orientation.
28 Ibid., note 26.
29 Maphalle, note 3 at 99.
30 Ibid., at 99–101.
31 The Civil Union Act 17 of 2006.
32 The Constitution of South Africa Act 108 of 1996.
33 Oomen, note 22 at 281.
34 Ibid.
35 The Constitution of South Africa, Section 28.
36 Mokotong, note 1 at 344.
37 Ibid.
38 Recognition of Customary Marriages Act 120 of 1998; see also *Kewana v Santam Insurance* 1993 4 SA 771; *Mpeti v Nkumanda* 2 NAC 43 1910; *Mkazelwa v Rona* 1950 NAC (S) 219; *Xolilwe v Dabula* 4 NAC 148; *Mbulawa v Manziwa* 1936 NAC (C&O) 76); *Myaki v Qutu* 1961 NAC 10 (S); *Gujulwa v Bacela* 1982 AC 168 (S).
39 The Constitution of South Africa, Section, 211(3).
40 *Thibela v Minister van Wet en Orde* 1995 3 SA 147 (T).
41 *ML v KG* Case no 15078/2012 [2013] ZAGPJHC 87.
42 Mokotong, note 1 at 345.
43 Recognition of Customary Marriages Act 120 of 1998, Section 3.

44 Himonga & Nhlapo, note 14 at 91.
45 Himonga C & Moore E, *Reform of Customary Marriage, Divorce and Succession in South Africa* (2015). Cape Town: Juta & Co Ltd at 63–68.
46 Maphalle, note 3 at 73.
47 Mokotong, note 1 at 348.
48 The applicant was a former Chief Executive Officer of the Telkom Foundation.
49 Himonga & Moore, note 32 at 111–128.
50 Ibid., at 113.
51 Himonga & Nhlapo, note 14 at 105.
52 Maithufi I P & Bekker J C, "The Recognition of Customary Marriages Act of 1998 and Its Impact on Family Law in South Africa" (2002). *The Comparative and International Law Journal of Southern Africa* 35(2): 182–197 at 196–197.
53 Himonga & Moore, note 32 at 111–128.
54 Ibid., at 128.
55 Ibid., at 249–250.
56 Department of Home Affairs Manual BI 1699 (November 2000).
57 Department of Home Affairs "Circular No. 53" (20 November 2000).
58 Recognition of Customary Marriages Amendment Bill GN 416 GG32198 of 8 May 2009.
59 De Souza M, "When Non-Registration Becomes Non-Recognition: Examining the Law and Practice of Customary Marriage Registration in South Africa" (2013). *Acta Juridica* 239–272 at 245–246.
60 Kovacks R J, Ndashe S & Williams J, "Twelve Years Later: How the Recognition of Customary Marriages Act of 1998 Is Failing Women in South Africa" (2013). *Acta Juridica* 273–291 at 278.
61 *Baadjies v Matubela* 2002 (3) SA 427 (W); Road Accident Fund v Mongalonkabinde 2003 (3) SA 119 (SCA).
62 *Road Accident Fund v Mongalonkabinde* 2003 (3) SA 119 (SCA).
63 De Souza, note 46 at 246.
64 The financial status of the applicant made payment and procurement of services possible.
65 The Civil Union Act 17 of 2006.
66 Himonga & Moore, note 32 at 128.
67 Griffiths J, "What Is Legal Pluralism?" (1986). *Journal of Legal Pluralism* 24: 1–55 at 1.
68 Merry S E, "Legal Pluralism" (1988). *Law and Society Review* 22(5): 869–896 at 869.
69 Himonga & Nhlapo, note 14 at 46.
70 von Benda-Beckmann F, "Who Is Afraid of Legal Pluralism?" (2002). *Journal of Legal Pluralism* 47: 37–42 at 37.
71 Ibid.
72 Rautenbach C, "Deep Legal Pluralism in South Africa" (2010). *Journal of Legal Pluralism* 60: 143–177 at 145.
73 Himonga & Nhlapo, note 14 at 46–47.
74 The Constitution of South Africa, Sections 8, 9, 31, 39, and 211.
75 See generally Seymour S M, *Native Law in South Africa.* (1970). Cape Town: Juta & Co Ltd.
76 For example, Ghana, Kenya and South Africa.
77 The Constitution of South Africa, Sections 31(1) and 211(3).
78 Higgins T E, Fenrich J & Tanzer Z, "Gender Equality and Customary Marriage: Bargaining in the Shadow of Post-Apartheid Legal Pluralism" (2007). *Fordham International Law Journal* 30: 1653–1708 at 1662.
79 Children's Act 38 of 2005.
80 Mokotong, note 1 at 345.

81 See also *Metiso v Padongelukfonds* 2001 3 SA 1142 (T); *Kewana v Santam Insurance* 1993 4 SA 771 (TkA); *Thibela v Minister van Wet en Orde* 1995 3 SA 147 (T); *Maneli v Maneli* 2010 7 BCLR 703 (GSJ).
82 This is applicable to Pedi and Lobedu marriages, where it is said, "*ngwana ke wa dikgomo*" – that a child belongs to he who has paid the bride price.
83 Children's Act 38 of 2005, Section 1, under definitions.
84 Ibid.
85 Mönnig H O, *The Pedi.* (1967). Pretoria: Van Schaik, 103.
86 *Maneli v Maneli* 2010 7 BCLR703 (GSJ).
87 *Metosi v Padongelukfonds* 2001 3 SA 1142 (T).
88 Supra note 72, para 40.

Bibliography

Bennett, T W (1991). *A Sourcebook of African Customary Law for Southern Africa.* Cape Town: Juta & Co Ltd.

De Souza, M (2013). "When Non-Registration Becomes Non-Recognition: Examining the Law and Practice of Customary Marriage Registration in South Africa" *Acta Juridica* 2013(1):239–272.

Griffiths, J (1986). "What Is Legal Pluralism?" *Journal of Legal Pluralism* 24:1–55.

Higgins, T E, Fenrich, J and Tanzer, Z (2007). "Gender Equality and Customary Marriage: Bargaining in the Shadow of Post-Apartheid Legal Pluralism" *Fordham International Law Journal* 30:1653–1708.

Himonga, C and Moore, E (2015). *Reform of Customary Marriage, Divorce and Succession in South Africa.* Cape Town: Juta & Co Ltd.

Himonga, C and Nhlapo, T (2014). *African Customary Law in South Africa: Post-Apartheid and Living Law Perspectives.* Cape Town: Oxford University Press.

Kovacks, R J, Ndashe, S and Williams, J (2013). "Twelve Years Later: How the Recognition of Customary Marriages Act of 1998 Is Failing Women in South Africa" *Acta Juridica* 2013(1):273–291.

Maithufi, I P and Bekker, J C (2002). "The Recognition of Customary Marriages Act of 1998 and Its Impact on Family Law in South Africa" *The Comparative and International Law Journal of Southern Africa* 35(2):182–197.

Maphalle, K A (n.p.). Succession in Woman-to-Woman Marriages under Customary Law: A Study of the Lobedu Kingdom (LLM thesis, University of Cape Town, 2017).

Merry, S E (1988). "Legal Pluralism" *Law and Society Review* 22(5):869–896.

Mokotong, M (2015). "O e Gapa le Namane Customary Law Parenting (Step-Parent Adoption from an African Perspective)" *THRHR* 78:344–355.

Mönnig, H O (1967). *The Pedi.* Pretoria: Van Schaik.

Oomen, B (2000). "Traditional Woman-to-Woman Marriages and the Recognition of Customary Marriages Act" *Tydskrif vir Hedendaagse Romeins-Hollandse Reg* 63(2):274–282.

Rautenbach, C (2010). "Deep Legal Pluralism in South Africa" *Journal of Legal Pluralism* 60:143–177.

Seymour, S M (1970). *Native Law in South Africa.* Cape Town: Juta & Co Ltd.

von Benda-Beckmann, F (2002). "Who Is Afraid of Legal Pluralism?" *Journal of Legal Pluralism* 47:37–42.

Part II

Women – violence and vulnerability

5 Integrating gender and access to justice into the public policy of the African Union

Paloma Duran[1]

Introduction[2]

Across Africa, gender inequality remains a widespread issue, with much of the discrimination faced by women on the continent centred on their participation in political life and decision-making (UNDESA, 2007). Over the past few years, though, the trend has been changing, with increasing numbers of women getting the chance to take part in politics.[3] One of the main areas where women in Africa face discrimination is access to justice, especially during conflicts (UNDP, 2014). This chapter analyzes the cases of gender inequality and access to justice within the African Union (AU),[4] and introduces a dual gender strategy, used by the Sustainable Development Goals (SDG) Fund with the aim of promoting gender equality. The chapter also examines issues of women's empowerment on the continent in the context of equal citizenship and participation in public affairs, as well as the challenges faced by the AU in trying to integrate gender and access to justice into its public policy. The need to address these issues at the level of the AU requires systematizing solutions that apply universally across a large and diverse continent. It is not therefore the intention of this chapter of address individual situations of countries within the AU.

Gender equality and women's empowerment in the AU

As was highlighted in Chapter 1, of this volume, gender-related constraints bear a high cost to society in terms of untapped potential in achieving poverty eradication, health, education, food and nutrition security, environmental and energy sustainability, and economic growth (FAO, 2014). The United Nations' (UN) Third World Conference on Women, which took place in Nairobi in 1985, represented the culmination of ten years' work on gender empowerment. It was the first World Conference on Women to take place on the African continent, and gathered approximately 1,400 official delegates from 157 countries, including representatives from the AU. Governments adopted the Nairobi Forward-Looking Strategies for the Advancement of Women, which outlined measures for achieving gender equality at the national level, and for promoting women's participation in peace and development efforts.[5] The outcome of this Conference was that Member States were urged to take constitutional and legal steps to eliminate all forms of discrimination against women, and tailor national strategies to facilitate the participation of women in efforts promoting peace and development. Additionally, there were specific recommendations for gender empowerment with regard to health, education and employment.[6]

The commitment of the AU to gender equality is rooted in the African Charter on Human and Peoples' Rights, adopted in Nairobi on 27 June 1981 and entering into force on 21 October 1986,[7] with Article 2 of the Charter recognizing that

> Every individual shall be entitled to the enjoyment of the rights and freedoms recognized and guaranteed in the present Charter without distinction of any kind such as race, ethnic group, colour, sex, language, religion, political or any other opinion, national and social origin, fortune, birth or other status.

In addition, Article 66 provides for special protocols or agreements, if necessary, to supplement the provisions of the Charter. Thus, the Assembly of Heads of State and Government of the Organization of African Unity, meeting in its Thirty-first Ordinary Session in Addis Ababa, Ethiopia, in June 1995, endorsed the recommendation of the African Commission on Human and Peoples' Rights to elaborate a Protocol on the Rights of Women in Africa.[8] This Protocol was adopted in Maputo in July 2003, eight years after the initial agreement, coming into force on 25 November 2005. The Maputo Protocol provided a comprehensive set of human rights for African women, while demonstrating the goodwill and commitment of AU Member States to investing in the development and empowerment of women.[9] The Protocol was possible due to a widespread acknowledgement of the importance of women's rights and their role in development.[10] Moreover, in 2000, the UN Security Council's Resolution 1325[11] referred to the role of Women in promoting peace and security, while New Partnership for Africa's Development's (NEPAD's) 2005 African Post-Conflict Reconstruction Policy Framework[12] also endorsed the role of women, with Article 42 stating, "Post-conflict reconstruction programmes should ensure creating an environment conducive to peace, justice and reconciliation; increasing the involvement of women at all levels."

In 2004, the AU Heads of State adopted a landmark commitment to reporting on progress made in gender mainstreaming: the "Solemn Declaration on Gender Equality in Africa" (SDGEA). The SDGEA incorporates the Protocol to the African Charter on Human and Peoples' Rights on the Rights of Women in Africa, and has become a major instrument for promoting gender equality and women's empowerment (GEWE) in Africa.

In 2009, the AU Gender Policy[13] was adopted in order to advance women's rights and gender equality. The main purpose of the Policy was to establish a clear vision and make commitments guiding the process of women's empowerment as regards policies and procedures impacting gender equality, gender justice, non-discrimination and fundamental human rights in Africa. Moreover, the Gender Policy took into account numerous other AU frameworks, strategies, decisions, declarations and instruments that had bearing on the advancement of gender equality.[14]

AU gender policy (2009): main targets and achievements

The AU's commitment to ensuring the implementation of its gender policy comes through in its own instruments on gender equality, as well as the international instruments it is signatory to, such as the Millennium Development Goals (MDGs) and UN Resolution 1325 on Security and Peace. The pledges to enact a more egalitarian gender policy are further reinforced through the documents adopted by the Regional Economic Communities (RECs), the AU Member States and the AU Organs, which have all individually committed to empower women and achieve gender equality. The AU's approach to gender policy is discussed below, using the framework of commitments outlined in the AU Gender Policy.

Creation of a stable and enabling political environment

The AU has adopted the AU 50/50 Gender Parity Principle, which has been described as the most inclusive global commitment given to the equal representation of men and women in decision-making practices.[15] The protocol was adopted in 2002 in South Africa, and acted as an illustration of the Union's commitment towards addressing persistent cases of gender inequality in the region. According to the Parity Principle, the AU Organs, Member States and the RECs have a responsibility to ensure that both men and women are equally represented. These institutions must therefore ensure they gear decisions and political declarations towards eliminating barriers to women's empowerment. The three bodies are also required to correct any situation that indicates non-compliance with programmes aimed at mainstreaming gender equality.

Additionally, the AU Organs are also supposed to ensure that experienced gender experts are utilized in the development of policies promoting the mainstreaming of gender equality and associated capacity building. Also, the AU Organs, Member States and the RECs are required to develop and implement gender policies that are in line with the principles of the AU and the UN in terms of emphasizing gender accountability, justice and transparency reforms. Such policies should aid the eradication of brutality, recognize the responsibilities of both genders and assist in gender mainstreaming.

For instance, in January 2009, the Heads of State at the Africa Union Summit held in Addis Ababa declared 2010–2020 the African Women's Decade[16] (AWD), which has been organized under the theme "Grassroots Approach to Gender Equality and Women's Empowerment". One of the main aims of the AWD is to advance gender equality through accelerated implementation of Dakar, Beijing and AU Assembly Decisions on GEWE, which incorporates both top-down and bottom-up approaches. As a result, there have been some encouraging signs regarding gender equality in Africa, with some states having made advances in protecting women from sexual violence and encouraging their participation in politics and election. According to MEWC's Annual Review of the African Women's Decade (MEWC, 2012), in October 2012, the Botswana High Court provided a boost to gender equality in Botswana by striking down a discriminatory customary law that only allowed men to inherit the family home. This is a significant step forward for women's rights not only in Botswana but across continent, where many women face similar discrimination. Another big step made on women's rights was the announcement in 2012 by Swaziland's deputy prime minister that the government intended to enforce the Child Protection and Welfare Act by prosecuting men who marry underage girls. In several countries, the presence of women in parliament has made a positive difference in the adoption of gender-sensitive policies. Also, as a result of pressure by women, some countries now have affirmative action policies, such as quotas, to increase the number of women in decision-making positions.

Legal measures against discrimination

One factor which is key to implementing the protocols adopted by the AU is a robust legal framework. Despite some progress made in strengthening the legal status of women in the region, much remains to be done. Multiple legal frameworks that combine religious, customary and traditional practices can be major obstacles when it comes to promoting women rights in Africa. The frequently conflicting systems hinder the empowerment of women, as many traditions impinge on women's agency, rights and access to justice. Other barriers include weak institutional infrastructure and legal frameworks that hinder the implementation of laws promoting gender justice (see Bond, 2010).

The AU is committed to providing legal education to the public, as well as taking affirmative action protecting both genders.[17] Jurisprudence on women's rights and the SDGEA provide for the accelerated popularization and enforcement of legislation addressing issues of gender-based abuse or discrimination. The SDGEA also promotes awareness-raising regarding the legal standing of the AU on matters involving gender equality. The Member States, the RECs and the AU Organs are all committed to ensuring that legal measures against discrimination are implemented in cross-cutting ways. First, the declarations or decisions of any of the parties involved need to be made gender in mind. Second, Member States should implement gender-sensitive conventions immediately after the AU adopts them.

As a result, some achievements can be noted across Member States. For instance, in 2012 Benin passed a law preventing domestic violence, forced marriages and female genital mutilation (FGM). Other countries to have adopted laws against domestic violence[18] include Angola, Guinea-Bissau and Liberia. Rwanda's parliament provides a positive example to the world, with at the time of writing more than 61% of its members being women.[19]

Mobilization of all stakeholders

The involvement of all actors, advocates and partners involved in implementing the AU Gender Policy are necessary if it is to be put into practice. The AU is committed to facilitating tactical partnerships with various stakeholders, such as governments, international organizations, development partners, women's groups and civil society promoting gender equality in Africa. Other important interest groups include the private sector and faith-based movements. To this end, the Member States and the Organs of the AU are committed to strengthening civil society, facilitating campaigns for empowering women, and engaging in dialogue with a variety of interlocutors across Africa. The AU Organs must also focus on developing strategies for disseminating information about the AU's decisions and resolutions to various groups, raising awareness of gender rights as envisaged in the African Charter.

Validation and harmonization of RECs' Programmes and policies on gender

The AU's Constitutive Act recognizes the RECs as the foundational blocks towards achieving a united region,[20] meaning gender policy implementation in the Member States can be promoted by harmonizing programmes from different RECs in the AU.[21] The AU Organs can also show their commitment through building requisite capacity in the regions, by collaborating with civil society movements in empowering women and mainstreaming gender, and organizing forums and conferences, the themes of which relate to gender discrimination in the region.

Africa's RECs include eight sub-regional bodies.[22] These are the building blocks of the African Economic Community established in the 1991 Abuja Treaty, which provides the overarching framework for continental economic integration. Africa's RECs not only constitute key building blocks for economic integration in Africa but represent key actors in ensuring peace and stability in their regions, working in collaboration with the AU.

Resource mobilization

In 2004, through Article 11 of SDGEA, the AU committed to the creation of a Trust Fund for African Women to ensure adequate financial resources for organizations working on women's empowerment. The Fund became operational in January 2010, mobilizing resources to support programmes and institutions promoting gender equality. In its Gender Policy, the AU also commits to increasing resource allocation facilitating women's empowerment across the continent. This commitment extends to strengthening the AU's partnerships with global financial institutions in order to provide the financial support and technical expertise necessary for gender policy implementation.

In addition, the African Women's Development Fund (AWDF),[23] the first pan-African foundation supporting the work of women's rights organizations, makes grants on an annual basis to over 100 groups, organizations and institutions supporting the rights of African women. Since 2001, the AWDF has provided more than $34 million dollars to over 1,200 women's organizations in 42 African countries.

Capacity building for gender mainstreaming

The AU is committed to building the capacities of the various Organs of the AU, the Member States, and the RECs, in order to facilitate efforts aimed at gender mainstreaming.[24] The AU Organs and Member States are responsible for creating gender-sensitive organizational structures, procedures and systems. To this end, in 2000 the AU Commission created the Women and Gender Development Directorate (WGDD) to serve as the lead agency in promoting women's empowerment programmes, and ensuring capacity building for gender mainstreaming in all AU Organs, the RECs and Member States by 2020 (Mutasa & Paterson, 2015:72). Additionally, the WGDD is also responsible for ensuring that gender is mainstreamed into all AU programmes, as per the directions of the Decision on Mainstreaming Gender and Women's Issues within the AU (Gawanas, 2009).

For instance, in 2010 the WGDD put forward a bold vision in the form of the previously mentioned African Women's Decade (2010–2020), identifying ten themes which were intended to set the agenda for the coming decade, addressing one theme a year.[25] Twice a year, the WGDD convenes what is known as the AU Gender Pre-Summit, bringing together various relevant stakeholders (civil society organizations, women's rights advocates and development partners) and incorporating a much-needed gender perspective into the highest-level meeting in Africa.

In addition to mainstreaming gender in all AU Organs, Member States and RECs, the AU Commission is committed to gender mainstreaming in sectors such as social, political and economic affairs; human resources; peace and security; trade; the rural economy; and infrastructure.[26] At the level of the Member States, policies have been adopted to end discrimination against women and ensure gender mainstreaming in all these sectors (Gardner, 2007).

Promoting women's participation in peacekeeping and security

Lastly, the AU is committed to enhancing the role of women in peacebuilding activities, including conflict prevention, conflict management, conflict resolution and post-conflict reconstruction and development.[27]

This commitment echoes the one made in Article 2 of the SDGEA, which calls for,

> Ensuring the full and effective participation and representation of women in peace processes including the prevention, resolution, management of conflicts and post-conflict reconstruction in Africa as stipulated in UN Resolution 1325 (2000) and to also appoint women as Special Envoys and Special Representatives of the African Union.

The reason behind this oft-repeated commitment is that during conflict and post-conflict situations, violence against women usually escalates as well as has adverse effects on women's access to education, employment and human rights.

While subsequent policies have prioritized women's roles in peacebuilding, the reality is that Member States have shown "limited commitment or capacity … to integrate gender perspectives into conflict prevention, management and resolution processes" (Economic Commission for Africa, 2009). Despite follow up resolutions to UN resolution 1325,[28] in the years leading up to 2010, "less than 10% of peace negotiators have been women; [and] less than 6% of reconstruction budgets specifically provide for the needs of women and girls" (UN Women, 2011).

The AU Women Gender and Development Directorate has collaborated with several other commissions in the AU, including working with the Department of Peace and Security in order to develop a gender-training manual mainstreaming gender in peacekeeping operations. Also, in partnership with women's networks, the Directorate advocated with governments in order to ratify all the international African legal instruments (e.g. the Protocol to the African Charter on Human and People's Rights) on the Rights of Women. This included spearheading the process by which government officials review and amend guidelines for reporting on the SDGEA, and successfully advocated for improved reporting.

Gender equality in the AU in the context of the 2030 agenda

The 2030 Agenda is an ambitious roadmap for economic, social and environmental development, adopted unanimously by all 193 member states of the UN. The declaration made at the United Nations Headquarters in September 2015 called for "combatting inequalities within and among countries; to build peaceful, just and inclusive societies; to protect human rights and promote gender equality and the empowerment of women and girls".[29] This agenda, for the first time, specified sustainable development as the collective responsibility of governments, the private sector, civil society and citizens, in developed as well as developing countries.

There is interlinkage between Goal 5 and the other SDGs of the 2030 Agenda. For example, closing gender gaps is an important element in addressing important problems related to poverty, food insecurity, social inclusion, rural development, water and sanitation, and other issues. While there has been some progress towards improved gender equality, there is much more still to be done. Gender inequality is deeply rooted in economic, social and cultural structures; therefore, sustainable development can never truly be attained without the empowerment of women and girls. Therefore, regarding the 2030 Agenda, women's equality and empowerment is both the objective and part of the solution. All this being said, it is important that Member States put special emphasis on mainstreaming and monitoring the results of Goal 5 in particular.

To achieve the SDGs, and especially Goal 5, a human rights-based strategy is required to support women's movements and their participation in politics and public affairs (Danish Institute for Human Rights, 2016). The empowerment of women, as stated in Goal 5, includes reproductive, sexual, legal, political and economic rights.[30] The goal also advocates reducing disparities in education, which are widely experienced in Africa today. While the AU is currently integrating gender and access to justice into its public policy, the implementation of Goal 5 would further ensure the elimination of all forms of brutality towards women and strengthen efforts towards gender justice.[31] In order to further accelerate gender equality in the AU, its leaders in 2013 adopted Agenda 2063. This aspirational document sets out a vision for African society based on common destiny and shared values. The Agenda recognizes effective citizen participation in public policy processes, government accountability, openness and transparency at all levels of governance – national, regional and continental – as prerequisites for the continent's transformation. Crucially, it states,

> Investment in the empowerment of women and girls is a well-recognized development priority in Africa. Aspiration 6 of the African Union's Agenda 2063 underlines the potential of Africa's people, especially its women. The Ten-Year Implementation Plan of Agenda 2063 is committed to full gender equality and the significant empowerment of African women by 2023 at the national, regional and continental levels.

The implementation process of Agenda 2063 was designed to include public and private partnership, and is divided into different levels (including national, regional and continental levels). The Agenda envisages that achieving these interwoven goals will make a significant contribution to promoting gender equality across the continent. This vision is encapsulated in Aspiration 6, which envisages an AU where women are fully empowered in all spheres, whether socially, politically or economically.

Experience of the SDG Fund in promoting gender equality

The SDG Fund is a multi-donor, multi-agency, development cooperation mechanism created in order to implement the SDGs.[32] Since 2014, the year when it was created, the Fund has implemented joint programmes in more than 20 countries, working with 14 UN agencies to improve the lives of some 3.5 million people across the world. The main objective of the SDG Fund is to bring together UN agencies, national governments, academia, civil society and business to accelerate achievement of the SDGs, and in the process it has placed GEWE at the heart of its efforts. By directly empowering women and bringing a gender perspective to all development work, the SDG Fund has promoted gender equality as a multidimensional issue to be addressed by a range of solutions and actors. Thus, SDG Fund joint programmes are designed to address gender-related inequalities by factoring in their fundamental causes and prioritizing concrete interventions to empower the most excluded and vulnerable.

Implementing a dual strategy[33] helps advance gender equality by changing institutions, legislation, policies, behaviours, attitudes and social norms across all joint programmes. Joint programmes have, to some extent, improved legal systems with respect to women's rights, particularly those of marginalized indigenous and ethnic minority groups. Moreover, the joint programmes have addressed discriminatory practices across multiple sectors by ensuring the inclusion of women, particularly those living among the world's most vulnerable groups. The dual strategy has also contributed to raising public awareness about the importance of gender equality as a component of aid and development effectiveness, and to improving institutional structures and resource allocations in this regard.

Promotion of gender equality can be done through education, capacity building, employment and political representation, as well as by ensuring women's access to health and credit. However, there is no universal solution, and this is why gender equality programmes need to take into account national settings and needs. As a result, a wide range of innovative solutions and development partners (including academia and the private sector) are needed in order to address gender in a broad and holistic manner, as set out in the 2030 Agenda. Taking a closer look at this, the following case studies describe the experiences of four AU countries (Côte d'Ivoire, Ethiopia, Mozambique and Tanzania) regarding the SDG Fund.

Côte d'Ivoire[34]

Sociopolitical instability caused by the Civil War that started in Cote d'Ivoire in 2002, and the post-election crises of 2010, has created a situation of insecurity and vulnerability. In 2011, Human Rights Watch reported that the post-election crisis evolved from a targeted campaign of violence to an armed conflict in which forces from both sides committed grave crimes. Since then, peace deals have alternated with renewed violence, as the country has edged towards a political resolution of the conflict. This has led to the collapse of the judicial and prison system, worsening poverty and heightened inequalities, including access to basic social services and civil registration. As a result, problems of identification, discrimination and inter-community violence have risen. People, especially women, lack knowledge of key legal provisions protecting property and persons, and have poor access to institutions of justice. For example, in the case of 86% of married women in the San Pedro region, it is the husband who, without consulting his wife, decides on how household income is spent. At the national level, 32% of women who have an income cannot make their own decisions on the use of that income. Aggravating this situation are significant levels of interpersonal violence affecting women and minors, further hindering their ability to fulfil their potential. To address these challenges, the SDG Fund – along with relevant UN agencies, the national Government and local organizations – launched a joint programme[35] on poverty reduction in the San Pedro region, providing basic needs for the at-risk population, as well as assisting in their being able to gain equitable access to justice services (see Box 1).

Box 5.1 The SDG Fund in Côte d'Ivoire

The programme in Côte d'Ivoire is especially focused on providing support to women, who can access legal information and individualized counselling through legal clinics and a community network. These juridical clinics, run by the Association of Female Jurists of Côte d'Ivoire (Association des Femmes juristes de Côte d'Ivoire), offer legal aid and judicial services to women, with particular attention paid to those who have children at risk of abuse, negligence, violence or exploitation. The organization has also run radio programmes and other legal awareness campaigns. Since January 2015, approximately 13,000 people have benefited from free consultations on their legal rights in areas such as property ownership, rural land tenure, employment law, inheritance law, civil registrations and child support.

This joint programme provides a small but important glimpse into the potential of targeted local interventions in promoting gender equality and access to justice for women. Vulnerable women are now more aware of income-generating issues such as rural land tenure, commercial law, labour law, tax law and the operation of civil and judicial administrations. Such efforts have improved the social inclusion of vulnerable populations and poverty reduction in the San Pedro region, and in Côte d'Ivoire more generally. The AU will need many such successes on the ground to carry forward the momentum of more sweeping legal and institutional reforms.

Ethiopia

The 2015 Gender and Development Index (GDI) placed Ethiopia 174 out of 188 countries, with men favoured over women with regard to food, health care, education and formal sector employment. Agriculture is a livelihood source for the majority of those living in rural areas, both women and men, but while women farmers perform up to 75% of farm labour, they only hold 18.7% of agricultural land. Additionally, while women possess equal rights to access bank loans, mortgages and other forms of financial credit, they have not been able to use them effectively.

The SDG Fund programme on Rural Women's Economic Empowerment[36] has been developed to accelerate economic empowerment of rural women in two regions: Afar and Oromia (see Box 2). It has been developed as a differentiated component of the Joint Programme on Gender Equality and Women Empowerment, implemented by the Government of Ethiopia and UN agencies, and coordinated by UN Women. The programme in its design places particular emphasis on SDG Goal 5 ("Achieve gender equality and empower all women and girls").

Box 5.2 The SDG Fund in Ethiopia

The programme in Ethiopia targets 2,000 pastoralist women, and indirectly affects 12,000 household members; over 14,000 community members; 80 rural women-run producers' cooperatives (which adds up to 5,000 members); and 3,000 women members of rural savings and credit cooperatives. The aim of the programme is to improve food security, nutrition, social protection, and coping mechanisms, creating gender-responsive policy and an institutional environment for women's economic empowerment.

The programme uses the following multifaceted approaches to achieve its goals: providing inputs such as fertilizers, extension services, technology and information to women; supporting beneficiaries to manage local food security reserves and organize into cooperative groups; promoting savings and leadership; providing women with new skills in order to expand production in small-scale agribusiness; and strengthening policies and programmes promoting rural women's voices in rural producer associations, financial cooperatives, and unions.

At a community level, the inclusion of spouses and general male engagement has been employed as a central strategy to ensure women's empowerment. This has resulted in some husbands in Oromia allowing their wives to go to meetings and training sessions whenever they are invited to attend. As the targeted women also witnessed, their spouses appeared to have a better awareness of the women's rights, despite not being seen to fully change their practices. In practice, male spouses are often sceptical of their wives' attempts to go to public gatherings and training sessions, considering them a threat to their patriarchal influence and household control.

To address policy and institutional gaps on gender equality, the joint programme has joined hands with UN Women Eastern and Southern Africa Regional Office and UNDP-UNEP Poverty-Environment Initiative Africa, initiating at a country level two evidence-based research programmes[37] aimed at informing policy development in the agricultural sector. Additionally, the partnership between the International Fund for Agricultural Development (IFAD), the UN Food and Agriculture Organization (FAO) and the International Food Policy Research Institute (IFPRI) on the Impact evaluation, using the Women's Empowerment in Agriculture Index (WEAI), will produce a report regarding rural women's economic empowerment in the agriculture sector.

Mozambique

Though Mozambique has experienced positive average gross domestic product (GDP) growth in recent years, this has failed to generate significant economic diversification, job growth, inclusion of women in the labour market, or social development. Mozambique's extractive industry is expanding yet is not generating sufficient local jobs and income, particularly for the rapidly growing youth population. The prospect of economic opportunities arising from the extractive industry boom offers a wide range of opportunities for the empowerment of women. However, as indicated by various studies, women are not fully benefiting from such opportunities. Historically, women and young girls, as well as being disadvantaged economically, tend to be more exposed to the many risks inherent in extractive sector operations.

According to the World Bank, it is rare to find extractive industries where women constitute 10% or more of its workforce, in spite of evidence that they take better care of equipment, and are better at enforcing health and security standards vital for business efficiency. It has also been acknowledged that women tend to spend the income from their jobs more productively than men, which is important for the economy and the well-being of their communities. Lack of relevant skills, limited capacity to access the extractive industry value chain, and role stereotyping are among the main obstacles to women's ability to leverage economic opportunities from the extractive industries present in Mozambique. Therefore, targeted skills development and support for entrepreneurship among women, as well as policy incentives for companies, are important strategies towards gradually bridging the job gap between women and men in the extractive sector and its related value chain. The SDG Fund programme[38] in Cabo Delgado and Nampula provinces has been developed to facilitate gender-sensitive employment policies and workforce skills, as well as to improve small business production and business linkages to selected multinational enterprises (MNEs) (see Box 3).

Box 5.3 The SDG Fund in Mozambique

The SDG Fund programme in Mozambique aims to create at least 1,500 direct jobs and 1,500 indirect jobs, of which at least 50% will be for women, and at least 25% for young men and women. Towards this end, the programme will support the start-up and/or expansion of at least 250 small- and medium-sized enterprises (SMEs), of which at least 35% will be run by female entrepreneurs.

The hoped-for outcomes of the programme are as follows:

- MNEs in extractive industries comply with policies on the local purchase of goods and services, as well as environmentally friendly business practices. They should apply gender- and age-sensitive recruitment policies to hiring nationals;
- A workforce, both within the extractive industry and other businesses in the value chain, with better vocational skills and opportunities in extractive firms;
- National/local businesses capitalize on opportunities to provide environmentally sustainable services and products to the extractive industry;
- National and international decision makers have better access to data in order to formulate job-creating measures and strategies regarding the extractive industry.

In essence, the joint programme aims to address local development challenges by facilitating gender-sensitive employment policies and work-force skills, as well as improving the productive capacity and business linkages of SMEs in partnership with selected MNEs operating in the provinces of Cabo Delgado and Nampula. It is anticipated that the results of this programme will inform policy and decision makers involved in the sector, promoting women's empowerment and gender equality in the extractive sector and demonstrating best practice that can be replicated in other AU countries.

Tanzania

Despite Tanzania recording economic growth of around 6–7% over the last decade, the absolute number of people living in poverty has grown over this period. Some 28.2% of mainland Tanzanians are poor, with the incidence of poverty higher in rural areas. Women and men encounter specific and differentiated obstacles with regard to well-being. Social norms governing responsibilities and roles limit women's opportunities in the labour market, putting them in a more vulnerable position in relation to unreliability of employment and loss of income. Also, unequal control over assets and resources, such as access to land and inheritance, render women more likely to be living in poverty than men. In Tanzania, about a quarter (24.7%) of households are headed by women. In addition, women tend to be disadvantaged in the event of major social or economic shocks. For example, girls are more likely than boys to be removed from school in times of increased hardship. Another factor that puts women at risk is power relations regarding intra-household decision-making. Decisions within the household tend to be taken by men, which impacts on women's strategies to mitigate risk, including their own health care.

In meeting the above challenges, social protection policies and programmes can contribute to women's economic empowerment by enhancing the participation of women in decent employment; easing resource constraints; facilitating women's access to assets and credit; enhancing women's decision-making power over financial resources; and facilitating their access to education, health and social services (see Box 4).

Box 5.4 The SDG Fund in Tanzania

The SDG Fund programme[39] supporting Tanzania's Productive Social Safety Nets (PSSN) has been developed to assist Tanzania in eradicating extreme poverty and hunger. It also seeks to improve use of essential health services by pregnant women and children under five, as well as increasing school enrolment and attendance. This joint programme also promotes gender equality and women's empowerment by supporting a gender-responsive approach to social protection.

At a policy level, the joint programme assists – both financially and technically – the design and implementation of gender-sensitive social protection policies and ensures that basic social protection coverage is extended to the poorest and most vulnerable women and children. At the institutional level, mechanisms are put in place to ensure proper governance. Moreover, the joint programme supports the development of gender-sensitive and economically sustainable livelihood models and labour-based approaches. This is done by first undertaking a gender analysis that unpacks the different roles, needs, vulnerabilities, and aspirations of women and men, girls, and boys. Via the mainstreaming of community sessions on nutrition, hygiene, and mother and child health, the programme also contributes to improving women's health status, thereby reducing their financial burden and enhancing their productivity.

The programme focuses on operationalizing the Tanzanian National Social Protection Framework in order to strengthen inter-sectoral coordination, thereby improving the efficiency and effectiveness of delivery systems. This will allow beneficiaries to accumulate human capital, in turn improving consumption and well-being. Through ILO recommendation 2012, (No. 202) and the mandate of UN agencies, the programme supports the Government of Tanzania in designing policy that provides minimum guarantees regarding basic income security and health care needs for vulnerable women, children and youth, the elderly, and those unable to work due to sickness, unemployment, maternity and disability.

Development of policy and legislative instruments that provide extensive social protection coverage (with a strong gender component), alongside stable institutions and governance mechanisms, will ultimately benefit the people of Tanzania. It will also hopefully provide an experience that can be replicated in other AU countries.

Conclusion

Ending discrimination against women and girls is not only a basic human need but has a multiplier effect across all other development areas. It is widely recognized that gender equality is both a development goal and a precondition for achieving other development outcomes (African Development Bank, 2014). While some progress has been made towards improved gender equality, there is much more still to be done. This chapter analyzed the African Gender Policy, SDGEA, the Maputo Protocol, and other legal instruments and political declarations providing a framework for gender equality in the AU. Though Africa is undergoing changes, and women are achieving increased recognition in public and political life, the continent is still some way from reaching a situation where women have equal opportunities or rights. Women are often subjected to violence, and in many cases have limited access to education, healthcare and justice. The denial of vital resources such as land, assets, credit and even time, due to misplaced beliefs, outdated traditions, misinterpreted culture, patriarchy and power-wielding tactics impedes women's ability to maximize their capabilities. Gender inequalities in employment and earnings also mean that women have lower incomes, often preventing them from being able to open accounts in formal financial institutions (UN Women/UPU, 2015).

Through partnering with different stakeholders, such as governments, civil society and the international community, the AU has committed to improving the role of women in African society. The African Women's Decade and Agenda 2063 represent positive visions for the continent's future, while the 2030 Agenda lays out an ambitious framework for sustainable development, with Goal 5 focused on empowering women across Africa. The 2030 Agenda also makes clear problems related to poverty, food security, education, health, employment, social inclusion and the environment will not be solved without first addressing gender inequality. With these building blocks in place the real tests will lie in the political will and creativity with which these ideals are pursued, how successfully the governments of the AU can set up mechanisms to push legal and institutional reform, and the quality of data (which will form the backbone of monitoring efforts and are crucial to course correction) such efforts are based on.

Notes

1 The views expressed here are her own.
2 This chapter was prepared during the time of the author working in the United Nations. Its analysis and recommendations do not necessarily reflect the official views of the UN or its Members. The author wanted to especially thank Ekaterina Dorodnykh (Knowledge Management and UN Relations Analyst), who revised the first outline of this chapter, and Raul de Mora (Communication Specialist), who suggested some changes.
3 From 9.8% women in parliament in Sub-Saharan Africa in 1995 to 22% in 2015. See IPU (2015).
4 The AU is a continental union consisting of all 55 countries on the African continent. On 25 May 1963, in Addis Ababa, Ethiopia, 32 African states that had at the time achieved independence agreed to establish the Organization of African Unity (OAU). A further 21 members subsequently joined, reaching a total of 53 by the time of the AU's creation in 2002.
5 See: www.unwomen.org/en/how-we-work/intergovernmental-support/world-conferences-on-women#nairobi
6 See: www.5wwc.org/conference_background/1985_WCW.html
7 African Charter on Human and Peoples' Rights. Retrieved from: www.humanrights.se/wp-content/uploads/2012/01/African-Charter-on-Human-and-Peoples-Rights.pdf
8 Protocol to the African Charter on Human and Peoples' Rights on the Rights of Women in Africa. Retrieved from: www.achpr.org/files/instruments/women-protocol/achpr_instr_proto_women_eng.pdf
9 Maputo Protocol on Women's Rights: A Living Document for Women's Human Rights in Africa. Retrieved from: https://au.int/sites/default/files/documents/31520-doc-maputo_protocol_on_womens_rights_a_living_document_for_womens_human_rights_in_africa_submitted_by_the_women_gender_and_development_directorate_wgdd_of_the_african_union_commission.pdf
10 This was affirmed in the UN's Plans of Action on the Environment and Development in 1992, on Human Rights in 1993, on Population and Development in 1994, and on Social Development in 1995.
11 United Nations Security Council's Resolution 1325. Retrieved from: https://documents-dds-ny.un.org/doc/UNDOC/GEN/N00/720/18/PDF/N0072018.pdf?OpenElement
12 African Post-Conflict Reconstruction Policy Framework (2005). Retrieved from: www.chs.ubc.ca/archives/files/African%20Post-Conflict%20Recontrustion%20Policy%20Framework.pdf
13 African Union Gender Policy. Retrieved from www.un.org/en/africa/osaa/pdf/au/gender_policy_2009.pdf
14 These included the AU's Migration Policy Framework for Africa (2006); the Nutrition Strategy (2005–2015); the Plan of Action on the Family in Africa (2004); the African Common Position on Social Integration and the Social Policy Framework For Africa (2009); the Maputo Plan of Action (PoA) for the

Operationalisation of the Continental Policy Framework for Sexual and Reproductive Health and Rights 2007–2010; the African Youth Charter (2006); the outcome of the African Development Forum on Gender Empowerment and Ending Violence Against Women (2008); and the Comprehensive Africa Agricultural Programme (2003).

15 See www.un.org/en/africa/osaa/peace/women.shtml

16 The Road Map for the African Women's Decade: 2010–2020. Retrieved from: www.makeeverywomancount.org/images/stories/documents/AU_Road_map_for_the_AWD_2010.pdf

17 Protocol to the African Charter on Human and Peoples' Rights on the Rights of Women in Africa, Article 2(2). Retrieved from: www.achpr.org/files/instruments/women-protocol/achpr_instr_proto_women_eng.pdf

18 See http://evaw-global-database.unwomen.org/en

19 See http://data.worldbank.org/indicator/SG.GEN.PARL.ZS?year_high_desc=true

20 See www.un.org/en/africa/osaa/peace/recs.shtml

21 Constitutive Act of the African union. Retrieved from: www.achpr.org/files/instruments/au-constitutive-act/au_act_2000_eng.pdf

22 These are the Arab Maghreb Union, the Economic Community of West African States, the East African Community, the Intergovernmental Authority on Development, the Southern African Development Community, the Common Market for Eastern and Southern Africa, and the Economic Community of Central African States.

23 See http://awdf.org/our-work/

24 AU Gender Policy, Commitment 6.

25 The ten thematic areas are fighting poverty and promoting economic empowerment of women and entrepreneurship; agricultural and food security; health, maternal mortality and human immunodeficiency virus/acquired immune deficiency syndrome; education, science and technology; environment, climate change and sustainable development; peace, security and violence against women; governance and legal protection; finance and gender budgeting; women in decision-making positions; and the promotion of young women's movements.

26 AU Gender Policy, Commitment 7.

27 AU Gender Policy, Commitment 8.

28 Specifically Resolutions 1888, 1889 and 1960.

29 A/RES/70/1. Retrieved from: www.un.org/ga/search/view_doc.asp?symbol=A/RES/70/1&Lang=E

30 See https://sustainabledevelopment.un.org/sdg5

31 See https://unchronicle.un.org/article/goal-5-achieving-gender-equality-and-empowering-women-and-girls-sdg-5-missing-something

32 See www.sdgfund.org

33 See Dual Strategy, Report prepared by the SDGF 2015.

34 The statistics provided in the can be found on the official web page of the SDG Fund: www.sgdfund.org

35 See www.sdgfund.org/current-programmes/cote-d-ivoire/joint-programme-poverty-reduction-san-pedro-region

36 See www.sdgfund.org/joint-programme-gender-equality-and-women-empowerment-rural-women-economic-empowerment-component

37 These are Gender Gap in Agricultural Productivity in Ethiopia; and Budget Tracking of Agriculture Sector from Gender Perspective.

38 See www.sdgfund.org/more-and-better-jobs-cabo-delgado-province-and-nampula-province-harnessing-opportunities-new-economy

39 See www.sdgfund.org/joint-programme-support-tanzanias-productive-social-safety-nets-pssn

40 Additionally, please check the official web pages of the United Nations (www.un.org); UNDESA (www.un.org/development/desa/en); AU (www.au.int); as well as the SDG Fund (www.sdgfund.org) and UN agencies and Funds and programmes working for SDGs and Gender implementation.

Bibliography[40]

African Development Bank (2014). Investing in Gender Equality for Africa's Transformation. Retrieved from: www.afdb.org/fileadmin/uploads/afdb/Documents/Policy-Documents/2014-2018_-_Bank_Group_Gender_Strategy.pdf

Bond, J. (2010). Gender Discourse and Customary Law in Africa. *Southern California Law Review* 83:509.

Danish Institute for Human Rights (2016). Human Rights in Follow-Up and Review of the 2030 Agenda for Sustainable Development. Draft Paper February 2016. Retrieved from: http://www.un.org/esa/socdev/unpfii/documents/2016/National-HR/DIHR-FuR-paper_final-draft_29_02_16-Danemark.pdf

Economic Commission for Africa (2009). African Women's Report 2009 – Measuring Gender Inequality in Africa: Experiences and Lessons from the African Gender and Development Index. Retrieved from: www.uneca.org/sites/default/files/PublicationFiles/awr09_fin.pdf

FAO (2014). Gender-Specific Approaches, Rural Institutions and Technological Innovations: Identifying Demand- and Supply-Side Constraints and Opportunities in Access, Adoption and Impact of Agricultural Technological Innovations. Retrieved from: www.fao.org/3/a-i4355e.pdf

Gardner, T. MacKinney (2007). The Commodification of Women's Work: Theorizing the Advancement of African Women. *Buffalo Human Rights Law Review* 1:33.

Gawanas, B (2009). The African Union: Concepts and Implementation Mechanisms Relating to Human Rights, in Human Rights in Africa. Retrieved from: www.kas.de/c/document_library/get_file?uuid=6e7446b1-0662-d706-50c6-53879e22f65f&groupId=252038

IPU (2015). Women in Parliament: 20 Years in Review. Retrieved from: http://www.ipu.org/pdf/publications/WIP20Y-en.pdf

MEWC (2012). African Women's Decade 2010–2020: Annual Review 2012. Retrieved from: www1.uneca.org/Portals/awro/Documents/African-Women-Decade-2010–2020.pdf

Mutasa, S. and Paterson, M. eds (2015). *Africa and the Millennium Development Goals: Progress, Problems, and Prospects*. Lanham: Rowman & Littlefield.

UNDESA (2007). Online Discussion on Women, Political Participation and Decision-making in Africa. Retrieved from: www.un.org/womenwatch/daw/Technical Cooperation/docs/Online%20Discussion%20Report%20Africa%20FINAL.pdf

UNDP (2014). Improving Women's Access to Justice – During and After Conflict: Mapping UN Rule of Law Engagement. Retrieved from: www.undp.org/content/undp/en/home/librarypage/womens-empowerment/improving-women-s-access-to-justice.html

UN Women (2011). Annual Report 2010–2011. Retrieved from: www.unwomen.org/-/media/headquarters/attachments/sections/library/publications/2011/8/unwomen_annualreport_2010-2011_en%20pdf.pdf?vs=1505

UN Women/UPU (2015). Gender and Financial Inclusion Through the Post. Retrieved from: www.upu.int/uploads/tx_sbdownloader/genderAndFinancialInclusionThroughThePostEn.pdf

6 Access to justice, gender and customary marriage laws in Malawi

Lea Mwambene and Robert Doya Nanima

Introduction[1]

The impact of customary (marriage) laws and practices on women's access to justice in Africa has received a lot of attention in scholarly literature (see Bekker et al., 2006; Bennett, 1999; Mwambene, n.p. a; Mwambene, n.p. b; Ndulo, 2011; Seymour et al., 1982:11). As widely observed, customary laws are embedded in traditions or cultures that tend to promote a hierarchical or class system, and this in turn promotes the rights of men at the expense of women. For example, at the family level, only an adult man or husband is imbued with authority, which can be invoked to solve disputes and access property.[2] Women or wives, within marriage, are not equally entrusted with the same authority (Maluleke, 2012). The effect of such a system is an institutionalised mode of discrimination targeted at women.[3] In addition, the right to access justice is significantly affected by poverty, as well as the bureaucratic administrative and legal procedures of formal courts which are unfamiliar to a lot of rural women governed by customary laws.

This chapter, however, is forward looking; it contextualises poverty and critically analyses the legal strategies currently being used to promote equal access to, and positive outcomes from, justice processes for rural women who are governed by customary marriage laws in Malawi. The chapter highlights the fact that access to justice for women in a rural setting has to be evaluated against the customary and statutory law's ability to grant appropriate remedies. In this regard, access is not only limited to the existence of courts in rural areas, but also the ability of rural women to appreciate the laws and the means of enforcing their rights. It is argued that the ability of Malawi's substantive laws to enable rural married women to enjoy their rights within, and at the dissolution of, a marriage forms the yardstick with which to gauge access to justice.

Contextualising poverty, gender and access to justice for rural women in Malawi

According to a 2011 report from the Gender, Equity and Rural Employment Division of the Food and Agricultural Organisation, women who live in rural areas in Malawi are heavily impoverished. The report estimated that 78% of Malawian households are rural, and that of these 25% are female-headed (FAO, 2011:21). This is despite statistics showing that 95% of rural women are engaged in subsistence agriculture locally referred to as *mlimi*, compared to 85% of rural men (FAO, 2011:21). Furthermore, rural women do not receive remuneration for either domestic chores or farming.

With regard to patterns of mobility, the report estimated that 55% of rural women migrate to another rural or urban area because of marriage, compared to only 24% of men who migrate for the same reason (FAO, 2011:49). In their search for better employment, only 11% of rural women move to urban areas, compared to 37% of men (FAO, 2011:49). These gender disparities may also be linked to education statistics, which generally show that men enjoy a higher level of education than women.[4] As a result, women in rural areas are economically disadvantaged and find themselves restricted in terms of breaking out of the poverty gap.

The legal capacity of women in customary marriages

Malawi embraces both matrilineal and patrilineal customary marriage systems in various parts of the country (Chigawa, 1987). In order to understand how accessing justice in Malawi is gendered, it is instructive to evaluate the legal capacity of women in these two marriage systems. In a matrilineal society, three characteristics inform the customary marriage. First, the woman's lineage is used to trace the children who are born in the marriage (Phiri, 1983:258); second, the woman's lineage is used to trace inheritance of property (Cook, 1994); third, the women have custodial ownership of land (Mwambene, 2010:89; see also von Benda-Beckmann, 2007:89; Ngwira, 2005:6; Ntata & Sinoya, n.p.:14); and fourth, some societies require that upon the celebration of the marriage, the man moves to the wife's place of abode.[5]

Regarding patrilineal societies, the characteristics above are instead imbued in the man, with some modifications.[6] First, the man's lineage is used to trace the children who are born in the marriage to his kinsmen, unlike in matrilineal marriages where it is traced to the woman's eldest brother. Second, although the man's lineage is used to trace the inheritance of property, the payment of bride wealth offers the man more extensive authority over the woman, property, children, and inheritance rights (Mwambene, 2010).

On the face of it, the patrilineal system offers more benefits to a man compared to the benefits offered a woman in a matrilineal setting. For instance, empirical research by Peters and Kambewa show that in matrilineal societies the women are the owners of land, and men are limited to borrowing it for use (Peters, 2010; Peters & Kambewa, 2007). Furthermore, where a father buys land, he apportions it to his daughter(s) as the owners, and not the sons(s) (Peters & Kambewa, 2007:472). This research is, however, limited to lineage as a factor in land ownership in Malawi.

However, in both marriage systems, men often retain positions of power and authority within the kin group (Lowes, n.p.). This is because while patriarchy thrives on men having power and influence over others, matrilineality and patrilineality speak to the roles both men and women carry out due to the prevailing lineage. It follows that despite the existence of matrilineal societies the patriarchal nature of African society still places the man in a domineering position. This distorts the gender balance in society and can lead to a lack of adequate access to justice for women in customary marriages.

The Constitution and customary marriages

As widely observed, the institution of marriage is a key area where a woman's right to access justice is threatened within the sphere of customary law (Bekker & Buchner-Eveleigh, 2017). Several provisions in the Constitution are significant in this context. For example, the Constitution bars a person from being forced into marriage, [7] without consent from both parties entering into the union required. This section of the Constitution is further supported by provisions elucidating the rights of women in and after the dissolution of a marriage. For example, the Constitution requires that women enjoy the full and equal protection of the law on the one hand, as well as the right not to be discriminated against on the basis of their gender or marital status on the other.[8]

With regard to equal protection, the Constitution requires that women are accorded the same rights as men in civil law. This includes equal capacity to enter into contracts, as well as to acquire and maintain rights in property, independently or in association with others. This equality extends to other areas, such as the custody, guardianship and care of children, including the right to make decisions that affect their upbringing. Most importantly, this equality extends to the dissolution of a marriage, where the woman is entitled to a fair disposition of property held jointly with a husband; as well as to fair maintenance, taking into consideration all circumstances and, in particular, the means of the former husband and the needs of any children.[9] In addition, other sections of the Constitution refer to equality for all people in areas of economic activity, work and the pursuit of livelihoods in Malawi.[10]

Furthermore, the principles of national policy require that government adopt and implement policies embracing gender equality, ensuring the full participation of women on the basis of equal opportunities with men.[11] Equality extends to implementing the principles of non-discrimination, as well as policies addressing domestic violence, personal security, economic exploitation, and rights to property.[12]

In addition, the Constitution states that "Any law that discriminates against women on the basis of gender or marital status is invalid."[13] In order to offer preventive measures against invalid laws, Parliament is required to pass legislation aimed at eliminating customs and practices – including sexual abuse, harassment and violence; and discrimination in the economic sphere of life – that discriminate against women. Parliament exercised this mandate in the passing of a law providing for equality and non-discrimination against women in the marriage space. This is instructive in establishing how the constitutional provisions on access to justice have informed the formulation and application of legislation in Parliament.

Furthermore, section 10(2) of the Constitution requires that in the application and formulation of any Act of Parliament, and in the application and development of the common law and customary law, the relevant organs of State shall have "due regard to the principles and provisions of the Constitution".[14] This section requires the executive, the legislature and the judiciary of Malawi to be conscious of the provisions of the Constitution when applying or formulating laws. More relevant to this discussion, it speaks to the requirement for access to justice by rural women in situations of customary marriage (Singh & Bhero, 2016:3).

In addition, this provision requires the judiciary, when applying a customary law, to ensure it is subject to the provisions of the Constitution. As noted earlier, customary law in Malawi incorporates patrilineal and matrilineal systems, with the patriarchal nature of both marriage systems offering men significant power over women. As such, the judiciary is expected to balance the application of customary law in a way that ensures equal access to justice for men and women. This can be done by engaging with the constitutional principles of equality enunciated in the Constitution, which are illustrated later in this chapter.

Section 110 of the Constitution is also important, as it requires Malawian courts to exercise jurisdiction in the application of customary law in limited instances. Specifically, "... the jurisdiction of such courts shall be limited exclusively to civil cases at customary law and such minor common law and statutory offences as prescribed by an Act of Parliament."[15] This is an indication that not all customary laws are constitutionally recognised. As the court jurisprudence below illuminates, this position arguably stands in the way of improving equal access to justice, as many processes that impact on the right to access justice by women are not recognised by the formal justice system. As such, while traditional authority may apply customary law, Parliament has a role to play in passing legislation guiding the application of customary law.[16] However, as it will be shown later, the court's application of these provisions is crucial to developing jurisprudence that improves access to justice for women in customary marriages.

Furthermore, the application of customary law limits the recognition of constitutional rights, with the former seemingly embracing the values of a community rather than recognising the constitutional rights of an individual. This poses a potential limitation to access justice for women if the subsequent legislation that governs customary law does not expressly aid a woman's access to justice. Furthermore, where the judiciary does not proactively deal with customary law to the benefit of a woman's rights, the latter's access to justice is further choked.

As such, the constitutional provisions in Malawi generally point to the need for access to justice by women under customary law. This can only effectively come about through other enabling legislations passed to deal with the rights of women with regard to marriage under customary law. Such legislations are discussed in the following section.

The legal framework on customary marriages

In Malawi, customary marriages are regulated by the Marriage, Divorce and Family Relations Act (Marriage Act), [17] which consolidated all the other laws regulating marriage through the repeal and amendment of certain sections.[18] The Marriage Act provides for various forms of marriage and recognises that these different forms have the same legal status before the law.[19] This recognition informs the equal access to justice that women who are parties to the different forms of marriage systems are theoretically able to enjoy. The point of departure, however, lies in the process of recognition for some marriages, such as marriages of repute. In these cases, it is clear that court action is required. This involves consideration of various factors, such as the duration of the relationship and whether there has been cohabitation.[20]

In the context of women found in customary marriages, Section 14 of the Marriage Act sets the minimum age for entering marriage at 18 years. This is a direct response to the customary law that puberty be used as a pointer to determine when an individual is ready for marriage.[21] Abolishing puberty as a requirement, is a positive development that may go a long way in ensuring equal access to needs for both men and, particularly, women and girls found in these marriages.

In addition, the defining feature of the Marriage Act is that it accords equal rights to parties to any form of marriage, including customary law. The relevant section states, "[a] party to a marriage is entitled to equal rights as the other in their right to consortium".[22] It further states that these rights include the right to "consummation, companionship, care, maintenance and the rights and obligations commensurate with the status of marriage".[23] While this is a welcome gesture towards equal access to justice, it does not provide a framework within which to employ the principles, through a formally recognised court that has the sole purpose of exercising customary law. This leaves the application of these principles regarding women in customary marriages to the informal traditional courts, which may not be knowledgeable about current legal developments on customary laws and women's rights.

Court jurisprudence on access to justice and customary marriages

Various cases under customary law have been brought before the Malawian courts, most of which have been adjudicated on the basis of prevailing customary law. A look at the 2009 case of *Marko Mapsyele v Joyce Mapsyele* is instructive in this regard.[24] Here, the appellant and the respondent had married under customary law, with the marriage lasting 20 years before the appellant sought a divorce on the grounds of cruelty by the respondent.[25] On appeal, the High Court of Malawi held that a customary marriage placed a duty on the part of the appellant to provide a house for the respondent. As such, it was ordered that the appellant built a house for the respondent, since the lower court's order that the respondent should leave the matrimonial home would render her and her children homeless. Furthermore, the court set aside monetary compensation in lieu of a house, ordering that the respondent stay in the matrimonial home pending the appellant's construction of said house.

This case is instructive because, perhaps due to it relating to a customary marriage, it presents a rather simplistic approach to issues of access to justice and gender equality. The case relates to the requirement that a man provide his wife with a home to stay in during the term of a marriage, and at its dissolution. However, no reference is made to the existing jurisprudence on equality, freedom from discrimination, and the rights of a woman at the dissolution of a marriage. This lack of engagement with key constitutional provisions arguably waters down the prospective development of jurisprudence relating to women's access to justice, and gender equality in the context of customary marriages. Instead, the approach adopted by the court in this case demonstrates an embracing of patriarchy, with it being used as a tool to ensure the man still provides for the woman at the termination of the customary marriage.

In *Malewezi v Malewezi*,[26] a subsequent case with similar material facts, the judge took a different approach. In this case, the appellant had filed for divorce in the magistrates' court on the grounds that the customary marriage had irretrievably broken down due to infidelity by the respondent. In his approach, the judge, just as in *Mapsyele,* did not refer to any constitutional or statutory provisions. Instead, an engagement with decided cases was used to buttress the judgment. For instance, with regard to the need to share property arising out of a dissolution of marriage, cases such as *Gwanda Chakuamba v Electoral Commission* were used.[27] In addition, with regard to the implication that joint ownership is deduced from the fact there was a subsequent marriage, reliance was placed on *Malinki v Malinki.*[28] This approach indicated a shift from the substantive fact-based situation in *Mapsyele*, to a more principle-oriented stance in *Malewezi*. The principle used, however, was borrowed from common law and civil law, leading to a static interpretation that did not develop customary law in any way.[29] In a similar vein, regarding the lack of engagement with the Constitution, its key provisions should have been addressed in light of Malawi's patrilineal and matrilineal marriage systems having implications for equal access to justice.

A drastic point of departure came in the 2014 case of *Kishindo v Kishindo.*[30] Following the dissolution of their marriage by a magistrate's court, the appellant requested the court dispose of matrimonial property acquired during the marriage. The parties to the appeal had amassed various houses in addition to the matrimonial home, and the court grappled with the question of how many homes the wife should be entitled to at the dissolution of the marriage. The court held that it was unfair, upon the dissolution of marriage, to consider the intention of the parties at the time of acquiring the property, unless it was expressly stated that the property would not be affected by a divorce.

In the context of this chapter, it is important to highlight how the court dealt with issues of access to justice by a woman, and gender equality. In this case, the court opted to apply the constitutional principles of equality as the yardstick for applying customary law. This was in line with the notion that the application of customary law has to be subject to the constitution.[31] As such, it is correct to state that the use of fairness should be a subjective standard based on the principles of reasonableness, comity, proportionality and solidarity.[32] Although the court did not offer a definition of these concepts, the effect of earlier decisions indicated the bounds of their application as an adumbration rather than a limitation of the right to matrimonial property.[33] This decision therefore represents an expansive application of the right to equality and the rights of women to own property under customary law.

More importantly, the court contextualised the existence of matrilineal and patrilineal societies in the wake of the constitutional recognition of women's right to full and equal protection by the law, the right to non-discrimination on the basis of their gender or marital status, and to a fair disposition of jointly held property. The court was of the view that under customary law a man has an obligation to provide his wife with a house when he marries, and a divorce does not absolve him of that responsibility.[34] In the *chitengwa* matrilineal custom, the husband is obliged to build a matrimonial house in his village, rather than another place where the woman might wish to live. The decision in *Kishindo* applies equality on the basis of fairness and reasonableness, with due regard to the husband and surviving children. It is suggested that this purposive or generous approach seeks to ensure that equality is not given a blanket application, but rather a cautious approach which balances both the rights of the woman and the man.[35] It is because, under the *chitengwa* matrilineal custom, the man is still obliged to build the customary home for the wife.

Conclusion and recommendations

This chapter critically set out to contextualise poverty and analyse the legal strategies currently being used to promote equal access to and positive outcomes from justice processes for rural women in Malawi. The constitutional framework shows an intent to ensure equality and non-discrimination as a basis for creating an enabling environment for equal access to justice processes within the context of customary marriages. This intent can be seen in the latest court jurisprudence, which seeks to improve women's access to justice and gender equality in the context of customary marriages.

This intent is thwarted by legislative strategies that seem to be directed at elite women engaged in customary marriage rather than rural local women in typical customary marriages. Borrowing from Durojaye and Oluduro's (2016:315) proposition, we therefore advocate that legal interventions seeking to improve women's right to access justice should ask questions that speak to African rural woman's situational challenges. As such, any legal strategy addressing challenges to accessing justice and gender issues in the context of customary marriages should be informed by the justice needs of rural women.

In a similar vein, enforcement of the constitutional right to equality requires that rural women in customary marriages have access to justice and gender equality processes. This is because poverty, low levels of education, patriarchal power relations and limited mobility exacerbates such women's status in a rural setting. Therefore, the emphasis should shift to taking stock of the impact of legal strategies on women affected by patriarchal customary practices. This can be enforced through empirical studies, mass mobilisation and sensitisation workshops in communities governed by customary laws.

Notes

1 This chapter is based on research supported, in part, by the National Research Foundation of South Africa (NRF), Unique Grant No. 99216, and the Senate Research Funds from the University of the Western Cape. Any opinion, finding and conclusions or recommendations expressed in this material is that of the author and the NRF does not accept any liability in this regard.

2 see *Gumede v President of the Republic of South Africa and Others* Case No 4225/2006 Durban and Coast Local Division, 13 June 2008, unreported para 18.

3 see *Bhe and Others v Khayelitsha Magistrate and Others* 2005 (1) SA 580 (CC).

4 The Malawi Demographic and Health Survey 2015–2016, carried out by the National Statistical Office, indicates that 12% of women and 5% of men have no education. A close look at the statistics shows the perception of education level is attributed to primary school education. See the Malawi 2015–2016 Demographic and Health Survey, available at https://dhsprogram.com/pubs/pdf/SR237/SR237.pdf (accessed 15 August 2018).

5 This is the position in some communities in Malawi that practice *chikamwini* matrilineal marriages. The point of departure is in *chitengwa* matrilineal marriages; in which case where the woman moves to the man's village, the children still belong to the lineage of the woman.

6 These differences play a key role in where the matrimonial home is constructed, which is an issue that Malawian Courts have had to grapple with.

7 Constitution of the Republic of Malawi, 2010, s 22(4).

8 Ibid., s 24(1).

9 Ibid.

10 This is in line with the need to look as livelihoods as an extension of the right to live that emerging jurisprudence from similar jurisdictions, such as Uganda, point to. For a discussion on this, see *Salvatori Abuki and Another vs. The Attorney General,* Constitutional Court Case 2 of 1997.

11 Principle 13 (a) (i) of the national principles of the Constitution.
12 Principle 13 (a) (ii)-(iii) of the national principles of the Constitution.
13 Constitution of the Republic of Malawi, 2010, s 24(2).
14 Ibid., s 10(2).
15 Ibid., s 110(2).
16 Section 212 (1) states that the National legislation may provide for a role for traditional leadership as an institution at local level on matters affecting local communities.
17 Marriage, Divorce and Family Relations Act No. 5 of 2015.
18 The laws that have been repealed include the Marriage Act, Cap 25-1, the African Marriage (Christian Rites) Registration Act, Cap 25-02, the Asiatics (Marriage, Divorce and Succession) Act, Cap 25-3, the Divorce Act, Cap 25-4, the Married Women (Maintenance) Act, Cap 25-5, and the Maintenance Orders (Enforcement) Act, Cap 26-4.
19 Under section 12, a civil, customary, religious marriage; and marriage by reputation or permanent cohabitation, have the same legal status.
20 Marriage, Divorce and Family Relations Act No. 5 of 2015, s 13.
21 Ibid., s 14, and the memorandum to the section.
22 Ibid., s 48.
23 Ibid., s 48(2)
24 *Mapsyele v Mapsyele* (67 of 2007) [2009] MWHC 41 (25 March 2009).
25 While cruelty was a ground given for divorce in a customary marriage, the same was not required in other (e.g. civil) marriages. This represented a lack of equality with regard to the grounds for divorce available to women under customary marriages and other kinds of marriages.
26 *Malewezi v Malewezi* [2009] MWHC 37.
27 *Gwanda Chakuamba v Electoral Commission*, Civil Cause No. 74 of 1998.
28 *Malinki v Malinki* 9 Malawi Law Reports 441.
29 This approach is dangerous when used to distribute land, as customary law principles on land and property ownership lead to consequences that are different under statutory or common law. See discussion in this chapter regarding *Kishindo v Kishindo* High Court Civil Case 397 of 2013 [2014] MWHC 2 (8 October 2014). Furthermore, see persuasive jurisprudence from South Africa in *Bhe and Others v Khayelitsha Magistrate and Others* 2005 (1) SA 580 (CC); in which the Constitutional Court of South Africa stated that

> When dealing with indigenous law every attempt should be made to avoid the tendency of construing indigenous law concepts in the light of common law concepts or concepts foreign to indigenous law. There are obvious dangers in such an approach. These two systems of law developed in two different situations, under different cultures and in response to different conditions.

30 *Kishindo v Kishindo* High Court Civil Case 397 of 2013 [2014] MWHC 2 (8 October 2014).
31 see Constitution of the Republic of Malawi, 2010, s 10(2).
32 In *Kishindo*, the Court was of the view that these principles are wider than those stipulated in Section 24 (1) (b) (i) of the Constitution and are therefore an adumbration of the right, not a limitation.
33 see *Matimati v Chimwala* (1964–1966) ALR (MAL) 34; *Regina v Damaseki* (1961–1963) ALR (Mal) 69.
34 see *Matimati v Chimwala* (1964–1966) ALR (MAL) 34, 36, lines 26–37.
35 Questions with regard applying equality as an objective or subjective standard come to the fore. An engagement of these is, however, beyond the scope of this chapter.

Bibliography

Bekker, J. C., and Buchner-Eveleigh, M. (2017). The legal character of ancillary customary marriages. *De Jure*, *50*(1), 80–96.

Bekker, J. C., Rautenbach, C., and Goolam, N. M. (2006). *Introduction to legal pluralism in South Africa*. Durban: LexisNexis Butterworths.

von Benda-Beckmann, F. (2007). *Legal pluralism in Malawi: Historical development 1858–1970 and emerging issues* (No. 24). Zomba: Kachere Series.

Bennett, T. W. (1999). *Human rights and African customary law under the South African constitution*. Cape Town: Juta.

Chigawa, M. (1987). Report on customary law and social development: De jure marriages vis a vis de facto marriages at customary law in Malawi. Chancellor College, Malawi.

Cook, R. J. (1994). State accountability under the convention on the elimination of all forms of discrimination against women. In: Cook, R. J. (ed.) *Human rights of women: National and international perspectives* (pp. 1–36). Pennsylvania: University of Pennsylvania Press.

Durojaye, E., and Oluduro, O. (2016). The African commission on human and people's rights and the woman question. *Feminist Legal Studies*, *24*(3), 315–336.

FAO (Gender, Equity and Rural Employment Division) (2011) Gender inequalities in rural employment in Malawi: An overview. Available at: www.fao.org/docrep/016/ap092e/ap092e00.pdf (accessed 15 August 2018).

Lowes, S. (n.p.). Matrilineal kinship and spousal cooperation: Evidence from the matrilineal belt. Unpublished manuscript. Available at: https://scholar.harvard.edu/files/slowes/files/lowes_matrilineal.pdf (accessed 25 July 2018).

Maluleke, M. J. (2012). Culture, tradition, custom, law and gender equality. *Potchefstroom Electronic Law Journal/Potchefstroomse Elektroniese Regsblad*, *15*(1), 1–22.

Mwambene, L. (n.p. a). Divorce in matrilineal Customary Law marriage in Malawi: A comparative analysis with the patrilineal Customary Law marriage in South Africa. Unpublished LLM Thesis, University of the Western Cape, 2005.

Mwambene, L. (n.p. b). The impact of the Bill of Rights on African Customary Family Laws: A study of the rights of women in Malawi with some reference to developments in South Africa. Unpublished PhD Thesis, University of the Western Cape, 2008.

Mwambene, L. (2010). Marriage under African customary law in the face of the Bill of Rights and international human rights standards in Malawi. *African Human Rights Law Journal*, 10(1), 78–104.

Ndulo, M. (2011). African customary law, customs, and women's rights. *Indiana Journal of Global Legal Studies*, 18(1), 87–120.

Ngwira, N. (2005). Women's property and inheritance rights and the land reform process in Malawi. Institute for Policy Research and Analysis for Dialogue. Available at: https://sarpn.org/documents/d0000585/P522_Malawi_property_rights.pdf (accessed 23 August 2018).

Ntata, P., and Sinoya, C. (n.p.). Customary Law and the UN Convention on Women and Children's Rights. Unpublished, 1999.

Peters, P. E. (2010). "Our daughters inherit our land, but our sons use their wives' fields": Matrilineal-matrilocal land tenure and the New Land Policy in Malawi. *Journal of Eastern African Studies*, 4(1), 179–199.

Peters, P. E., and Kambewa, D. (2007). Whose security? Deepening social conflict over 'customary' land in the shadow of land tenure reform in Malawi. *The Journal of Modern African Studies*, 45(3), 447–472.

Phiri, K. M. (1983). Some changes in the matrilineal family system among the Chewa of Malawi since the nineteenth century. *The Journal of African History*, 24(2), 257–274.

Seymour, W. M., Bekker, J. C., and Coertze, J. J. J. (1982). *Seymour's customary law in Southern Africa*. Juta: Cape Town.

Singh, A., and Bhero, M. Z. (2016). Judicial law-making: Unlocking the creative powers of judges in terms of section 39 (2) of the Constitution. *Potchefstroom Electronic Law Journal/Potchefstroomse Elektroniese Regsblad*, 19(1), 1–22.

7 Justice for women in traditional and customary courts in Sierra Leone

A feminist analysis

Aisha Fofana Ibrahim

Introduction

It can be argued that historical events, ideologies and globalization require that access to justice in Sub-Saharan Africa be viewed through both a narrow lens (access to legal advice, legal services and other methods of dispute resolution) and a wider lens (access to social justice, including the fair distribution of health, housing, welfare, education and legal resources in society). However, access to formal justice systems – which are expensive, bureaucratic and cumbersome – is in reality beyond the reach of the majority of Africans. Traditional and informal justice mechanisms, which by contrast are more swiftly implemented and accessible both culturally and physically, therefore remain the dominant form through which they seek redress (Scanlon & Muddell, 2009; Fombad, 2014). Despite social justice activism creating the space for the delivery of legal services by non-state funded bodies, the literature on access to justice suggests that lack of infrastructure, distance as per the rural/urban divide, and an emphasis on retribution continue to make formal justice systems less attractive compared to traditional and informal justice systems, which focus on restoring social cohesion within the community by promoting reconciliation between disputing parties (Penal Reform International, 2000; Scanlon & Muddell, 2009).

Navigating the justice system has always been a herculean task for Sierra Leoneans, who not only have to deal with a bifurcated legal system that recognizes both a formalized common law and informal customary law but also with issues related to patrimony, competence, corruption and locatedness. The majority of Sierra Leoneans live in rural areas with limited access to the formal justice system. Thus, even though the authority of the informal justice system has declined significantly over the years due to governance and other reforms, the majority of Sierra Leoneans (over 80%) still seek redress from informal justice structures such as local chiefs, local courts and traditional/religious leaders (Alterman et al., 2002). This is because informal justice systems operate within local value systems and align with the perspectives of citizens, as well as often being cheaper, faster, more accessible and easier to understand, with proceedings usually avoiding legalese and being conducted in local languages (Alterman et al., 2002, World Bank Group, 2006). Through a number of governance reforms, such as decentralization, chiefdom and justice reform processes, the Local Court Act of 1963, which was bestowed with the power to address civil cases, has been revised severally to what is now the Local Court Act of 2011.

The Local Court Act 2011 was enacted "to introduce better provisions to strengthen the administration of justice in Local Courts which form part of the Judiciary of Sierra Leone" (Sierra Leone Gazette, 2011). In tandem with the justice reform programme that began after the civil war, the act aims to both formalize and professionalize the role of the local courts, making them more accountable to the populations they serve. Central to this reform is removing local courts from the control of chiefdom councils and instead placing them under the jurisdiction of the judiciary. However, the many challenges which existed before the reform – such as exorbitant fines, patrimony and gender injustice – remain. Women, who are often at a geographical and financial disadvantage when seeking justice in the formal system, often resort to informal mechanisms for conflict resolution and justice. However, they "are often not able to easily challenge and influence a change in the deeply entrenched patriarchal roots of customary law, especially at the level of the customary courts" (Fombad, 2014:487). The growing influence of women in all aspects of social, economic and political life is not adequately reflected in informal justice systems, as they are not active participants in traditional dispute resolution processes, especially in local courts. For example, though every community has a *mammy queen* (female traditional chief) and/or *Sowei* (circumciser/traditional birth attendant), women make up less than 1% of panel members in local courts in Sierra Leone.

With between one and four local courts in each of the 149 chiefdoms in Sierra Leone, they de facto represent the constitutionally recognized informal justice mechanism, and have the legal authority to adjudicate cases governed by customary law. Unlike the Local Government Act, which specifies women should have 50% representation at the ward level, the Local Court Act 2011 makes no provision for the representation of women on local court panels. These courts are presided over by a chairperson, together with a panel of elders or members, and are supported by the court clerk, all of whom are predominantly male. Thus, in a society infused with patriarchal norms and beliefs, and in which men have more access than women – whether politically, socially and economically – justice for women becomes extremely difficult to attain. This is exacerbated by local courts failing to recognize unequal power relations and the social circumstances that give rise to them, instead treating "culture as inert and homogenous rather than as an evolving reflection of living practice" (Vincent, 2009:62).

Tasked with the responsibility of interpreting customary laws, judgments in these courts often conflict with international conventions and constitutional commitments to gender equality, protection and human rights. This is because "customary legal systems in many countries pose a serious threat to women's equality rights by legitimizing and enforcing gender discriminatory rules with respect to marriage, divorce, property, and a host of other issues" (Williams, 2011:65). As can be seen in the 1991 constitution, issues that greatly affect women – such as divorce, marriage, adoption, land tenure and succession – are left in the purview of customary law, which is defined in the constitution as "the rules of law which, by custom, are applicable to particular communities in Sierra Leone" (Sierra Leone, 1991). This continues to be problematic for women and has been a central aspect of women's activism regarding the constitution review process.

Status of women

In Sierra Leone, as in most societies, there are differences and inequalities between women and men regarding assigned responsibilities, activities undertaken, access to and control over resources, as well as decision-making opportunities. Gender becomes a site of oppression greatly affected by laws and customs, given its relation to sexuality, marriage, divorce, child custody and family life as a whole. These laws and customs often contribute to lessening of women's power within their families and society more widely. Cultural barriers, such as customary laws around inheritance and property rights, as well as constitutional and religious laws, limit women's growth, leadership and access to justice, social services and economic empowerment, thus keeping them in poverty.

Preliminary results of the 2015 census place women at 50.9% of the population, with the majority living in rural and peri-urban areas. Despite women constituting a (small) majority in the country, they own less than 20% of the country's wealth and make up less than 30% of those in decision-making positions. Women still face structural and institutional barriers, coupled with a political culture that inhibits their full participation in governance. Institutional and normative structures such as family systems, infrastructure, gender ideologies and socio-cultural ideologies affect women's empowerment and gender equality in varied ways. The marginalization of women is manifested in harmful and discriminatory social practices, low levels of participation in politics and public life, low literacy levels, limited access to reproductive and sexual health resources, and restricted rights.

A majority of women in Sierra Leone continue to experience systemic abuse, as well as suffering from health complications and the constant shadow of violence in their homes, schools and communities. The frequency and severity of sexual and gender-based violence not only attests to the fact that many women lack basic human security but also points to the weakness of the justice system and rule of law. The impunity with which abuses of women's rights are perpetrated undermines national efforts to put an end to violence. Women's vulnerability to sexual and gender-based violence (SGBV) considerably undermines their productive capacities and cuts short their investments in education, which has devastating long-term consequences for development and peace. Even though local and chief courts are not supposed to adjudicate in criminal cases such as SGBV, in reality this is not the case. The majority of women and girls have limited access to magistrate courts, and instead seek justice in the customary and traditional justice system, where such cases are often judged from a gender-biased perspective.

Despite education often being recognized as a tool for changing the lives of the marginalized, women and young girls in Sierra Leone have unequal access to education due to early marriage and teenage pregnancy, as well as the priority being given to the education of the male child over the female in many rural communities. While the gap has been closing with regard to access to primary school education for boys and girls, it remains wide in the case of secondary school education. The prohibition of forced marriage and stipulation of 18 years as the minimum age for marriage in the Child Rights Act of 2007 is being violated, with evidence of "forced marriages" of young girls under 18 years old. Such cases taken to customary courts are always compromised by families making deals with families of perpetrators, ranging from financial/material compensations to offers of marriage, leaving girls with no justice whatsoever.

Between 2007 and 2009, parliament enacted three gender justice laws aimed at addressing the various forms of abuse faced by women in the country. These were the Domestic Violence Act (2007), which for the first time criminalized domestic violence and broadened the definition to include physical and sexual abuse, as well as economic, verbal, emotional and psychological abuse; the Registration of Customary Marriage and Divorce Act (2009), which raised the legal marriageable age and requires customary marriages to be registered, making it possible for women married outside of legal/formal institutions to register their marriages and divorces; and the Devolution of Estates Act (2007), which addressed issues of women's inheritance by allowing men and women to inherit equally and abolishing customary practices that contribute to the subjugation of women. In 2012, the Sexual Offences Act was enacted, criminalizing rape (including marital rape), indecent assault and harassment. The act imposes a maximum 15-year sentence for cases of rape and also entitles victims of sexual offences to free medical treatment, as well as a free medical report which is often necessary for prosecution. However, even with these progressive laws, the country's 1991 constitution, which is currently under review, has clauses denying women full equality in law. For example, Section 27 (4) D of the constitution exempts certain areas of the law – such as adoption, marriage and divorce – from protection against discrimination, giving preference to what prevails in tradition. This means that areas directly affecting women have been left to the discretion of tradition and culture. Thus, the majority of women seeking justice for issues related to marriage, divorce and adoption are dependent on the traditional norms of certain communities.

Situating traditional and customary justice systems

The traditional and customary justice system in Sierra Leone is inclusive of the state-recognized customary/local courts, as well as local- and tribal-chief courts, secret societies and religious leaders. This form of justice system is arguably a legacy of colonial indirect rule, in which the British, between 1896 and 1951, governed the Eastern, Southern and Northern parts of Sierra Leone indirectly through chiefs. During this time, courts of "Native Chiefs" were legally recognized as places where cases could be arbitrated. According to Fanthorpe and Gaima (2012),

> Chiefs had jurisdiction to hear and determine (a) all civil cases arising exclusively between 'natives' other than a case involving a question of title to land between two or more paramount chiefs or of a debt claimed by the holder of a store license and (b) all criminal cases arising exclusively between 'natives' other than cases of murder, culpable homicide, rape, pretended witchcraft, slave raiding, dealing in slaves, cannibalism, robbery with violence, or inflicting grievous bodily harm, matters or offences relating to secret societies, cases arising out of factional or 'tribal fights' and any other matters made offences under state law. A 'native' was legally defined *as any member of the aboriginal races or tribes of Africa ordinarily resident within the Protectorate.* Cases between 'natives' and 'non-natives' (the latter group included the Krios of the Sierra Leone Colony) were heard at a Combined Court presided over by the British District Commissioner and two or more paramount chiefs selected by him. All other adjudications were carried out in the first instance by the District Commissioner, who assumed the role of magistrate in a District Court.

In Freetown, the colonial authorities institutionalized a system of "tribal rulers" to supply day-to-day governance to the "native" African populations that had settled in the Colony. The Tribal Administration (Freetown) Ordinance of 1905 recognized these ethnic leaders as having responsibility for the social and economic welfare of their people and, especially, settling disputes among them according to customary law. "Tribal rulers" were allowed to charge fees for adjudication, and to levy fines for violations of regulations drawn up by the "tribal authority" (Fanthorpe & Gaima, 2012:7).

Traditional and customary justice systems have evolved over the years, with the enactment of laws that negotiate and contest the powers of paramount and local chiefs in these systems. The Chiefdom Councils Act of 1937 states that the primary duty of the chiefdom council is "to maintain order and good government in the area over which its authority extends and to interpose for the purpose of preventing, and to the best of its ability to prevent, the commission of any offence". The act also authorized the council to "make bye-laws as it may deem expedient for promoting peace, good order and the welfare of the people". This act was, however, modified in 1964 and transferred,

> bye-law making and other executive functions from the chiefdom council to a smaller chiefdom committee. The latter body comprises of the

> paramount chief (chair), chiefdom treasury/finance clerk (secretary), senior sub-chiefs (speakers and section chiefs) and a literate member (often the local MP).
>
> (Fanthorpe & Gaima, 2012:7)

The arbitrary imposition of fines by traditional authority goes back to colonial times, with the colonial authority trying to curb the problem by enacting laws curtailing such powers. According the Fanthorpe and Gaima (2012), the new legislation, in the form of the Tribal Administration (Colony) Ordinance of 1932, sought to strengthen government oversight over "tribal rulers", who were now re-named "tribal headmen". Among the provisions of this Ordinance was the stipulation that "no Tribal Headman shall exercise any jurisdiction, civil or criminal, of any nature whatsoever in respect of the members of his tribe".

Even though Sierra Leone is no longer described in terms of colony and protectorate, these vestiges of colonialism remain and are manifested in a legal system in which local courts exist outside of Freetown and tribal headmen/women still perform the functions of colonial "tribal rulers" in Freetown. Shortly after independence came the Local Court Act 1963, which brought local courts under the authority of the government, and vested the Minister of Justice with the power to appoint and dismiss local court chairpersons. As Fanthorpe and Gaima (2012:9) explain,

> Under this legislation, Native Courts were re-named Local Courts. They retained primary jurisdiction over customary law (with additional responsibilities for hearing minor cases under general law) and there were new provisions for appeals and referrals to higher courts. But their jurisdiction was now applied to territories (which remained legally undefined) rather than a category of persons ('natives'). This change prevented paramount chiefs from presiding over Local Courts, since their judicial authority, insofar as it was recognized by government, had always derived from their political sovereignty over their subjects (i.e. the 'native' inhabitants of their chiefdoms). Section 40(1a) of the 1963 Act safeguards this change by making it an offense for any person within the area of jurisdiction of a duly constituted Local Court to exercise or attempt to exercise judicial powers.

In 1974, the Local Court Act was amended, as a result of which local courts were delinked from the formal justice system and Ministry of Justice, and instead placed under the oversight of the Ministry of the Interior (now known as Ministry of Local Government and Rural Development). The 1980s and the years of civil war in the 1990s saw the highest levels of corruption in the local justice systems. There was considerable exploitation of people seeking justice, and this has even been attributed as a reason as to why so many of them joined the war. The amended Local Court Act 2011 can therefore be described as a product of post-war justice reform efforts. Other efforts include the setting up of the Justice Sector Coordination Office, the Justice Sector Development Project, the Access to Security and Justice Project, the Justice Sector Reform Strategy and Investment Plan 2008–2010, and the Legal Aid Bill 2012. The Local Court Act 2011 reverted oversight to the Ministry of Justice and the judiciary, stipulating in Section 15(1) that "a Local Court shall have jurisdiction to hear all civil and criminal matters arising within the local limits of its authority". Section 15(3a), meanwhile, states that "a Local Court shall have jurisdiction to hear and determine all civil cases governed by customary law". Furthermore, Section 44(1) states that "any person who within the area of the jurisdiction of any duly constituted Local Court exercises or attempts to exercise judicial powers [...] commits an offence and shall be liable to summary conviction". The act prohibits paramount chiefs from adjudicating and delinks local courts from chiefdom administration by stating in Section 10(a) "receive and pay into the consolidated Fund all fees, penalties, fines and other monies taken by the Court" and in Section 14(1) "the expenses of the court, including the salaries of the members and officials of the court, shall be a charge on the Consolidated Fund".

In the Western area (Freetown), there are many informal courts presided over by tribal and village heads, mostly men, even though they seem not to have any legal standing. Each ethnic group has its own tribal head who holds court to deal with issues from community members. According to the new Chiefdom and Administration Policy, the primary role of tribal heads is to promote harmony and understanding of tradition and customs among and between the ethnic groups in the Western Area. In that regard they are expected to promote social harmony and act to prevent and resolve conflict, and may mediate on traditional and customary matters. In performing their roles, the tribal heads should also comply with guidelines prepared by the Ministry responsible for local government in consultation with the Ministry of Justice (Fanthorpe & Gaima, 2012:12).

Local courts are the sole entity with the legal right to adjudicate cases governed by customary law. They are also mandated to try minor criminal offences and cases pertaining to divorce, debt, succession, defamation of character, breach of contract, witchcraft and land disputes. However, these courts face a lack of and irregular funding and therefore depend mostly on court fees and fines (Jackson, 2005). Even though the Local Court Act 2011 curtailed the powers of the paramount chiefs in local courts and abdicated the oversight of local courts to the judiciary, there have not been significant changes in how they are actually run. Excessive fees and fines that were common under paramount chiefs and court officials continue unabated, and this is directly connected to the endemic underfunding and irregularity of funding for these institutions. As a result, arbitrary fines and charges continue to be levied on those seeking redress. These arbitary fines, as well as the uncertainty of how much a court case might cost, deters many from seeking redress in these institutions. This is even more detrimental to women, who earn less and may be charged more for violating "custom/tradition" by taking someone to court.

Women's (in)access to justice in traditional and customary systems

Much of the literature on access to justice in Sierra Leone identify barriers as including bureaucracy, transparency, consistency in rulings, cost, fines, court infrastructure and gender discrimination (Fanthorpe, 2006, Manning et al., 2006). In a society in which men have more access – politically, socially and economically – than women, women's inequitable access to justice becomes particularly troubling. This is more apparent in the traditional justice system, which is mostly presided over by men and where patriarchal conditions couched in the discourse of "culture" prevail.

The association between women and tradition, inclusive of the colonial legacy, has been widely analyzed (Mani, 1990; Ahmed, 1992). This association has meant attempts at increasing or maintaining control over women have often been argued in cultural terms, using an uncritical notion of "culture". These arguments are often based on the "assumption that cultures are bounded, discrete units defined by ahistorical 'traditions' or 'customs'" (Walley, 1997:426). Such "hardened conceptions of 'culture' can suggest both insurmountable barriers between 'us' and 'them' and a predetermined 'authenticity' to which individuals are pressured to conform" (Walley, 1997:429). In essence, when women seek redress in customary courts, they are faced with deep-rooted patriarchal biases.

In a survey of users of local and chief courts conducted for this chapter, I found that more women sought justice in chief courts than in local courts, not because these courts are more gender responsive but because of proximity to residence, cost, and swiftness of judgement. Prevalent among the cases heard in these chief courts include use of abusive language, debt, domestic violence and maintenance/child support. In these courts, complainants are asked to pay "bora" (the traditional offering of "respect" towards or a chief) before their cases are heard. The local courts also charge a fee before any complaint procedure is started. Generally, people seeking redress start at the town chief level but can move their cases through the channel of town chief, section chief, paramount chief and up to the local court depending on the outcome at each stage of the process. However, this does not mean that the courts of section chiefs, paramount chiefs and local courts cannot be the first place people seek redress – it all depends on the nature of the case, proximity and cost.

In some cases, women seek justice through traditional and customary justice systems because they do not want to break filial bonds. As Akoto (2013:29) argues,

> the notion of resolving a (seemingly) internal family dispute to an external (and non-customary) forum such as a court would be perceived as a

> potentially transgressive act which would incur social opprobrium. State law is regarded as being appropriate for public and not private law issues.

This happens a lot in devolution of property cases. In traditional Sierra Leonean society, many widows are obligated to marry the brother or relative of their deceased spouse, who would take over the conjugal and other functions of the deceased, especially if the deceased left property. The rationalization for this is that the man's property, including his wife/wives and children, are better protected when the property stays within the family. In this way culture is treated as "inert and homogenous rather than as an evolving reflection of living practice" (Vincent, 2009:62). When widows refuse to adhere to such arrangements, they are ostracized and driven away from their homes. Then, when they seek redress from traditional authority, they rarely get the justice they deserve, irrespective of the fact that the Devolution of Estate Act 2007 has made such practices illegal. In essence, only women who are educated or aware of these gender justice laws are able to challenge such rulings in local courts.

Unequal power relations remain central to women's oppression in rural Sierra Leone, especially those in polygamous marriages. As Vincent (2009) argues, in many traditional marriages multiple partners are common, and the economic dependence of women on men, particularly when children are involved, is one of the key reasons why men are in a position to dictate the terms on which intimate partnerships are conducted. Gender-based violence thus becomes common in such arrangements. In Sierra Leone, many acts of gender-based violence, especially domestic abuse, are addressed through informal channels focused on restorative justice. This is very unlike the United States and other Western countries, where "suitability of restorative techniques in cases of domestic violence is strongly questioned because of power imbalances in the relationship and the fact that the relationship between offender and victim is often ongoing" (van Wormer, 2009:107). Where women are second-class citizens and where socio-cultural norms and practices relegate them to subordinate positions, it is rare for women to come out victorious in a case against a male, especially a spouse. Even when a man is found guilty of abusing his wife and is fined for the offence, or required to perform reconciliatory actions such as taking gifts to the wife's family, the adjudicator(s) will try to help the perpetrator save face by looking for an infringement committed by the wife, such as talking back or throwing things at the husband. In such cases, the woman is asked to apologize to her husband. As far as traditional culture is concerned, the husband cannot be made to feel emasculated, with the public apology by his wife reaffirming his position as head and master of the household. Even the reconciliatory action may not be effective because traditional systems do not have specific enforcement measures to back up their decisions: they are often non-binding and rely primarily on social pressure. In essence, women often do not get redress because social pressure is rarely imposed, especially on issues around domestic violence.

Traditional and customary justice systems often try to reconcile feuding parties and because many women seek to end the violence but not the relationship, they may agree to a reconciliation that is not necessarily in their best interests or those of their children. In many cases, the mental well-being of children in the household who witness the abuse is not taken into consideration during hearings of such cases. Often, women leave or are driven away from abusive homes only for their children to be left in the hands of their abusers and co-wives, who may not wish them well. Most women cannot take their children with them because of economic dependency.

Sierra Leone's civil war was characterized by its high rate of sexual and gender-based violence, which unfortunately has not abated in the post-war era. Incidences of rape and other forms of sexual violence remain unacceptably high, with survivors finding it challenging to get redress in both the formal and informal justice systems. Legally, the local and chief courts are not allowed by law to adjudicate in cases of murder, rape (including statutory rape) and assault causing blood injury. In reality, they do often adjudicate in rape cases due to a number of interrelated reasons, including distance from police stations and magistrate courts, court costs, and families wanting to avoid stigma. In many instances, perpetrators are asked to "pay damage" and /or marry the victim, contributing to underage marriage and revictimizing the victim. The rationale behind the act of marrying off rape victims to perpetrators (with claims that they are better off being married rather than living with the stigma of rape in their communities with limited opportunity for another suitor) is nothing but a continuum in the control of women's bodies. The rights of the woman/girl to her body and her moral and legal rights to justice are not considered in such decisions. This is because the body, especially the feminized body, is a site on which cultures write and inscribe their meanings, as well as a text through which cultural formations can be understood.

Cultural prescriptions of the body vary, and even though theoretical perspectives for understanding the creation of femininity differ in their emphasis on femininity as oppression or as cultural discourse, the focus remains on how these practices work to control or discipline women (Foucault, 1979; Chapkis, 1986; Bordo, 1989). Women and girls rarely get justice for the abuse of their bodies because, as Molyneux (2007:61) argues, male sexual rights over women's bodies "has usually been associated with a division between public and private matters of legal jurisdiction, in which the 'private' sphere of the family has been left 'outside justice' but where those within in it are subjected to masculine prerogative". Even though the newly introduced Sexual Offences Act 2012 prohibits child marriage and takes strong punitive action against SGBV offenders, providing an overall solid framework for the investigation and prosecution of such cases, it has had a limited effect on women and girls, especially those in remote areas of the country.

Cases of "Woman palava/damage", which Fanthorpe (2006) claims form the bulk of cases heard in customary courts, can be seen as the embodiment of women as property. A man, usually broke because of a bad harvest or business investment, will accuse his wife of adultery and take the alleged lover to court (chief or local) to claim "damage" for having sexual relations with his spouse. The rights and bodily integrity of women are ignored in this cultural practice, where the customary practice of women as chattel is unapologetically upheld and enforced. A woman, however, has no right to take another woman to court for having an affair with her spouse, nor can she be paid "damage" because customarily only a woman can be owned.

An understudied concept that also contributes to women's lack of access to justice is that of "stranger", as opposed to indigene, in rural communities. The concept, which Fanthorpe (2006) describes as the "extreme localization of criteria of identity and belonging", is complex and often inadvertently affects women who marry outside of their ethnic group or region. "Stranger" status comes with limited rights and community citizenship, can last for generations and depends on the patronage of the so-called indigenous inhabitants. Even though a woman's claim to citizenship and rights to the locale may come through her husband, this may not always be the case, as has happened on countless occasions when women wanting to run for political office are told to do so in their "hometowns". The indigenous hometown for many women has become a place of distant memory, as they have spent the better part of their lives in their husband's village. A woman denied political office in such a case and wanting to seek redress locally may not get justice, especially if the case is against a "son/daughter of the soil". Such women automatically fall within the general "stranger" category, even though their children are accepted as "local", as defined by patrimony.

Conclusion

It is quite apparent in Sierra Leone that accessing justice systems does not necessarily translate into getting justice. Informal justice systems are much easier to access but are often fraught with corruption and patrimony. Even though the local courts were placed under the jurisdiction of the judiciary and over ten million dollars spent in various projects to reform the justice system, the focus has primarily been on reforming the judiciary/formal justice system, with little or no attention to traditional and customary justice systems, which for the majority of Sierra Leoneans remain the most accessible in terms of location and cost. Women's lack of access to justice remains unacceptably high because customary law often legitimize and enforce gender discriminatory rules with respect to marriage, divorce, property and land issues.

Women's groups have in many ways challenged customary and religious traditions that marginalize women and oppose gender equality. Thus, the experience of living under different patriarchal conditions has led to the formation of a particular consciousness that questions the position of women in society. Women's activism for gender equality and equity, as well as the full attainment of sexual and reproductive health, has intensified over the years and borne fruit in the enactment of what is popularly referred to as the four gender justice laws: the Registration of Customary Marriages and Divorce Act 2009, the Devolution of Estates Act 2007, the Domestic Violence Act 2007, and the Sexual Offences Act 2012. However, implementation of these laws has been weak and often in conflict with customary law. For example, even though the Devolution of Estates Act 2007 has repealed the discriminatory provisions of law and practices against women, and has made men and women equal in the distribution of estate, it is still not uncommon for women – on the demise of their spouses – to be cheated out of the property accrued by herself and her husband in the name of tradition. Many women do not know their rights or how the act protects them, and as such fall victim to interpretations of customary laws that take no cognisance of the new law on devolution of estate. In addition, the Sexual Offences Act 2012 prohibits child marriage and takes strong punitive action against SGBV offenders, yet is contradicted by customary law, where a 16-year-old bride is permissible.

It is not that women are not able to get any justice in customary and traditional courts, but most of the time judgement is gendered, and couched in customary practices and laws that discriminate against women. Political accountability to women's empowerment remains elusive, and is reflected in the lack of women in leadership and decision-making positions, and the limited number of gender-sensitive governance reforms enabling elected officials to be more effective at promoting gender equality in public policy as well as ensuring their implementation. In general, women's rights and gender equality are regarded as a secondary priority, with tackling the abuse of women and their marginalization from public life not seen as vital to national development.

Bibliography

Ahmed, L. (1992). *Women and Gender in Islam*. New Haven, CT: Yale University Press.

Akoto, A. (2013). "Why Don't They Change?" Law Reform, Tradition and Widows' Rights in Ghana. *Feminist Legal Studies* 21:263–279.

Alterman, O., A. Ninienda, S. Rodella and K. Varzi (2002). *The Law People See: The Statute of Dispute Resolution in the Provinces of Sierra Leone in 2002*. Freetown: National Forum for Human Rights Publication.

Bordo, S. (1989). The Body and the Reproduction of Femininity: A Feminist Appropriation of Foucault. In: Alison Jaggar and Susan Bordo, eds. *Gender/Body/Knowledge*. New Brunswick: Rutgers University Press.

Chapkis, W. (1986). *Beauty Secrets: Women and the Politics of Appearance*. Boston, MA: South End Press.

Fanthorpe, R. (2006). On the Limits of Liberal Peace: Chiefs and Democratic Decentralization in Post-war Sierra Leone. *African Affairs* 105(418):27–49.

Fanthorpe, R. and E. Gaima (2012). Assessment of Traditional Dispute Resolution Mechanisms and Oversight of Informal Justice in Sierra Leone: Access to Security and Justice Programme. Consultancy Report.

Fombad, C. M. (2014). Gender Equality in African Customary Law: Has the Male Ultimogeniture Rule Any Future in Botswana? *Journal of Modern African Studies* 52(3):475–494.

Foucault, M. (1979). *Discipline and Punish.* New York: Vintage.

Jackson, P. (2005). Chiefs, Money, and Politicians: Rebuilding Local Government in Post-war Sierra Leone. *Public Administration and Development* 25(1):49–58.

Mani, L. (1990). Multiple Mediations: Feminist Scholarship in the Age of Multinational Reception. *Feminist Renew* 35:34–42.

Manning, R., P. Dale and L. Foster (2006). *Crime and Conflict Statistics from the GoBifo/ENCISS/Decentralization Survey.* Washington, DC: World Bank Group.

Molyneux, M. (2007). Refiguring Citizenship: Research Perspectives on Gender Justice in the Latin American and Caribbean Region. In: Maitrayee Mukhopadhyay and Navsharan Singh, eds. *Gender Justice, Citizenship and Development.* New Delhi: Zubaan Press.

Penal Reform International (2000). *Access to Justice in Sub-Saharan Africa: Role of Traditional and Informal Justice Systems.* London: Penal Reform International.

Scanlon, H. and K. Muddell (2009). Gender and Transitional Justice in Africa: Progress and Prospects. *African Journal on Conflict Resolution* 9(2):9–28.

Sierra Leone (1991). The Constitution of Sierra Leone, 1991. Chapter XII, Article 170(3). www.sierra-leone.org/Laws/constitution1991.pdf (accessed 1 March 2019).

Sierra Leone Gazette (2011) Vol. CXLII, No. 10 of 3rd March 2011, The Local Courts Act.

van Wormer, K (2009). Restorative Justice as Social Justice for Victims of Gendered Violence: A Standpoint Feminist Perspective. *Social Work* 54(2):107–116.

Vincent, L (2009). Polygamy in the Recognition of Customary Marriages Act. *AGENDA* 82:58–65.

Walley, C. J. (1997). Searching for "Voices": Feminism, Anthropology, and the Global Debate Over Female Genital Operations. *Cultural Anthropology* 12(3):405–438.

Williams, Susan H. (2011). Democracy, Gender Equality and Customary Law: Constitutionalizing Internal Cultural Disruption. *Indiana Journal of Global Legal Studies* 18(1):65–85.

World Bank Group (2006). World Development Report 2006: Equity and Development. http://documents.worldbank.org/curated/en/435331468127174418/pdf/322040World0Development0Report02006.pdf

8 Engendering access to justice in Nigeria

The role of public interest litigation

Basil Ugochukwu

Introduction

Anatole France's famous statement that "The law, in its majestic equality, forbids the rich as well as the poor to sleep under the bridges, to beg in the streets, and to steal bread" (France, 2015; Lynch, 2002; Sabella, 1989; Sepielli, 2013) is staggering not just for its durability, but for its relevance to the question of equal protection of the law and access to justice for all. The statement is neither bogus nor false, but this is only the case if it is interpreted formally and stripped of the specific context in which the law applies. The law purports to penalize or reward "any person" without erecting categories or making exceptions. However, it is in the practical application of seemingly neutral legal norms, often framed in impersonal and non-*ad hominem* language, that we can see context for France's statement and therefore judge these norms on a metric of justness and equality. Most of the time, the law in practice contradicts the appearance of formal fairness, justness, or equality, with its seeming neutrality and formality providing cover for the entrenchment of a latent hegemony of privileged interests.

This chapter examines access to justice in relation to the rights of women in Nigeria. It asks what, if any role, public interest litigation can play in ensuring that fairness and gender equality are integrated into access to justice measures, whether constitutionally prescribed or as collateral to the overall administration of justice policy. After explaining how the concepts of access to justice and public interest litigation are deployed in the chapter, the analysis looks at some examples of access to justice issues in the context of women's rights in Nigeria, the extent to which public interest litigation could be deployed to address them, and the impediments that are likely to be encountered in doing so.

Access to justice in a transitional context

It is important to clarify the concept of access to justice and how it animates and generally frames this chapter. In doing so, I will provide background perspective on how access to justice questions arise in transitional situations, as in Nigeria where civil rule was restored in 1999 after several years of military dictatorship. This is relevant for the simple reason that access to justice concerns tend to be heightened in dictatorial situations. Even so, extending the analysis in this manner gives room assessing whether the civil dispensation which replaced the dictatorship brought about any changes or simply papered over concerns.

Access to justice as a concept can be understood in various ways. Some scholars have suggested that it has both wider and narrower meanings. The wider meaning represents access to justice as an opportunity to exploit the entire political order in a given society, as well as sharing in the benefits derived from its social and economic development (Okogbule, 2005:96). In its narrower formulation, access to justice stands for no more than the opportunity to utilize law courts and gain access to the remedies that they can provide. The narrower sense therefore stands for "access to judicial adjudication of dispute" (Oba, 2003).

Context is therefore crucial for conceptualizing access to justice in a meaningful way. There is a cost dimension, such as being able to pay for legal representation, as well as capability factors, such as education and awareness. It cannot be assumed, as one scholar has noted, that those who lack access to justice are simply "unable to pay market rates for representation by lawyers" (Blasi, 2004). This amounts only to a reductionist definition of the concept. While the ability to hire the best lawyers for legal representation may form a major pillar of access to the courts in some legal systems, it may only amount to a minor detriment of access to justice in other contexts. Put another way, in developed societies legal representation may be a very prominent factor in analyzing the availability of access to justice in a way that this does not play out in developing environments. Prioritizing legal representation in this fashion might mean other factors are minimized, taken for granted, or simply erased from the list of variables.

In some contexts, legal representation may be an insignificant element in the equation of access to justice. This is because in such situations several other substantive and structural factors impede access even before victims can get to the front door of the courts. As will be shown later, these factors produce heightened negative impacts in developing/transitional situations, meaning that in situations where societies are transitioning to democratic/constitutional rule, making justice available to those who were once denied it is often a major socio-legal challenge. In relation to human rights, for example, while legal representation is necessary for launching formal legal complaints before the courts, it does not address "the narrowness, formalism, west-centrism, individualistic, capitalist and … superficial underpinnings and orientations of mainstream … norms, praxis and discourses [which makes] them part of the problem of subordination and impoverishment … rather than part of the solution" (Kennedy, 2002; Okafor & Ugochukwu, 2016:291).

Public interest litigation

A major challenge facing many legal systems is how to establish mechanisms aimed at ensuring that all persons, regardless of status or gender, have equal access to justice both in terms of the formal structures of legal administration, such as the courts, and the overall mechanisms for social and political inclusion. While this is a worthy aspiration, it is hardly ever realized in practice, thus necessitating government intervention through legal aid schemes or non-governmental institutions acting in the public interest (Salman & Ayankogbe, 2016). In recent times, social justice advocacy in many domestic legal regimes has proceeded alongside public interest or impact litigation activities.

While there is no generally agreed definition of public impact litigation, or what some have referred to as "social action litigation" (Agbakwa & Okafor, 2009; Cummings & Rhode, 2008;), for the purposes of clarity, it is useful to explain what is meant by "public interest" and "public impact litigation", and how the concepts are employed in this chapter (see Box 8.1).

Box 8.1 Defining public interest and strategic impact litigation

Public interest litigation

In this chapter, public interest litigation is used in the sense of litigation launched in pursuit of a worthwhile public interest. This interest could arise in a variety of ways. It could be litigation pursued on behalf of poor and marginalized individuals, or social categories whose voices and concerns might otherwise be drowned out by the legal system. In India, for example, its "distinctive brand of public interest litigation" has been deployed on subjects such as women's rights, poverty, indigenous rights, labor (bonded and child), and protection of the environment (Dasgupta, 2008). In Nigeria, cases have been launched to test the constitutionality of the death penalty[1] and the holding charge,[2] enforce environmental protection through project impact assessments,[3] trigger interim measures at the domestic level prior to consideration of a complaint to the African Commission on Human and People's Rights,[4] and to challenge forced evictions.[5]

Strategic impact litigation

Public or "strategic impact" litigation is a more procedural incarnation of litigation in the public interest. The emphasis here moves from "interest" to "impact", and the framing of the case is what distinguishes cases organized around the former from those organized around the latter. While public interest litigation focusses on the "interest" being pursued through a lawsuit, strategic litigation is more about the "impact" expected from a single judicial decision. It is often anticipated that strategic cases will generate an impact that goes well beyond the actual outcome of the individual case (Okafor & Ugochukwu, 2014:439). In strategic impact cases, a litigant or a cause could win out in the public space even while actually failing inside the court room (NeJaime, 2011). Victory here could come in two forms. The first form that victory could take is when the litigant wins the case such that the jurisprudence established positively impacts a trail of future cases. The second form is when the case is lost in court but the advocacy and public information around it generates sufficient pressure to force the hand of policy makers to implement reform.

From the definitions of public interest and strategic impact litigation offered in Box 8.1, it is clear that in some instances there can be a convergence of the two in specific lawsuits. This is often the case when, on the one hand, there is a clear objective to serve the legal need of a target vulnerable person or group and, on the other, the outcome of the case produces a ripple effect on the administration of the justice system that extends well beyond that single case. In the Nigerian context, an example would be the case of Bayo Johnson.[6] In this case, the objective of assisting a vulnerable suspect that the system had victimized coincided with the altogether different goal of solving a lingering concern in the criminal justice administration process, that is, the holding charge phenomenon. The case dealt with the constitutional guarantee of presumption of innocence, as well as broader questions regarding the right to a fair trial in criminal proceedings. The court had to decide whether it was lawful for the police to bring criminal suspects before courts which lacked the jurisdiction to try the substantive allegations on the "holding charge", merely to secure detention orders upon which suspects could then be held indefinitely awaiting trial.

The Nigerian Constitution of 1999 does not provide for public interest litigation, even though one might conclude it shows some sensitivity to the issue of access to justice. Regarding public interest litigation, the constitution is clear that before a person can challenge an alleged action violating one or more human rights enshrined in the constitution, the person raising the challenge must show how the alleged action affected him/her personally.[7] Therefore, public interest litigators had to present their cases in the names of actual victims of alleged violations, or their actions would be barred for want of *locus standi*. This orientation is changing in Nigeria following the promulgation of new fundamental rights enforcement rules in 2009.

Patriarchy as an obstacle to access to justice for women in Nigeria

Nigeria falls into the category of societies described as patriarchal. Patriarchy in this context means no more than the dominance of men and their values in a given society (Foord & Nicky Gregson, 1986:194). As a Weberian concept, it described a system in which men ruled societies through their position as heads of households. Patriarchy has, over time, become more widely understood as a "system of social structures, and practices in which men dominate, oppress and exploit women" (Walby, 1989:214). A more comprehensive definition of patriarchy sees it as,

> a group organization in which males hold dominant power and determine what part females shall and shall not play, and in which capabilities assigned to women are relegated generally to the mystical and aesthetic and excluded from the practical and political realm, these realms being regarded as separate and mutually exclusive.
>
> (Rifkin, 1980)

Law is a powerful tool in constructing social order and has a very strong and intimate relationship (some scholars describe this relationship as "uneven") (Gavigan, 2012:273) with the production and perpetuation of patriarchy. It is a symbol and vehicle of male authority as well as a form of hegemonic ideology (Gavigan, 2012:84). Law has also "served as a bastion of male privilege and female subjection" (Conagahan, 2013:3). Historically, there is no better evidence of this than the fact that women were treated as property under the law in England. Married woman could not own property separately from her husband or control her own wages and profits up until 1870, when the Married Women's Property Act[8] was passed (Combs, 2005; Shanley, 1989).

Patriarchy and the subordination of women in Nigeria occurs both as a secular issue and as a cultural phenomenon. On the one hand, some jurisprudence, laws and protocols allowed by the state perpetuate the subordination of women, while, on the other hand, local cultural practices are often used as cover to achieve the same outcome. In terms of laws, for example, Section 55(1) of the Nigerian Labour Act, 1990, prohibits women from being employed on night work in any public or agricultural undertaking (Ekhator, 2015:286). Section 55(7), however, excludes nurses and women occupying management positions from this prohibition. Also, under Section 127 of the Police Act, married women cannot seek enlistment in the Nigerian Police Force. An unmarried police woman who gets pregnant is immediately discharged from force and can only be reinstated on the approval of the inspector general of police. A woman police officer who intends to get married is required under Regulation 124 of the Police Act to first apply in writing for approval to the Commissioner of Police under whose command she is serving. None of these rules apply to men.

Court jurisprudence, on the other hand, could arise in the context of the interpretation of statutes or the application of customary rules. In the case of *Nwanya v Nwanya*,[9] for instance, the Nigerian Court of Appeal sitting in its Enugu Division refused to recognize the contributions of an estranged wife in the acquisition of matrimonial property, simply because she had brought no documentary evidence of the claimed contributions. Regarding cultural practices, the plight of women among Nigeria's various ethnic groups is worsened in relation to rules governing inheritance. Under Nigerian law, if a man made a will prior to death, his property is distributed according to the terms of the will. However, if he dies intestate (without making a will), the property is distributed according to the applicable customary rules, which in most cases are discriminatory to women. The discriminatory aspects of property inheritance under Nigeria's many customary/cultural laws are expressed in various guises, including "primogeniture rules, rights of spouses, rights of adopted children and rights of illegitimate [children]" (Onuoha, 2008:81).

The case of *Mojekwu v Iwuchukwu*[10] offers the clearest illustration of a situation where jurisprudence and cultural interpretation can unite to further erode the rights of women. In the case, the appellant Augustine Mojekwu pleaded the *Ili-Ekpe* custom of Nnewi town in southeastern Nigeria, which he claimed entitled him to inherit Caroline Mojekwu's late husband's property. Under the custom in question, if a man dies without male surviving children, any daughters he might have cannot inherit his property. Instead, the deceased's closest male relative is the beneficiary of the inheritance. Through this case, the Court of Appeal had an opportunity to filter a typical Nigerian customary practice relating to inheritance through the lens of human rights. It ruled in favor of Mrs. Mojekwu, stating that *Ili-Ekpe* custom was repugnant to natural justice, equity and good conscience. The court also struck it down for being contrary to the constitutional prohibition on discrimination. The Supreme Court, for its part, while agreeing that the *Ili-Ekpe* custom was repugnant, concluded that this should not extend to all customs that failed to recognize the "role" of women.

Cases such as *Mojekwu* justify public/strategic impact litigation to the extent that the decision in that single litigation could result in positive consequences across the entire legal system. The Supreme Court's reluctance to allow this case to impact other contexts indicates the judges were potentially sympathetic to other customs that may contradict the anti-discriminatory stance of the constitution. More than that, it illustrates one of the major limitations of litigating in the public interest in a legal and judicial system that is deeply conservative and patriarchal.

Engendering access to justice and public interest litigation in Nigeria: the current situation

Given the many forms that the subordination of women under the Nigerian legal system takes, this makes for fertile ground for public interest/impact litigation to enable women more access to justice. There are strong constitutional grounds upon which all the discriminatory laws and protocols highlighted above could be challenged in the Nigerian law courts. While not exhaustive, they represent specific examples of how these issues manifest in practice. And while the *Ili-Ekpe* custom that triggered the *Mojekwu* case was exposed as a result, there are many such customary practices that discriminate against women across Nigeria's ethnic groups that rarely face public or judicial scrutiny. Such practices raise serious legal and constitutional questions that deserve to be brought before the courts. They also highlight, apart from the public interest issues involved, a separate concern regarding access to justice for women who, as a societal segment, lack the education or resources to present these questions before the courts without legal assistance.

Compared to men, women in Nigeria are more economically deprived. They are victims of what a scholar has referred to as "economic violence", that is, a state in which an abuser (who in most cases is male) has complete control of the victim's (mostly female) money and other economic resources or activities (Fawole, 2008:168). Based on this definition, some married women in Nigeria could be described as victims of this kind of violence. Husbands in such situations not only prevent their wives from working, thereby depriving them of economic independence, but also seize their earnings under the threat of physical abuse. On a different level, there is also the concept of feminization of poverty, which captures the Nigerian reality that poverty is more prevalent among households headed by women than those headed by men. Some of the reasons advanced for this include discrimination against women in the labor market, lower levels of educational attainment by women, and lower salaries for women compared to men even when they perform comparable tasks within an organization (Anyanwu, 2010). All of this goes to show that there is a "gendered" dimension to the problem of poverty in Nigeria (Aniekwu, 2002; Okafor & Ugochukwu, 2015:399).

Given that women suffer serious acts of discrimination and cultural abuse, and that this interacts with their apparently lowly economic conditions, it can only mean they have all the more reason to seek legal redress. It also shows they are more in need than men of the legal assistance necessary to gain access to the procedures of legal justice. This returns us to the statement of Anatole France that opened the chapter. While that statement may be considered more appropriate in the criminal law context, it can be extended to the civil sphere if it is applied to the same issue of deprivation and lack of access.

In the criminal sphere, the poor are more likely to have to defend themselves in court for having done what the law has forbidden, such as sleeping under the bridges, begging in the streets, and stealing bread. In the civil sphere as well they are more likely than the rich to be denied their rights, be physically abused with impunity, and be victimized in various other ways previously described. In addition, the poor are also more likely to lack the resources required to pursue redress in order to have their violated rights vindicated through the judicial process. If the majority of women in Nigeria are poor, how are they ever going to be able to use the law as a resource to challenge the causes and justifications for their impoverished condition? They will require help that can come either through officially sanctioned legal aid measures, or through nongovernmental institutions by way of public interest litigation.

The fact remains that there does not seem to be a great deal of litigation launched to redress violations of the rights and livelihoods of Nigerian women as a public interest law issue. This is irrespective of the fact that some nongovernmental legal advocacy groups have mounted a variety of interventions on behalf of women the legal system has discriminated against or victimized in other ways. Before providing some instances of these interventions, it is helpful to note that by virtue of Section 46(4)(a) of the 1999 Constitution, the Nigerian National Assembly is empowered in all necessary and desirable ways to enable High Courts to exercise their jurisdiction to redress human rights violations. The Assembly is further empowered under Section 46(4)(b)(i) to make legal provisions for rendering legal assistance "to any indigent citizen of Nigeria where his right under [the Constitution] has been infringed or with a view to enabling him to engage the services of a legal practitioner to prosecute his claim".

The Legal Aid Council

At present, the Legal Aid Council is the federal institution through which the government implements the above constitutional provisions. Its assistance covers both criminal and civil cases. The law establishing the Council mandates it to provide legal assistance when a defendant is charged with certain identified offences such as murder, manslaughter, malicious or willful wounding, and assault occasioning actual bodily harm (McQuoid-Mason, 2003:111). The civil category was introduced by an amendment to the law in 1994, meaning that legal aid through the Council was extended to cover civil claims related to accidents and violations of fundamental human rights guarantees in the Constitution.

There is limited publicly available information on the depth and effectiveness of the official legal assistance mechanism, and there is also little to go on by way of scholarly research on the activities of the Nigerian Legal Aid Council. However, from its mandate above, it is clear its effectiveness is hindered by a narrow focus, which takes place in the midst of widespread legal abuses that ought to warrant its intervention. While violations of the rights of women recognized by the constitution are within the Council's area of competence, there is nothing to suggest it has carried out any worthwhile legal assistance measures in this area. In addition, the limit on its areas of focus precludes it from acting on some widely prevalent legal problems in which the rights of women are implicated. An example is oil-related litigation in Nigeria's Niger Delta region. These are not the kinds of cases covered under the Legal Aid Council Act but are deserving of being the subject of litigation nonetheless (Frynas, 2001:407).

Legal advocacy groups

The ineffectiveness of the public legal assistance program opens the door for private actors to step in and fill the gap. At least in one sense of the concept of public interest litigation – the provision of basic legal services – private actors have performed this role to a relatively good level. As will be shown below, some of the groups have been very visible in providing legal assistance to women who have faced human rights denial, discrimination, or victimization.

However, before proceeding, it has to be stated that in relation to the application of strategic/public impact litigation, a great deal is left to be desired on the part of legal advocacy groups. Apart from the *Mojekwu* case mentioned previously, which produced a relatively revolutionary overthrow of cultural practices discriminating against women, there has been no similar cases or judgments of the same level of relevance since Nigeria restored civil rule in 1999. Even then, the *Mojekwu* case was presented or argued not by a nongovernmental legal advocacy institution but by private legal practitioners. It was also launched long before the transition to civil rule, even though the final Supreme Court decision was issued some years thereafter. The fact that public impact cases relating to the rights of women are not coming before the courts for adjudication, even when there are strong reasons why they should, is difficult to explain. Some reasons for this situation are offered in the latter parts of this chapter.

Let me now return to the few cases where nongovernmental advocacy groups provided legal defense services to women who otherwise might have been denied such on account of their poverty, lack of education, or lack of understanding of the legal process. The more famous cases in this regard occurred in the context of the ultimately flawed attempt by some state governments in Northern Nigeria to institute the aspects of Islamic Sharia'h law in their administration of justice regimes. Starting in Zamfara state in 2000, it soon spread to 12 other states in Nigeria's mainly Islamic north (Ibrahim & Lyman, 2004; Laremont, 2010; Nmehielle, 2004; Ojielo, 2010). A magazine compiled a list of persons convicted under the new Sharia'h laws and the often-bizarre reasons they were found guilty in a special edition entitled "Living with Sharia'h" (Ojielo, 2010:142). The list of offenses included carrying a Muslim woman on a motor bike and having sex with one's mother-in-law. Others included stealing, "indecent" dressing, consuming alcohol, and approaching a female hostel in a private car. The punishments ranged from lashing with a cane to amputation of arms to stoning to death (Umar, 2007).

In 2001, the Sharia'h court in Sokoto state sentenced Safiya Hussaini, divorced and the mother of four children, to death by stoning for having a child outside marriage. Meanwhile, the man whom Safiya claimed had raped her and got her pregnant was found not guilty due to the prosecution not being able to produce the four male Muslim witnesses needed to prove rape (Okekeocha & Ewoh, 2013). In Katsina state, Amina Lawal was also sentenced to death by stoning for being pregnant while not married. The grounds for conviction were her confession and the fact she was physically pregnant (Ibrahim, 2004). She had no legal representation at the initial trial and was not informed of her constitutional right to a lawyer (Okekeocha & Ewoh, 2013). As a result, the court did not have the information that her alleged offence occurred before the law under which she was tried was promulgated. In fact, both women were described as "poor and uneducated rural women", lacking any kind of intellectual judgment about the legal fate that had befallen them (Umar, 2007:40).

The Sharia'h Court of Appeal reversed convictions in these two cases. In Safiya's case, the appeal court held that she could not face retroactive punishment on the basis of a law that did not exist at the time she committed the alleged offense. In Amina's case, the earlier judgment was reversed on several grounds, including that there had been insufficient evidence to convict and that the defendant had a right to withdraw her confession (Human Rights Watch, 2004). Aside from these two cases, several other Sharia'h trials involving women were completed and punishments carried out. This included the case of Bariya Magazu, convicted of having a child outside marriage and sentenced to 180 lashed. The sentence was later reduced to 100 lashes after Bariya recanted an earlier allegation that she had been raped. None of the three men she accused of raping her were therefore brought to trial. The sentence was executed long before it should have been under Sharia'h law, given that Bariya was still weaning her child at the time (Howard-Hassmann, 2004:4).

Returning to Safiya Hussaini and Amina Lawal, in both cases the conscience of many Nigerians as well as domestic and international human rights advocacy groups was stirred. While Bariya did not have an opportunity to mount an appeal against her punishment, Safiya and Amina were luckier. Not only were they able to launch appeals, but the appeals were successful owing largely to the legal representation that was mobilized through the actions of committed civil society actors such as BAOBAB for Women's Human Rights (see Box 8.2).

Box 8.2 Legal advocacy groups involved in women's rights in Nigeria

BAOBAB for women's human rights

A comprehensive list of cases in which BAOBAB provided legal representation to defendants could not be found, as the organization's website was down at the time of writing. From what could be gleaned by desktop research, the organization provided legal representation to a number of women caught up in the Sharia'h debacle in Northern Nigeria. For example, in 2004 they provided legal representation to Daso Adamu who had been sentenced to death for adultery. The conviction was quashed on appeal.[11] They also assisted Hafsatu Gwiwa (Sokoto, adultery), Aisatu Musa (Sokoto, fornication), Hauwa Garuba (Sokoto, adultery), Maryam Abubakar Bodinga (Sokoto, adultery), and Fatima Usman (Niger, adultery) during this period.[12]

Project alert on violence against women

Lagos-based Project Alert on Violence Against Women which describes itself as "a non-governmental women's rights organisation set up in January 1999 to promote and protect the rights of women and young girls."[13] Besides running a home for battered and abused women and girls, the organization provides legal counselling and representation services for poor women and victimized girls. Its legal services portfolio extends to such issues as divorce, custody of children, rape, physical assault, and abduction.

Women's Law Clinic

Legal clinics in a handful of faculties of law in Nigerian universities teach students practical professional skills they can use to provide legal services to segments of the society including women and girls. One such clinics is the Women's Law Clinic (WLC) at the University of Ibadan, which was inaugurated in 2007. It is described as a specialized clinic focusing on women issues (Bamgbose, 2015:387). Its goals are "to provide legal services to less advantaged women in society … with the aim of improving the lives of women, securing justice, and advancing civil, political, economic, social and cultural rights" ((Bamgbose, 2015:389). A report of the Clinic's accomplishments from 2008 to 2013 show that its officials offered legal advisory services to several indigent women. The cases in which they intervened included claims for maintenance of children, widows seeking legal protection from in-laws seeking to deprive them of family property, and settlement of landlord and tenant disputes (Bamgbose, 2015:389–393).

Impediments to public interest litigation

Locus standi

Regardless of the modest victories, groups like BOABAB have recorded in enhancing access to justice for women, there remain a number of obstacles to making these gains sustainable over the long term. One obstacle, in particular, stands out, in the manner in which it also seems to undermine the rule of law. Legal standing, or *locus standi*, to bring forward legitimate human rights questions before the court, is critical to judicial intervention in such cases. Before the passage of the Nigerian Fundamental Rights (Enforcement Procedure) Rules of 2009, an individual needed to demonstrate personal injury in order to be able to present a valid human rights complaint. If such an individual could not show personal injury, the doctrine of *locus standi* barred her or him from presenting the case.

A brief history of the development of the *locus standi* doctrine in Nigeria's legal, and especially human rights, jurisprudence may be helpful at this point. It was the main issue in the case of *Adesanya v President of the Federal Republic of*

Nigeria,[14] which arose from the interpretation of provisions in the 1979 Constitution that were similar to those contained in the Constitution of 1999. The questions, as formulated by the Nigeria Supreme Court, were as follows: If a legislative enactment appears to be *ultra vires* the Constitution, or if an act infringes any of its provisions dealing with fundamental human rights, who has *locus standi* to challenge its constitutionality? Does any member of the public have the right to sue? Or should *locus standi* be confined to those persons whose vested legal rights are directly interfered with by the measure, or to persons whose interests are liable to be specially affected by its operation? In its majority decision, the court held that "standing will only be accorded to a plaintiff who shows that his civil rights and obligations have been or are in danger of being violated or adversely affected by the act complained of."[15]

Where this reasoning should have yielded recognition of the plaintiff's standing to present their claim in Adesanya's case, the court concluded otherwise. Instead, it held that the plaintiff lacked standing because he had participated in the process (a senatorial confirmation hearing) from which his complaint arose. This conclusion was later described as being "at complete odds with [the Judge's] reasoning" (Ogowewo, 1995:7), because the court conflated the court's discretion in terms of the remedy that could be applied (which judges possess in declaratory applications) and the justiciability component of the standing principle. The question was whether the plaintiff's complaint was justiciable as a matter of constitutional significance and therefore not requiring of a personal injury or stake. The court also made indirect reference to the possibility of opening the floodgates of litigation if it expanded the corridor of standing more than it had done in this case (Ogowewo, 1995:8).

For many years after this judgment, Nigerians, in order to be granted standing, had to show what exceptional burden the application of any law or exercise of an action would place on them. Such burden had to be above and beyond what other Nigerians might experience. In other words, if it was a general law or action affecting all persons, to be able to merit legal standing to challenge the law or action, a person needed to prove a personal interest beyond that which all other persons had in redressing the specific grievance. This effectively nullified the possibility of public interest litigation, as almost all cases litigated on this basis invariably stumbled due to this condition. It should come as no surprise that *locus standi* restrictions featured prominently on the list of impediments to effective human rights litigation throughout this period (Nwauche, 2010:507).

It was because of these long-standing complaints that the need arose to redress them by establishing new rules. The new rules came in the shape of the 2009 proclamation of the Chief Justice of Nigeria, which was aimed at addressing the procedural shortcomings in the 1979 rules (Ekhator, 2014:77). The 2009 rules contain an expansive preamble laying down its broad objectives, and the role of judges and lawyers in ensuring they are achieved. Not only does it require the courts to interpret the constitution, and in particular its human rights provisions, in an expansive and purposeful manner, but it also enjoins them to respect domestic, regional and international human rights instruments called to their attention.[16]

Moreover, the new rules encourage enhanced access to justice for all classes of litigants, especially the poor, illiterate, uninformed, vulnerable, incarcerated, and unrepresented. To further affirm this objective, the rules require courts to encourage and welcome public interest litigation in the human rights field. In particular, human rights activists, advocates, or groups and nongovernmental organizations may institute human rights actions on behalf of any potential applicants. No human rights case may be dismissed or struck out for want of *locus standi*.[17] By this specific provision, the new rules appeared to revolutionize the regime of legal standing in human rights litigation in Nigeria. In addition, the rules seemed to respond to almost all the much-highlighted issues of the 1979 rules.

Even so, there have been criticisms of the 2009 rules as well. It was argued that under the guise of the new rules, the Chief Justice usurped the powers of the National Assembly and conferred "additional powers on the High Court for the purpose of enabling the court to exercise its jurisdiction more effectively" (Sanni, 2011:526; see also Dakas, 2012). The author takes particular issue with the requirement of the new rules that Nigerian courts "respect" international instruments in dealing with human rights cases, as this would seem to be at variance with the provision of Section 12(1) of the Constitution requiring such instruments to have first been domesticated by parliament before being applied in the Nigerian legal system.

Having such an expansive standing regime is, nevertheless, welcome on many levels, regardless of the 2009 rules still being untested concerning their effectiveness (or lack thereof), and the fact that courts remain reluctant to move beyond the definition of *locus standi* as formulated in the Adesanya case. There is concern that the anticipated benefits of an expanded standing qualification provided by the 2009 rules have not materialized due to the rules themselves being viewed in some quarters as unconstitutional. Specifically, the argument is that the provisions requiring recognition of regional and international human rights instruments, as well as permitting public interest litigation, are not consistent with the constitutional provisions relating to the competence of constitutional litigation. As such, the argument continues, they are null and void (Dakas, 2012:528; Ekeke, n.p.). The courts seem to have bought into this argument given that they (including the Supreme Court) have simply ignored the 2009 rules, and have instead persisted with the strict interpretation of the standing doctrine (Ekeke, n.p.:48). What this means in reality is that the human rights of the poor and marginalized, including a good proportion of women in Nigeria, continue to be violated without redress, as the process excludes public interest litigation that could have spoken out on their behalf.

Other impediments

While *locus standi* remains an obstacle to improved access to gender justice in Nigeria, it is by no means the only one. As suggested previously in the chapter, there is pervasive abuse of the rights of women across Nigeria, with most of these abuses not redress. It is also the case there are only very few institutional groups actively helping women seek remedies in the courts. There is a shortage of institutions (such as BAOBAB) providing legal assistance to victims of discriminatory laws. In addition, as clearly demonstrated by BAOBAB's experiences, even where such groups do exist, they may not have sufficient resources to provide legal representation to all, or at least most, women in need. This lack of resources can arise in a variety of ways.

First, there is only so much a handful of organizations can do to help hundreds of thousands of women requiring legal assistance. As someone who worked in the Nigerian nongovernmental sector for years, the author is aware that there are few staff available to conduct litigation in these organizations. A legal and judicial system in which ethical considerations are often sacrificed for personal gratification is clearly discouraging to lawyers minded toward social justice. Corruption is very much rooted in the fabric of Nigerian society, and by extension its judicial system (Langseth & Michael, 2003; Ugochukwu, 2011:70). This presents a twofold dilemma to public interest and social justice organizations. First, they do not have the resources to bribe court officials for favorable decisions. Second, it makes litigation harder to win because, in most cases, they are up against government agencies that have a clear advantage before judges schooled in a political tradition that believes the government can do no wrong (Nwabueze, 1977).

Even should there be sufficient litigation staff to pursue more cases than is currently happening, other resources – such as those needed to cover filing fees, transportation, documentation, additional costs because of delays, etc. – may still be lacking. Over the years, the costs of pursuing legal redress through Nigerian courts have risen exponentially (Okafor & Ugochukwu, 2015:433). In the case of *General Oil Ltd v Oduntan*, [18] which was decided in the difficult years of military rule in Nigeria, Justice Niki Tobi, then of the Nigerian Court of Appeal, stated it was common knowledge that litigation had become a very expensive venture in the country. He added that the economic situation prevailing at that time worsened the situation, due to rising court filing fees as well as fees for the hiring of lawyers. Not a lot has improved since, and the situation may in fact have degenerated (Okogbule, 2005:101).

Connected to the issue of costs is the no-less-frustrating challenge of delays in the disposal of cases. Rather than counting the costs in terms of the amount paid to get the litigation off the ground, the costs here shift to maintaining the case until judgment is entered. The obvious consequence of this is that the longer it takes to pursue a case to its conclusion, the more the litigant pays by way of time and resources. Physical and financial exhaustion are therefore inevitable in most instances. If appeals become necessary after the initial case has been heard, this adds further to the costs. The financial resources needed to file or defend appeals are far greater than those required at lower court levels.

While nongovernmental groups can raise donor funding for advocacy and research, it is harder to raise the funds needed for litigation. This is due to the simple reason that what counts as measurable success in a litigation context is more difficult to calculate. Funders therefore often view litigation in Nigeria as throwing resources into a bottomless pit. For this reason, many social justice nongovernmental organizations, including women's groups, are constrained in providing legal services to those most in need. Sadly, this an ongoing frustration, with nothing to suggest the situation is likely to change any time soon.

Conclusion

While there are opportunities to apply public interest litigation strategies in defense of the rights of women in Nigeria, this chapter has shown how this can be fraught with challenges owing to a variety of factors. Not even a constitutional regime recommending equal treatment before the law, and non-discrimination based on gender, has been able to reform a patriarchal society in which women bear an unusually heavy burden within the legal system. Other challenges include, at the general level, the financial cost and cultural barriers of accessing justice.

In this chapter, I have given examples of the ways in which the rights of women could make for strong public interest litigation causes, as well as the institutions within the legal system that could pursue these causes. The chapter also addresses obstacles specific to each of those institutions in the context of public interest litigation and access to justice, such as a lack of resources, delays in the administration of justice system, the small number NGOs committed to public interest litigation, and the question of legal standing. Whether these challenges will be overcome with time is an open question. However, the unsatisfactory state of the rights of women in securing access to justice means that those already in the field cannot give up the struggle in the near future.

Notes

1 *Peter Nemi v Attorney General of Lagos State & Another* (1996) 6 NWLR [Pt 452] at 42; this case was argued on behalf of the appellant by a nongovernmental organization named Human Rights Law Service.
2 *E.A. Lufadeju & Another v Evangelist Bayo Johnson* (2007) 3 S.C. [Pt 2] 134; also argued by Human Rights Law Service.
3 *Oronto Douglas v Shell Petroleum Development Company Limited* (Unreported) Suit No M/474/2003, in which the applicant was an environmental rights activist seeking legal protection of the right to a livable environment in Nigeria's Niger Delta region; see also Ibe (2007:243).
4 *The Registered Trustees of Constitutional Rights Project v President of Nigeria* (Unreported) Suit No M/102/92
5 *Aiyeyemi & Others v The Government of Lagos State and Others* (Unreported) Suit No M/474/2003; see also Ibe (2007:243).

6 *E.A. Lufadeju & Another v Evangelist Bayo Johnson* (2007) 3 S.C. [Pt 2] 134.
7 *Attorney General, Adamawa State v Attorney General, Federation*, [2005] 18 NWLR (Pt 958) 581 at 604, where the Supreme Court held, "It is not enough for a plaintiff to merely state that an Act is illegal or unconstitutional. He must show how his civil rights and obligations are breached or threatened."
8 *Married Women's Property Act 1870.*
9 *Nwanya v Nwanya* [1987] 3 NWLR (Pt. 62) 697.
10 *Mojekwu v Iwuchukwu* [2004] 4 Sup Ct (Pt 1) 1.
11 GlobalAdvocacy.Com, "Daso Adamu has been Discharged and Acquitted"; online at http://globaladvocacy.com/baobab_daso_adamu_discharged.html.
12 Baobab for Women's Human Rights, "Sharia Implementation in Nigeria: The Journey So Far"; online at http://iknowpolitics.org/sites/default/files/sharia_nigeria_baobab.pdf.
13 Project Alert on Violence against Women, "About Project Alert"; online at http://www.projectalertnig.org/about.html.
14 *Adesanya v President of the Federal Republic of Nigeria* [1981] 1 All NLR 1.
15 Ibid., at 39.
16 Fundamental Rights (Enforcement Procedure) Rules, 2009 para. 3(b) of the Preamble.
17 Ibid.
18 *General Oil Ltd v Oduntan* [1990] 7 NWLR (Pt. 63) 433.

Bibliography

Agbakwa, Shedrack and Obiora Okafor (2009). "Social Action Litigation and Access to Justice in Nigeria: A Critical Case Study" Pages 207 – 255, in Ayesha Kadwani Dias and Gita Honwana Welch eds., *Justice for the Poor: Perspectives on Accelerating Access* (New Delhi: Oxford University Press).

Aniekwu, Nkoli (2002). "Gender and Human Rights Dimension of HIV/AIDS in Nigeria" *African Journal of Reproductive Health* 6:30.

Anyanwu, John C. (2010). "Poverty in Nigeria: A Gendered Analysis" *Journal Statistique Africaine* 11:38.

Bamgbose, Oluyemisi (2015). "Access to Justice through Clinical Legal Education: A Way Forward for Good Governance and Development" *African Human Rights Law Journal* 15:378.

Blasi, Gary (2004). "How Much Access? How Much Justice?" *Fordham Law Review* 73:865.

Combs, Mary Beth (2005). "A Measure of Legal Independence: The 1870 Married Women's Property Act and the Portfolio Allocations of British Wives" *Journal of Economic History* 65(4):1028.

Conagahan, Joanne (2013). *Law and Gender* (Oxford: Oxford University Press, 2013).

Cummings, Scott and Deborah Rhode (2008). "Public Interest Litigation: Insights from Theory and Practice" *Fordham Urban Law Journal* 36(4):603.

Dakas, Dakas C. J. (2012). "Judicial Reform of the Legal Framework for Human Rights Litigation in Nigeria: Novelties and Perplexities" in Epiphany Azinge and Dakas C. J. Dakas eds., *Judicial Reform and Transformation in Nigeria* (Lagos: Nigerian Institute of Advanced Legal Studies).

Dasgupta, Modhurima (2008). "Public Interest Litigation for Labour: How Indian Supreme Court Protects the Rights of India's Most Disadvantaged Workers" *Contemporary South Asia* 16(2):160.

Ekeke, Alex (n.p.). "Access to Justice and *Locus Standi* before Nigerian Courts" [LL.M Thesis submitted to the Faculty of Law, University of Pretoria, April 2014], online at http://repository.up.ac.za/dspace/bitstream/handle/2263/43108/Ekeke_Access_2014.pdf?sequence=3&isAllowed=y.

Ekhator, Eghosa O. (2014). "Improving Access to Environmental Justice under the African Charter on Human and Peoples' Rights: The Roles of NGOs in Nigeria" *African Journal of International and Comparative Law* 22:63.

Ekhator, Eghosa O. (2015). "Women and the Law in Nigeria: A Reappraisal" *Journal of International Women's Studies* 16(2):285.

Fawole, Olufunmilayo (2008). "Economic Violence to Women and Girls: Is It Receiving the Necessary Attention?" *Trauma, Violence, Abuse* 9(3):167.

Foord, Jo and Nicky Gregson (1986). "Patriarchy: Towards a Reconceptualization" *Antipode* 18(2):186.

France, Anatole (2015). *The Red Lily* (London: Forgotten Books).

Frynas, Jedrzej George (2001). "Problems of Access to Courts in Nigeria: Results of a Survey of Legal Practitioners" *Social & Legal Studies* 10(3):397.

Gavigan, Shelley (2012). "Something Old, Something New? Re-Theorizing Patriarchal Relations and Privatization from the Outskirts of Family Law" *Theoretical Inquiries in Law* 13(1):271.

Howard-Hassmann, Rhoda (2004). "The Flogging of Bariya Magazu: Nigerian Politics, Canadian Pressures, and Women's and Children's Rights" *Journal of Human Rights* 3:3.

Human Rights Watch (2004). "V. Human Rights Violations under Shari'a in Northern Nigeria" in "Political Shari'a? Human Rights and Islamic Law in Northern Nigeria". 21 September 2004, online at https://www.hrw.org/report/2004/09/21/political-sharia/human-rights-and-islamic-law-northern-nigeria#.

Ibe, Stanley (2007). "Beyond Justiciability: Realising the Promise of Socio-economic Rights in Nigeria" *African Human Rights Law Journal* 7:225.

Ibrahim, Hauwa (2004). "Reflections on the Case of Amina Lawal" *Human Rights Brief* 11(3):39, online at www.wcl.american.edu/hrbrief/11/3ibrahim.pdf.

Ibrahim, Hauwa and Princeton Lyman (2004). *Reflections on the New Shari'a Law in Nigeria* (New York & Washington, DC: Council on Foreign Relations).

Kennedy, David (2002). "The International Human Rights Movement: Part of the Problem?" *Harvard Human Rights Journal* 15:101.

Langseth, Peter and Bryane Michael (2003). "Foreign-Sponsored Development Projects in Africa: The Dialogue between International and African Judicial Integrity Projects" *Journal of Sustainable Development in Africa* 5:3.

Laremont, Ricardo Rene (2010). "Islamic Law, Muslim-Christian Relations, and the Transition to Democracy in Nigeria's Fourth Republic" *Journal of the Middle East and Africa* 1:25.

Lynch, Philip (2002). "Begging for Change: Homelessness and the Law" *Melbourne University Law Review* 26:609.

McQuoid-Mason, David (2003). "Legal Aid in Nigeria: Using National Youth Service Corps Public Defenders to Expand the Services of the Legal Aid Council" *Journal of African Law* 47(1):107.

NeJaime, Douglas (2011). "Winning through Losing" *Iowa Law Review* 96:941.

Nmehielle, Vincent O. (2004). "Sharia Law in the Northern States of Nigeria: To Implement or Not to Implement, the Constitutionality Is the Question" *Human Rights Quarterly* 26(3):730.

Nwabueze, Ben O. (1977). *Judicialism in Commonwealth Africa: The Role of Courts in Government* (London: C Hurst).

Nwauche, Enyinna (2010). "The Nigerian Fundamental Rights (Enforcement) Procedure Rules 2009: A Fitting Response to Problems in the Enforcement of Human Rights in Nigeria" *African Human Rights Law Journal* 10:502.

Oba, Abdulmumini (2003). "Improving Women's Access to Justice and the Quality of Administration of Islamic Criminal Justice in Northern Nigeria" in Joy Ezeilo ed., *Shari'a Implementation in Nigeria: Issues & Challenges on Women's Rights and Access to Justice* (Enugu: Women's Aid Collective & Women Advocates Research & Documentation Centre).

Ogowewo, Tunde (1995). "The Problem of Standing to Sue in Nigeria" *Journal of African Law* 39:1.

Ojielo, Ozonnia M. (2010). "Human Rights and Sharia'h Justice in Nigeria" *Annual Survey of International & Comparative Law* 9(1):135.

Okafor, Obiora Chinedu and Basil Ugochukwu (2014). "Inventing Legal Combat: Pro-Poor 'Struggles' in the Human Rights Jurisprudence of Nigerian Appellate Courts, 1999–2011" *African Journal of Legal Studies* 7:429.

Okafor, Obiora Chinedu and Basil Ugochukwu (2015). "Raising Legal Giants: The Agency of the Poor in the Human Rights Jurisprudence of the Nigerian Appellate Courts, 1990–2011" *Africa Human Rights Law Journal* 15:397.

Okafor, Obiora Chinedu and Basil Ugochukwu (2016). "Poverty in the Human Rights Jurisprudence of Nigerian Appellate Courts (1999–2011)" *Journal of African Law* 60:289.

Okekeocha, Chinelo and Andrew Ewoh (2013). "Questioning the Constitutionality of Sharia Law in some Nigerian States" *African Social Science Review* 6(1):15.

Okogbule, Nlerum (2005). "Access to Justice and Human Rights Protection in Nigeria: Problems and Prospects" *SUR – International Journal of Human Rights* 2:94.

Onuoha, Reginald Akujobi (2008). "Discriminatory Inheritance under Customary Law in Nigeria: NGOs to the Rescue" *International Journal of Not-for-Profit Law* 10(2):79.

Rifkin, Janet (1980). "Toward a Theory of Law and Patriarchy" *Harvard Women's Law Journal* 3:83.

Sabella, Rosalie (1989). "The Social and Legal Paradigms of Equality" *Windsor Review of Law & Social Issues* 1:5.

Salman, R. K. and O. O. Ayankogbe (2016). "Denial of Access to Justice in Public Interest Litigation in Nigeria: Need to Learn from Indian Judiciary" *Journal of the Indian Law Institute* 53(4):594.

Sanni, Abiola (2011). "Fundamental Rights Enforcement Procedure Rules, 2009 as a Tool for the Enforcement of the African Charter on Human and Peoples' Rights in Nigeria: The Need for Far-reaching Reform" *African Human Rights Law Journal* 11:511.

Sepielli, Andrew (2013). "The Law's 'Majestic Equality'" *Law and Philosophy* 32:673.

Shanley, Mary Lyndon (1989). *Feminism, Marriage, and the Law in Victorian England* (Princeton, NJ: Princeton University Press).

Ugochukwu, Basil (2011). "The Pathology of Judicialization: Politics, Corruption and the Courts in Nigeria" *The Law and Development Review* 4 [Article 4]:59–87.

Umar, Muhammed S. (2007). "Gender Issues in Application of Islamic Law in Nigeria" *Al-Jami'ah* 45(1):30.

Walby, Sylvia (1989). "Theorizing Patriarchy" *Sociology* 23(2):213.

9 Without land, without justice

How women's lack of land rights impedes access to justice

Aparna Polavarapu

Background

In Sub-Saharan Africa, where many households rely on agriculture for their basic livelihoods, access to land is key to economic empowerment (FAO, 2011:23–24) and, accordingly, access to justice. While the actual rights available to women and men vary from country to country, a common theme is that women struggle to obtain meaningful access due to a combination of state laws and customary norms (Polavarapu, 2013:110–119). Without meaningful land rights, women in agricultural societies lack secure access to the most important available source of wealth and livelihood, risking not just poverty but legal disempowerment. This chapter explores how such problems are driven in part by community resistance to improving women's access to land, and argues that interventions to create exercisable land rights for women must engage with community members.

The causal relationship between lack of economic resources and difficulty accessing justice is well understood: those who are economically disempowered have greater difficulty overcoming the financial requirements of accessing courts and legal representation. However, there are other ramifications to the lack of recognized land rights. Even where statutory law grants equal rights to purchase, sell, inherit, or otherwise access, use, or dispose of land, women face obstacles exercising these formal rights in communities that continue to enforce customary gendered norms of access. Where women are not granted equal access to land, they are unable to exercise other rights due to the vulnerability created by a lack of secure land rights.

Though women face significant problems of access due to inadequate legal frameworks, reform of the legal framework, though necessary, is an insufficient means of resolving such problems. As this chapter demonstrates, problems of access are driven in part by community resistance to improving women's access to land. Interventions seeking to create exercisable land rights for women must therefore engage with community members.

Access to land and poverty reduction

The right of access to land is not a singular right. Rather, it is more accurately described as a bundle of rights, several of which bestow economic benefits important for basic subsistence and primary income generation. Rights to use and remove crops, or natural resources such as lumber or water, from the land provide a means of subsistence and primary income generation. Additionally, rights to dispose of or encumber the land create opportunities for investment and additional income generation. These additional opportunities to extract capital from land can provide economic security in times of drought or other hardship. The strength and durability of these rights are thus tied to food security and poverty reduction (Meinzen-Dick, 2009).

Though the relationship between land rights and poverty reduction – as well as the understanding that many women suffer discriminatory laws and policies denying them equal access to land – is widely accepted, land-reform policies have typically focused on assuring security of land rights at the household level. Data pertaining specifically to women's land rights and poverty reduction therefore remains scant. An assumption underlying this emphasis on the security of land rights at a household security is that household assets are shared among members (Lastarria-Cornhiel et al., 2014:118). However, discriminatory laws and gendered norms ensure that household land is not equally available to each member. Even as this gendered phenomenon has become increasingly documented, there is little empirical data examining the link between women's land rights and poverty (Meinzen-Dick et al., 2017). This may, in part, be due to a failure to account for legal pluralism, normative structures influencing land rights, and the various types of tenure arrangements (Meinzen-Dick et al., 2017:8).

A legal analysis makes evident that in Sub-Saharan Africa many women's rights to land, particularly in rural areas, are fragile and limited. When these rights are threatened, a woman's economic security is therefore also at risk. Access to justice is often considered a necessary precondition for the effective implementation of new rights. In order to exercise new or improved land rights, rights holders must be able to access justice. The relationship, however, goes both ways. When land rights are neglected, access to justice may also be undermined.

Customary land tenure and land law in Sub-Saharan Africa

Since gaining independence, many Sub-Saharan African states have struggled to adequately engage with existing legal pluralism relating to land tenure. States transitioning from colonial regimes to independence were given counsel by various international organizations and western state governments, and were encouraged to embrace western policy approaches. The World Bank, for instance, favored the adoption of a system of formal title,[1] which would regularize and systematize the hodge-podge system that existed under colonial rule. Among other things, this system was meant to wipe out customary tenure, and would arguably produce economic and social benefits. Unfortunately, the attempt to deny the legitimacy of alternative tenure arrangements increased vulnerability and confusion.

During the precolonial period, land tenure systems were developed based on the needs of the communities they served. Thus, tenure arrangements could vary dramatically based on how the land was used, as well as on the social system of the community. Actual rights granted depended on whether land was being used for lumber, grazing, crop cultivation, some other purpose, or a combination thereof. In addition, the rights granted to an individual or family could be determined by a single leader or small group of leaders, by recognized family relationships, as part of a feudal system, or through societally recognized practices (Kajoba, 2002).

Though any discussion of custom must come with the caveat that it is very community-specific and one cannot make a universal pronouncement regarding all things custom in a single geographic region, it is safe to say that women typically had rights inferior to men when it came to land ownership, access, use, or decision-making. A woman's rights were often understood in terms of her relationships to men. If unmarried, separated, or divorced, a woman's father or his clan was expected to provide for her, sometimes by giving her land to live on and cultivate in order to support her family. A married woman could expect to be cared for by her husband and his family. In some communities a widow was permitted to remain on marital property until her children came of age. If she had no minor children, she could stay on the property by marrying a male relative of her husband, a practice referred to today as "widow inheritance." This practice has been described as a protective one, in that it gave a widow an opportunity to access land she otherwise would have been denied. However, it is understood today as forcing a woman to decide between impoverishment and marrying a person she did not freely choose (Polavarapu, 2013:111–112).

Under customary law, where land rights were passed down through lineage, a woman could not expect to inherit property, as giving land to a woman was viewed as losing clan land. Women were transient members, moving from the clan of their natal family to the clan of their husbands. For clans to maintain their land, it needed to remain in the hands of men, who were considered permanent clan members.

The colonial experience disrupted customary norms and relationships with land. In their quest for land and resources, colonial governments alienated land from the native populations. They also, in some cases, altered local populations' relationships with land that had not been alienated. The British, for example, attempted to apply and enforce customary norms in cases involving "personal law" between local Africans. However, if the customary norm was unconscionable to the British adjudicator (i.e., deemed "repugnant" to their morals and justice), it was set aside.[2] The use of the repugnancy tests was a blatant attempt to change certain customary norms, but norms were also altered inadvertently. The attempt to name and apply customary norms was done through a British legal lens, not a local one. The western approach treated what should have been more flexible legal norms as rigid rules. Norms were thus stripped of the ability to change to adapt to community changes, though whether and how they would have changed more organically is a matter of speculation.

In yet other cases, colonial authorities, in their attempt to affix a structure of governance and rules they understood, empowered individuals to make pronouncements on customary norms. In some communities, this power was already concentrated in men or in certain families. But in cases where norm negotiation was a community event, this dramatically altered power relationships. Newly empowered individuals or groups could, and often did, reinforce norms that maintained their power and resisted norms that diffused it (Polavarapu, 2013:112–113).

With the coming of independence, customary law was further adulterated, as newly formed governments attempted to cope with legal pluralism while asserting the dominance of state law. Some countries attempted to obliterate customary approaches to land tenure, requiring everyone to title their land. Others attempted to maintain a plural approach, but the intervention of formal legal systems in issues of customary tenure changed customary norms.

In Sub-Saharan Africa, states continue to take varied approaches to granting and guaranteeing rights to land. Rwanda exemplifies the purely statutory approach. In its land reforms, it amended the land law, marriage law, and inheritance law, among others. These laws are important because they explicitly grant equal rights to women and men to, among other things, inherit, own, control, and sell land (Polavarapu, 2011:118–123). Rwanda is in the minority with this approach (Polack et al., 2013:20). Other Sub-Saharan African countries have acknowledged or protected customary forms of tenure, even while their laws are beginning to make application of discriminatory norms illegal (Polack et al., 2013:22–23). An increasing number of constitutions hold customary law accountable to constitutional rights guarantees. In addition, statutes and courts are requiring that women be allowed access to marital property, be granted inheritance rights, and otherwise experience security of tenure. However, while many argue for the intervention of formal law in implementing gender equality, formal law has – in at least some cases – served to reinforce or even exacerbate existing gender inequality.

In some cases, state law undermines the very rights it grants to women. In Kenya, for example, the Law of Succession Act grants women rights to shares of an intestate estate, while denying these rights to certain women. Though the Act does not grant women rights equal to men, it does grant rights that have historically been at risk. For example, a surviving spouse, whether male or female, is entitled to the personal and household property of the decedent, and a life interest in the remainder. However, if the surviving spouse is female, then her interest is subject to change if she remarries. No such restriction is placed on widowers. Still, these particular provisions do take some steps toward improving the situation of widows, who might otherwise face immediate eviction on their husbands' deaths. However, the Act also excludes certain "agricultural lands" from its provisions on intestacy and instead maintains customary law in those areas. The result is that in these areas, customary law, the governing law, does not need to ensure women gain the rights granted by statutory law.[3]

By its very nature, customary law should be adaptable to women's needs, but in many places it has been shaped to undermine women's rights rather than protect them. In Kenya and Tanzania, the act of documenting customary law in the 1960s has contributed to the inflexibility of norms denying women equal rights to men. In Tanzania, the Judicature Act includes schedules laying out, in detail, the substantive content of each district's customary law relating to marriage, custody, guardianship, and, to some degree, succession.[4] These provisions, drafted in 1963 and purportedly reflecting the substance of customary norms at the time of drafting, severely limit women's rights. In Kenya, a judge authored the Restatement of African Law in 1969, which is still referred to by courts when they have occasion to apply customary law.[5] The writing down of customary norms has the potential to alter the very nature of customary law, which is supposed to be flexible and subject to negotiation. In both Kenya and Tanzania, communities are now bound by rules that were written decades ago, in a way they might not have been had customary law been permitted to function naturally.

On the other hand, there can also be problems with unwritten customary norms. In theory, customary law should undergo alterations if half its beneficiaries are not adequately benefitting from its operation. However, in addition to the changes created by colonialism, customary norms were also impacted by economic and global changes. For example, the rise of cash crops and increasing demographic pressure are sometimes blamed for clan members seeking to utilize any norms possible to justify the taking of land from others (Lastarria-Cornhiel, 1997:1328–1329). While norms regarding fairness may previously have dictated that clan members set aside a plot of land for a vulnerable community member, economic pressures now make that plot of land significantly harder to part with.

Additionally, even where statutory law requires that woman be granted access to land, some communities simply ignore the formal law in favor of norms denying women such rights. In Uganda, for example, the practice of "widow eviction" – forcible eviction of a widow from the marital home and property by the husband's family after his death – continues to be a tremendous problem. Pursuant to statutory law, widows have rights to remain on the marital property. However, relatives often claim that the land cannot possibly belong to the widow, citing the customary concern of keeping land within the clan (International Justice Mission, 2014:11). In Rwanda, where statutory law grants women inheritance rights equal to those of men, communities still express a preference that only men inherit (Polavarapu, 2011:133–135).

Across Sub-Saharan Africa, both statutory and customary laws have largely fallen short of the obligation to protect women's rights to land. Many statutory laws take the step of granting some rights to women, but fall short of granting full equality in land rights. Some of these laws create exceptions for customary law, allowing communities to avoid altering norms to benefit women. Even where such exceptions are not written into law, in some cases the statutory law is simply ignored. In each of these cases, women – particularly those living under customary law – lack meaningful land rights, and their ability to access justice is compromised.

Hurdles to accessing formal courts

In agricultural economies, a lack of access to land can be devastating in many ways, primarily because lack of access to land is not just a source of income but also of power and social standing (FAO, 2011:23–24). In addition, consistent with traditional gender norms, while women tend to bear the burden of cultivating the land, they are commonly denied control over the fruits of the labor. In such a situation, women do not have the economic and social wealth necessary to effectively access justice.

Accessing formal courts requires overcoming multiple financial obstacles. Filing a complaint and seeing a proceeding through to completion requires the payment of various fees. Finding an advocate is optional, but doing so requires money or the luck to find one willing to work pro bono. Presenting any witnesses typically requires paying for their transportation.

Women in rural areas often face even greater obstacles than their urban counterparts. Courts are further away, sometimes requiring hours of travel to reach. Court processes may take multiple days, requiring repeat travel. Case backlog, a problem experienced and acknowledged by many countries' judiciaries (See Chioma, 2018; World Bank, 2009:38),[6] lengthens the time required to complete a court process. In addition to paying for the travel itself, a woman will lose the value of any work she could have done that day. If she has children, she will also need to provide for childcare. However, these are costs faced by any woman in rural poverty. The lack of meaningful and recognized rights to land has far more dire effects. For many, insecurity of land access translates to food insecurity. A lack of decision-making power relating to land also means a lack of decision-making power with respect to the fruit of the land, regardless of the time spent cultivating it. In these circumstances, women must rely on the strength of their kinship and social networks. However, when justice is being sought outside the community, women risk losing their social capital and face a potential backlash.

Customary law is not just about the norms governing a community but also the institutions developing and enforcing those norms. Community members typically bring disputes to the nearest authority, which may include a family head, clan head, or local elder. Some countries have attempted to formalize these customary dispute resolution structures. Uganda's constitution and Local Council Courts Act create and empower Local Council Courts to preside over a select number of matters for which customary law governs.[7] South Africa is attempting to do something similar with a Traditional Courts Bill.[8] Regardless of whether these informal courts or councils are made formal, they tend to hold greater legitimacy for local communities than formal state courts. The decision-makers are members of the tribe, clan, or community and are well versed in local practices and norms.

Women seeking to change the operation of a norm or assert rights granted under statutory law (but not available under historic custom) can and often do go to a customary institution first. Even for those unhappy with the norms as they currently operate, the community institution is often viewed as the more legitimate institution. The formal court is not only a more foreign body, but attending such a court is also a risky proposition. Seeking justice at a court means choosing an outside institution and potentially alienating family and clan members. This is particularly dangerous for those with relatively less power, including women, whose economic health depends on social relationships. Endangering those social relationships means endangering her access to land, and potentially losing whatever income or crops she has already cultivated. In these cases, the greatest roadblock to accessing justice in a formal court is the risk of losing everything in the aftermath.

Lack of effective remedy

Even after overcoming obstacles of access, women face another significant problem when trying to enforce legal judgments in their favor. Court opinions matter only insofar as people decide they matter. When compliance is lacking, the state is required to step in. However, seeking the state's involvement a second time not only requires additional work on the part of the person seeking enforcement, including additional investments of time and money, but it is also not guaranteed to be effective.

To ensure enforcement of her rights in an area where customary law is still an important force, a women's optimal result is a favorable decision from a customary institution. Customary bodies are often authorized to ensure that communities act in accordance with both customary and statutory law. In addition, such bodies are typically viewed with respect by the community, and their decisions are more likely to be adhered to. However, such bodies are populated by members of the community, who are bound up in the power structure that is reinforced by customary norms. Though there are instances of successful outcomes for women seeking to overturn norms that deny them land, there are also many failures (Claassens & Mnisi, 2009:493–502). Women struggle to assert their rights before such institutions.

On the other hand, when a formal court is used as an option, in addition to the potential loss of important social capital a woman also faces the possibility that a judgment in her favor will have no real effect. Refusal to comply with court decisions is often justified by arguments citing the judgment's illegitimacy due to it contradicting customary norms, or because it is the product of a non-community-based approach to resolving the dispute. In Uganda, for example, the practice of "widow eviction" persists even when widows have received court orders affirming their right to remain on marital property.[9] A paper order adds nothing to a woman's arsenal if her relatives and community members simply ignore it. In this case, she must seek help from outside actors if she is to exercise her rights.

Enforcing such judgments against resistant actors is exceedingly difficult. Local officials residing in the noncompliant community are often just as resistant as other community members to enforcing decisions that are contrary to local norms. A woman can also seek assistance from police officers closer to the court or from the court itself, but this requires encountering again many of the obstacles she faced when seeking to access the court in the first place.

Even after revisiting a court, enforcement might not be possible. Courts are often empowered to take follow-up action, such as imposing liens or making additional orders, but even those have no power if there is no enforcement behind them. Returning with a second order does not add any additional weight to an already resistant community. In the case of widow eviction in Uganda, a woman can seek the assistance of a bailiff, but doing so can overwhelm her with fees without guaranteeing enforcement (Polavarapu, 2019).

Some Ugandan judges have expressed that when they discover their orders are being ignored, they will intervene of their own accord. By meeting with local council members and the parties in dispute, they seek to lend some authority to their ruling. However, they also admit that while parties will promise to respect a woman's rights while in the presence of the judge, they are unsure what actions will be taken after they depart.[10]

Additionally, such follow-up is not always feasible, with budgets often barely covering cost of running courthouses. Difficulty of travel between remote rural locations and formal courts is a two-way problem. In order for such intervention to be systematic, the state would need to provide investment to cover the time and expense taken by such visits. Judges who visit sites now do so at their own discretion and on their own time.

Women's rights advocates in Uganda have also stated that they are sometimes able to assist with the enforcement of judgments. Like the judges, they visit the site in dispute, speak with both parties, as well as the local leaders, and are usually able to get individuals to agree to acknowledge the woman's right to the land. A key difference, though, is that these advocates suggest they have better long-term results because they are more able to follow up, and community members know that they will return.[11] However, this type of intervention is only available when adequately funded women's rights organizations that engage with customary law and institutions are located in the vicinity.

Lack of enforcement is an unsurprising problem. State law that conflicts with customary norms has had difficulty gaining traction throughout Sub-Saharan Africa. Even where rights are granted under state law, without buy-in from local community members with influence and power, that law is often ignored. Court judgments are only effective when people feel compelled to follow them, preferably out of a sense of obligation, but possibly also due to the knowledge that the state can compel them. However, where the state lacks either the interest or the capacity to ensure such follow-up, enforcement remains a rarely achieved aspiration.

Effect on women's other rights

The absence of land-related justice has a cascade effect on women's other rights, with violations of land rights sometimes accompanied by other rights violations. In addition, without effective land rights, women are inhibited from exercising their other rights. A particularly salient example is how domestic violence is intertwined with land insecurity.

Land insecurity is connected to economic, verbal, and physical forms of domestic violence. In the case of widow eviction, for example, family members seeking to grab land from a widow have employed threats or physical violence (International Justice Mission, 2014). In Busoga, Uganda, where domestic violence rates are extremely high, there are multiple reported instances of men evicting their intimate female partners, who often bear the burden of cultivating the land, as soon as harvest season is over. These women not only lose their shelter, but access to the fruits of their labor.[12]

In addition, land insecurity may prompt women to decide to live with domestic violence, rather than seeking a means of resolving it. A woman seeking to assert her right to be free from violence must weigh the value of fighting for that right against what she will lose by alienating those on whom she depends for economic support.

From the moment she makes the decision to push back against violence from her partner or family members, a woman risks significant loss for herself and any children she may have. A woman complaining about abuse from her husband, for example, potentially faces retaliation from her husband or his family members. In cases where she has no meaningful land rights, her access to any meaningful form of wealth is usually dependent on staying within the good graces of her kin or her husband's kin. Risking those relationships means risking losing her means of supporting herself and her children. Pressure from members of the kin network can be very persuasive because of the importance of those relationships. In Uganda, for example, many women are reported as backing down from pursuing complaints in part because of the constant pressure they receive from community members to find other ways to address the violence, or to simply accept it.[13] Any attempt to resolve a problem in a manner not accepted by the community thus also runs the risk of losing community support, and potentially losing any access to land.

Meaningful change requires community engagement

Women's lack of land security inhibits justice in multiple ways and in a manner that does not lend itself to improvement through simple legislation. Deeply entrenched norms, along with external motivators such as land scarcity and other economic factors, have proven difficult for the law alone to break down. However, advocates reporting some measure of success have described involved interventions that incorporate parties to a dispute, local leaders, and sometimes justice officials, to encourage normative change.

While in the past, customary norms were often viewed as something to be cast aside, they are now understood as something legal systems must engage with. Development actors recognize that these traditional systems of tenure may provide greater protections for those who are otherwise vulnerable (FAO, 2010:5–8), and in fact may be more efficient than a system of individual title (Deininger & Binswager, 1999:258). Formal title did not incorporate many of the rights recognized under customary tenure, and in some cases titling actually lost women what rights they did have under customary tenure (Polavarapu, 2013:113–115). Simply incorporating customary tenure into the legal framework, however, is inadequate to protect women's rights. Though some countries have required that discriminatory customary practices be discarded, women continue to be denied meaningful access to land.

While laws adequately protecting women's rights must be enacted, additional community-level engagement is necessary in order to encourage compliance with the laws. Activists and development actors already support awareness-raising and norm-changing interventions to address women's rights concerns including domestic violence, family planning, and land rights. In terms of land rights, some advocates have worked to help women advocate for themselves before traditional institutions (Claassens & Mnisi, 2009). Arguing for implementation of constitutional and international norms relating to equality, these women have, in some cases, convinced leaders to remember the norm of fairness and decide an issue in favor of them. However, there are also many examples of women failing to convince institutions to assert or recognize land rights for women. Still, in some of these cases, women even having the opportunity to meaningfully engage in norm negotiation is a success in itself.

Though engaging with the community in this way is not a guarantee of improvement, it is a more effective option than simply relying on the law alone. Of course, in any case where advocates and disputants seek to create positive normative change, the law is an important part of the negotiation. Along with community acceptance of new legal norms, women need to be able to rely on rights granted by the law.

Conclusion

In Sub-Saharan Africa, justice is hard to come by for those who lack access to land. Land is a key locus of status, power, and wealth, and the ability to own or access it is a great indicator of one's ability to obtain justice. Justice takes on different dimensions in legally plural systems that include customary and traditional justice mechanisms. Women suffering due to inadequate access to land may have technically accessed justice as provided for by the customary system, but have in reality failed to receive substantive justice due to their relatively inferior rights to land, the obstacles preventing them from effectively participating in norm-creation, and the impact a lack of land rights has on their ability to exercise other rights.

Though it is tempting to consider formalized law in the form of constitutions and statutes as the solution, state law has, in many cases, reinforced or even worsened women's relative inequality in terms of access to land. Even where statutory law has made attempts to remove obstacles preventing women from equally accessing land, negative norms remain. The law is only as effective as its enforcement, and this is virtually nonexistent when the population refuses to comply and the state cannot (or does not) allocate sufficient resources to ensure compliance. Thus, accessing justice – in its pursuit or its results – requires engaging with the community to create normative change. Statutory law remains important, with such laws serving an expressive function that can be used to persuade local norm influencers. State oversight is also necessary to track, measure, and ensure better treatment of women. However, state action alone is inadequate until local populations can be convinced of its legitimacy.

Land is the most important source of wealth in Sub-Saharan Africa, so much so that justice in connection with land or any other matter is severely restricted for those without land. With a significant percentage of land under the vise-like grip of men and kin groups seeking to abuse customary norms to maintain their control, adequate intervention requires engaging with community and customary institutions to facilitate normative change.

Notes

1 A 1975 World Bank land reform policy called for replacing communal tenure arrangements with a titling system. See Deininger and Binswager (1999:248).

2 Some of these repugnancy tests even survived the end of colonialism. See, for example, Polavarapu (2013:117); Kiye (2015:86).

3 The Law of Succession Act (2008), Cap. 160, §§ 32–42 (Kenya). Technically, custom must abide by the constitutional guarantee of equality, but in application, it often does not.

4 Local Customary Law (Declaration) Order, Government Notice 279/1963, Schedule 1, Laws of Persons [Sheria Zinazohosu Hali ya Watu], 2002, C. 358 (Tanz.); Local Customary Law (Declaration) Order, Government Notice 436/1963, Schedule 2, Laws of Inheritance [Sheria za Urithi], 2002, C. 358 (Tanz.).

5 Opinions authored as recently as 2017 cite the Restatement of African Law as an authoritative source of customary law. See, for example, In the Matter of the Estate of J.N.K., Succession Cause 897 of 1998 (Kenya).

6 See also David Maraga, Chief Justice, Supreme Court of Kenya, Speech During the Launch of the Blue Print (26 January 2017).

7 Local Council Courts Act (2006) (Uganda).

8 Traditional Courts Bill of 2017 (S. Afr.).

9 In Lira, Uganda, for example, judicial officers and attorneys report that families routinely "disinherit widows" by forcibly removing them from their land, regardless of the law. Attorneys and judicial officers (names and additional information withheld to protect confidentiality) in Lira, Uganda. Oral and taped

interviews, Lira, Uganda, June 29–30, 2015. Interviews by author in relation to grant-funded justice sector research involving interviews of more than 70 respondents in Eastern, Central, and Northern Uganda.

10 Judicial officer (name and title withheld to protect confidentiality) in Lira, Uganda. Taped interview, Lira, Uganda, 29–30 June 2015.

11 Women's rights advocate (name withheld to protect confidentiality), in Kampala, Uganda. Author interview, Kampala, Uganda, 23 June 2015.

12 Nakalembe, Judith (Coordinator, Kamuli Gender Based Violence Center and Legal Officer, UWONET). Taped interview. Kamuli, Uganda, July 8, 2015.

13 State attorney (name withheld to protect confidentiality) in Kampala, Uganda. Oral interview. Kampala, Uganda, June 25, 2015; Dorah Mafabi, Head of Mission, Avocats Sans Frontières Uganda. Taped interview. Kampala, Uganda, 1 July 2015.

Bibliography

Chioma, Unini (2018). Lagos Judiciary Embarks on Court Decongestion Project. *The Nigeria Lawyer*, 2 March 2018.

Claassens, Aninka and Sindiso Mnisi (2009). Rural Women Redefining Land Rights in the Context of Living Customary Law. *South African Journal on Human Rights* 25:491–516.

Deininger, Klaus and Hans Binswager (1999). The Evolution of the World Bank's Land Policy: Principles, Experience, and Future Challenges. *The World Bank Research Observer* 14(2):247–276.

FAO [Food and Agriculture Organization of the United Nations] (2010). Statutory Recognition of Customary Land Rights in Africa: An Investigation into Best Practices for Lawmaking and Implementation. FAO Legislative Study 105. http://www.fao.org/3/i1945e/i1945e00.pdf

FAO [Food and Agriculture Organization of the United Nations] (2011). The State of Food and Agriculture, 2010–2011: Women in Agriculture – Closing the Gender Gap for Development. http://www.fao.org/3/i1945e/i1945e00.pdf

International Justice Mission (2014). Property Grabbing from Ugandan Widows and the Justice System. Washington: International Justice Mission. Available at www.ijm.org/documents/studies/IJM-Propery-Grabbing-from-Ugandan-Widows-and-the-Justice-System.pdf (accessed 17 March 2019).

Kajoba, Gear M. (2002). *Land Use and Land Tenure in Africa: Towards an Evolutionary Conceptual Framework*. Africa: Council for the Development of Social Science Research in Africa.

Kiye, Mikano E. (2015). The Repugnancy and Incompatibility Tests and Customary Law in Anglophone Cameroon. *African Studies Quarterly* 15(2):85–106.

Lastarria-Cornhiel, Susana (1997). Impact of Privatization on Gender and Property Rights in Africa. *World Development* 25(8):1317–1333.

Lastarria-Cornhiel, Susana, Julia A. Behrman, Ruth Meinzen-Dick and Agnes R. Quisumbing (2014). Gender Equity and Land: Toward Secure and Effective Access for Rural Women. In: *Gender in Agriculture: Closing the Knowledge Gap*, edited by A. R. Quisumbing, R. Meinzen-Dick, T. L. Raney, A. Croppenstedt, J. A. Behrman and A. Peterman. Netherlands: Springer, 117–144.

Meinzen-Dick, Ruth Suseela (2009). Property Rights for Poverty Reduction? DESA Working Paper.

Meinzen-Dick, Ruth Suseela, Agnes Quisumbing, Cheryl Doss and Sophie Theis (2017). Women's Land Rights as a Pathway to Poverty Reduction: Framework and Review of Available Evidence. *Agricultural Systems* 172:72–82.

Polack, Emily, Lorenzo Cotula and Muriel Côte (2013). *Accountability in Africa's Land Rush: What Role for Legal Empowerment?* London/Ottowa: IIED/IDRC.

Polavarapu, Aparna (2011). Procuring Meaningful Land Rights for the Women of Rwanda. *Yale Human Rights & Development Law Journal* 14(1):105–154.

Polavarapu, Aparna (2013). Reconciling Indigenous and Women's Rights to Land in Sub-Saharan Africa. *Georgia Journal of International and Comparative Law* 42(1):93–132.

Polavarapu, Aparna (2019). Global Carceral Feminism and Domestic Violence: What the West Can Learn from Reconciliation in Uganda. *Harvard Journal of Law and Gender* 42(1):123–176.

World Bank (2009). *Uganda—Legal and Judicial Sector Study Report*. Available at https://openknowledge.worldbank.org/handle/10986/3088 (accessed 31 August 2018).

Part III

Advocacy and vulnerability for Sub-Saharan Africa's poorest

10 Conflict-related sexual violence and access to justice

The case of the Central African Republic

Isidore Collins Ngueuleu and Cristina Fernández-Durán Gortázar

Introduction

The United Nations (UN) Secretary-General's 2018 Report on conflict-related sexual violence (CRSV) focuses on 19 countries, of which nine are located in Sub-Saharan Africa. The report establishes a hypothetical correlation between sexual violence, countries affected by conflict and poverty, and the concentration of wars in Sub-Saharan Africa. It is well known that social, economic, political and environmental factors are all drivers of conflict, meaning that access to basic rights during wartime is often compromised. Therefore, the denial of basic rights, particularly access to justice, acts at both the cause and consequence of conflict. CRSV has only started to come under international scrutiny during the last three decades, despite sexual violence – whether for strategic purposes or not – having been linked to conflict historically.

Looking at the socio-economic dimension of conflicts, poverty and sexual violence appear intertwined in a vicious circle. Poverty increases women's vulnerability to sexual violence, while sexual and gender-based violence (SGBV) reduce women's socio-economic opportunities. In recent years, fighting poverty has become an important step to increasing access to justice for victims of CRSV.

In this chapter we aim to show what actual access to justice is available for victims and what role gender inequality plays in this. To this end, international, regional and domestic legal instruments and their applicability in Sub-Saharan African conflict settings will be explored. The chapter provides a legal definition of CRSV, which is then interrogated in the form of a case study on the Central African Republic (CAR). Ranked bottom of the Human Development Index and mired in protracted conflict, CAR is a paradigmatic example of the obstacles encountered by victims of CRSV to access justice.

Defining CRSV under international law

Despite numerous developments at the international level related to providing a legal framework on CRSV, there is still no clear definition of sexual violence (ICRC, 2015). This is the case for the four Geneva Conventions (GCs) and their corresponding protocols, as well as within the International Human Rights Law (IHRL). Only in International Criminal Law (ICL) has there been an observable effort at clarifying the concept.

The International Crime Tribunal for Rwanda (ICTR), in the *Akayesu* case, 1998, defined sexual violence as "any act of a sexual nature which is committed on a person under circumstances which are coercive", understanding coercion as not limited to physical "threats, intimidation, extortion and other forms of duress which prey on fear or desperation".[1] Furthermore, the Statute of Rome adopted by the International Criminal Court (ICC) includes "sexual slavery, enforced prostitution, forced pregnancy, enforced sterilization or any other form of sexual violence of comparable gravity"[2] as a crime against humanity. However, the terms used in these definitions above lack specificity and are wide-ranging. What exactly should be considered an "act of sexual nature"? Does it need to be physical? What would amount to "comparable gravity" when listing sexual violence acts?

It is also important to differentiate sexual violence from rape. Though they are generally understood as equivalent, rape is a more restrictive concept which falls *within* the definition of sexual violence. The International Criminal Tribunal for the former Yugoslavia offers a definition in the *Furundzija* case[3] applied – *inter alia* – by the ICC in the "Elements of crime".[4] The nuance between gender-based violence and sexual violence also becomes relevant when explaining this matter. Gender-based violence was defined by the Convention on the Elimination of all Forms of Discrimination Against Women (CEDAW) Committee as "violence directed against a woman because she is a woman or that affects to women disproportionately".[5] Gender-based violence includes violence that is not necessarily sexually based – as defined above – but gender-based, such as domestic violence, honour killings or forced marriage.

Finally, since we are specifically addressing sexual violence linked to conflict rather than general sexual violence, the question about what elements are needed to connect sexual violence with conflict is particularly relevant. Is it sufficient that an episode of sexual violence occurs during an armed conflict? The answer is not clear, but we could affirm that regarding the perpetrators, he/she must be an armed – State or non-State – actor (not a civilian) in order for the act to be considered CRSV (Wood, 2014). Regarding the purpose of violence, it is more difficult to draw clear criteria connecting sexual violence with armed conflict. It is commonly understood that sexual violence is used by armed actors as a weapon – that is, as a strategy of punishment, torture and terror – the practice not only being tolerated but purposefully implemented by armed organisations. However, some armed actors inflict sexual violence for individual purposes, with the organisation simply tolerating or even clearly forbidding such acts (Wood, 2014).

Ultimately, the nexus could be set by International Humanitarian Law (IHL) following the criteria that CRSV amounts to a violation of IHL.

However, this raises the question of whether all CRSV necessarily amounts to a violation of IHL or ICL. To what extent, then, does international law currently cover the case of CRSV?[6]

Prohibition of sexual violence under international law

The explicit prohibition of rape appears for the first time in the Lieber Code (1863),[7] a codification of international customary law regarding war, considered as the preamble to modern Humanitarian Law. However, after the Second World War, the Tokyo and Nuremberg Tribunals did not pursue rape or other forms of sexual violence that were generally not discussed. Progressively, some dispositions started to give legal protection to women and children, and subsequently some legal provisions began addressing sexual violence explicitly, but not linked to conflict. It was not until the early 1990s that awareness on wartime sexual rights' violations started to increase within the international community and thus be reflected in international law and soft law.

IHL: express prohibition but lack of definition

Rape and other forms of sexual violence are expressly prohibited in the GC IV, which provides that "women shall be specially protected against any attack on their honour, in particular against rape, enforced prostitution, or any form of indecent assault".[8] This provision is complemented by Additional Protocol I, which foresees that "outrages upon personal dignity, in particular humiliating and degrading treatment, enforced prostitution and any form of indecent assault (…) are prohibited (…) whether committed by civilian or by military groups".[9]

The prohibition of sexual violence is also reinforced under the interpretation of the prohibition of cruel treatment and torture in Article 3 common to all four GCs. This categorically protects – contrary to the previous disposition – both men and women, extending the prohibition not only to international armed conflicts but also to non-international armed conflicts. That said, the difficulty regarding the application of the GCs and the Additional Protocols is, as stated earlier, the lack of a precise definition of rape and/or sexual violence.

IHRL: prohibiting torture or cruel, inhuman or degrading treatment

Given that IHRL applies both in times of peace and war, it is pertinent to analyse the protection it provides and possible connections with the other instruments of international law. Furthermore, it is especially applicable to cases of sexual violence committed during armed conflict but not directly linked to conflict (as IHL requires).

Generally, International Human Rights treaties do not expressly mention the prohibition of rape or any other form of sexual violence. That said – as also occurs for IHL – it is through the prohibition of torture or cruel, inhuman or degrading treatment that the prohibition of sexual violence should be guaranteed: the UN Convention Against Torture (CAT) is the very cornerstone containing this prohibition and its consequent protection of victims.

Looking specifically at the African regional level, the Protocol to the African Charter on Human and Peoples' Rights on the Rights of Women in Africa (the Maputo Protocol) calls on all states to guarantee protection for women against all forms of sexual violence, with Article 11 ruling specifically on CRSV.[10] Although the definition is extensive and provides for women to be protected in armed conflict, its effectiveness at country level has often been questioned.

African Human Rights case law on CRSV is almost non-existent. This can be seen at the level of the African Commission on Human and Peoples' Rights, the African Court on Human and Peoples' Rights, and United Nations treaty monitoring bodies, as well as the courts of sub-regional intergovernmental organisations such as ECOWAS and SADC.[11] At the African Union(AU) level, the African Commission – despite its decisions not being formally binding for AU member states – is more active than the African Court. The *Democratic Republic of the Congo v. Burundi, Rwanda and Uganda, 2003* case is an example of this. The DRC alleged massive human rights violations during the Second Congo War, including mass rape, with the purpose of propagating HIV/AIDS in order to decimate the local population.[12]

International Criminal Law: rape and other forms of sexual violence as international crimes

The criminalisation of sexual violence was first recognised under the statutes of the International Criminal Tribunal for the Former Yugoslavia (ICTY) in 1993 and the International Criminal Tribunal for Rwanda (ICTR) in 1994 – and more widely interpreted through its jurisprudence – as a crime against humanity.

However, the central legal instrument regarding ICL is the ICC Statute which, coming later than the *ad hoc* tribunals above, offers a broader scope and more rigorous regulation on the matter, recognizing as criminal acts "rape, sexual slavery, enforced prostitution, forced pregnancy and enforced sterilization".[13] These violations are not only considered under the scope of crimes against humanity or genocide but are recognized as war crimes in their own right.

The first time the ICC recognised rape as a war crime was in the Jean-Pierre Bemba trial[14] (this point will be further developed later in the chapter) for crimes committed in CAR between 2002 and 2003. It is also important to mention the Special Court for Sierra Leone (SCSL), in which Liberian rebel leader (and future president of the country) Charles Taylor was sentenced for having been involved in subjecting the civil population of Sierra Leone to a campaign of terror, and particularly for using sexual violence as an instrument of terror. He was charged for with committing crimes against humanity by means of rape, sexual slavery and acts of terror, perpetrated through, inter alia, sexual violence.[15]

Soft Law in the fight against CRSV: UN resolutions

It is important to refer to the resolutions and declarations issued by the UN General Assembly and the Security Council, which have contributed *opinio iuris* to International Law on the prohibition of sexual violence. Several UN Resolutions have directly or indirectly contributed to the fight against sexual violence in relation to armed conflicts.[16] Resolution 1325 (2000) on Women and Peace and Security reaffirms the important role of women in the prevention and resolution of conflicts and is the base for further Resolutions specifically addressing CRSV, such as Resolution 1820 (2008), which links sexual violence as a tactic of war with women's peace and security issues, highlighting that sexual violence in conflict constitutes a war crime. UN Resolution 1888 (2009) – following resolution 1820 – mandates that peacekeeping missions protect women and children from sexual violence during armed conflict, and requests that the secretary-general appoint a special representative on sexual violence during armed conflict. In addition, Resolution 1612 (2005) on children in armed conflict explicitly condemns rape and other forms of sexual violence against children.

Actual access to justice for victims of CRSV

Despite the efforts made at an international community level, real cases show that there is a huge gap between law and practice. Mass rape and other acts of sexual violence continue to occur, with appalling numbers of victims reporting sexual abuses. Even more worrying are the numerous instances of impunity reported, as well as the many further victims who have not featured in reports. Data gathering remains a huge challenge. In 2010, the MARA (Monitoring, Analysis, and Reporting Arrangements) on CRSV was established by UN Security Council Resolution 1960 to ensure the systematic gathering of timely, accurate, reliable and objective information on CRSV against women, men and children.

A common pattern for Sub-Saharan African countries?

Focusing specifically on Sub-Saharan African armed conflicts, is there a common pattern regarding sexual violence offences? It is only in recent years that more consistent data on the matter[17] has been made available, which makes difficult a common characterization. Moreover, as Elisabeth Jean Wood suggests, it is not possible to define a pattern for CRSV as there is a big "variation in (the) repertoire, targeting and frequency of armed organisations"; specifically and concerning the purpose of the violence she suggests "widespread rape often occurs as a practice rather than a strategy" (Wood, 2014).

A pilot study (see Nordas, 2011) of CRSV in conflicts in 20 African countries and encompassing 177-armed conflict actors suggests – *inter alia* – that not all armed actors in African conflicts engage in sexual violence. This could mean that it is not necessarily part of their ideology or war strategy. This, in turn, would suggest that sexual violence is not inherent to these armed conflicts, and is therefore not inevitable. Regarding the overall number of victims per year, even if the number of actors reporting to have used sexual violence is decreasing, it is unclear whether the total number of victims per year is also decreasing. Those who are perpetrating acts of sexual violence are reported to be state actors in higher percentage than rebel groups or militias. The purpose of the violence perpetrated seems to be indiscriminate: in most of the conflicts, victims have not been selectively targeted. Concerning the relation between sexual violence and active conflict, the report suggests acts of sexual violence take place during the periods of war where there is relatively greater calm. Furthermore, the violations persist up to five years into the post-conflict period.

Access to justice for victims of sexual violence

International law instruments do not seem to be providing a satisfactory answer to the issues described above, with only individual perpetrators under International Criminal Law having been prosecuted. The numbers of those being prosecuted is extremely low, and convictions even lower. However, further developments in International Law dispositions are not needed. Rather, what is required is the correct application of these provisions in domestic law. As Seelinger (2014) points out, national courts should address the "accountability gap" by taking responsibility for the prosecution of international crimes.

Beyond implementing international rules in domestic law, strong institutions capable of properly and efficiently applying these rules, as well as working on prevention and strengthening potential victims' empowerment, are essential. This is underlined by the fact that most African countries affected by CRSV show fragile institutions at all levels in basic sectors such as health, education, the military and the judiciary, even during peacetime.

The UN secretary-general has raised the issue that many victims do not report the offences they have suffered, estimating that "for each rape reported in connection with a conflict, 10 to 20 cases go undocumented".[18] Various reasons – that will be further developed later in the chapter with relation to the CAR case study – prevent victims from reporting. These include: adding to the physical and psychological trauma already suffered, low levels of education, cultural taboos, economic barriers, and generalised gender-based discrimination leading to fears of being stigmatized. The consequence perpetrators evading prosecution and conviction by national systems of justice is a lack of confidence in state institutions – including the police and the judiciary – by the wider population.

CRSV in the CAR

Since gaining independence from France in 1960, the CAR has been characterized by recurring tensions, with periods of relative stability alternating with numerous crises. In recent decades the country has faced numerous *coup d'états* and rebellions that have caused its institutions to become fragile. This has had a big impact on the country's social fabric, generating inequalities and exclusions. CAR, which is ranked by UNDP as the poorest country in the world (PNUD, 2016:28), is a fragile State where 62% of its population live in poverty, and women are the most exposed to violence and marginalization. In recent years CAR has faced several conflicts in which sexual violence has been perpetrated. The question of whether these crimes are conflict-related or not will – accordingly to the aforementioned definitions – will be addressed hereafter, as well as the issue of access to justice.

In late 2013, a dramatic conflict erupted in the already fragile CAR, leading to a chaotic humanitarian situation involving forced displacement, destruction and looting of houses, thousands of killings, and various violations and exactions against men and women, including horrific sexual violence. The country was already recovering from a long series of crises, including a *coup d'état* and the 2003 conflict which had involved a similar level of violence and suffering. Today, almost 2.7 million people out of a total population of 4.6 million are in need of humanitarian assistance. Meanwhile, since the start of the 2013 crisis, over 600,000[19] people have been internally displaced across the country, over 570,000[20] have fled to neighbouring countries, and more than 5,000 people have been killed (OCHA, 2015). In this chapter, we will focus on the 2003 and 2013 CAR conflicts.

On 5 May 2014, the Special Representative on Sexual Violence in Conflict briefed[21] the Security Council Committee on the situation in CAR, noting that all warring parties had used sexual violence to subjugate and humiliate opponents. Many acts of sexual violence were documented, presenting either Fulani Mbarara communities or members of ex-Séléka, Anti-balaka, and *Révolution et Justice* or the *Front Démocratique du Peuple Centrafricain* armed groups as the authors. In 2014, for instance, "2,527 cases of conflict-related sexual violence cases were documented in the Central African Republic, including rape perpetrated to terrorize civilians, with many victims being assaulted in their homes, during door-to-door searches and while sheltering in fields or the bush".[22]

The link with the conflict

When considering the alleged aggravating circumstances relevant to rape in the *Bemba* case,[23] the Chamber took into account, *inter alia*, "whether the victims were armed, the location of crime, the victims' ages, particularly in cases of sexual violence; the duration and repeated nature of the acts; the perpetrators' motives; and the violent and humiliating nature of the acts".[24]

In 2015, almost 58% of the 30,000 cases of sexual violence reported to humanitarian actors were perpetrated by armed groups in circumstances of active conflict, or occurred within their area of influence during periods of instability and State failure (MISAC, 2015). The highest rate of violence occurred between September and October 2015 in Bangui, affecting mostly women. Not all acts of sexual violence, even in the context of conflict, are to be considered conflict-based. The United Nations Multidimensional Integrated Stabilization Mission in the Central African Republic (MINUSCA) verified 79 cases of CRSV. These were committed by former Séléka, Anti-balaka and Lord's Resistance Army elements; armed youth and self-defence groups; and *gendarmes* and the police.[25] It therefore appears from the UN secretary-general reports that the sexual violence recorded in the current CAR conflict is directly related to it either because belligerents used sexual violence as an instrument of war, or because of the unstable context in which the acts occurred.

Among the various acts of sexual violence perpetrated apart from rape, many cases of forced marriage and sexual slavery were reported. Married women were abducted from their homes and forced to marry former Séléka fighters, and allegations arose of women and girls being used as sex slaves by Anti-balaka elements.[26] Lewis Mudge, Africa researcher at Human Rights Watch, claimed in a report that "holding civilians captive, killing children, and sexually enslaving women and girls are shocking tactics by anti-balaka and amount to war crimes" (Human Rights Watch, 2015).

Perpetrators' motivation

Looking at the perpetrators' motivation in the *Bemba* case, the ICC concluded that there were aggravating circumstances, with the Chamber finding that the MLC troops (who perpetrated the crimes) did not receive adequate financial compensation and, in turn, self-compensated through acts of sexual violence, including rape. They also committed acts of rape in order to punish civilians who were suspected of being rebels or rebel sympathizers. That is how the connection between the acts themselves and the conflict was established, which would mean they constituted CRSV. Even if Jean-Pierre Bemba was acquitted of war crimes and released by the appeal chamber of the ICC,[27] all the testimonies show that the cases of sexual violence he was accused of were conflict-related.

Rape has been the most common crime in the 2013 conflict, and in many cases has been used to punish women suspected of trading with people on the other side of the sectarian divide.[28] It also involves the rape of minors, sexual slavery and sex demanded from women fleeing war zones as a form of "payment of passage".[29] Meanwhile, with regard to the 2003 conflict that led to the Bemba indictment, Dr André Tabo, expert on post-traumatic stress disorder ("PTSD") and sexual violence in armed conflict, testified during the trial that MLC soldiers used sexual violence as a weapon of war.[30]

For the first time, the reality of rape committed against men was properly discussed and addressed in an international court. Through the case, the ICC became the first international court prosecute and convict (though the accused was later acquitted) an individual for male rape under the specific charge of rape (Ruiz, 2016:17).

Sexual abuses by peacekeeping forces

In recent years, allegations of sexual exploitation and abuses (SEA) by peacekeepers were reported during conflicts, and sometimes in the course of military operations. It is complex to say whether such SEA is CRSV or not since, in general, peacekeepers are not part of the conflict. It is, nevertheless, clear that sexual abuses committed by peacekeepers are sexual violence. In 2015, "there was also a disturbing pattern of sexual exploitation and abuse by international peacekeepers, with the MINUSCA Conduct and Discipline Team addressing 23 cases".[31] In addition, almost 100 girls in CAR reported sexually abuses by international peacekeepers and French soldiers in 2014.[32]

Some of the abuses occurred during military operations and thus, by definition, can be said to amount to CRSV: "evidence strongly suggested that a 12-year-old girl was raped by a MINUSCA soldier during the operation, while two civilians were killed after UN soldiers apparently shot indiscriminately down an alleyway" (Amnesty International, 2016). As a result of these accusations, Congolese peacekeepers have been tried in their country for rape or attempted rape. It will be interesting to see if the conflict will be considered an aggravating circumstance and if the victim will participate in the trial.

The legal framework in CAR

In CAR, the legal framework protecting civilians against sexual violence has improved significantly in recent years (see Box 10.1). International instruments have been ratified, recommendations implemented, new institutions created and laws adopted or revised. However, access to justice in conflict-affected areas is not limited to legal changes and reforms. In most post-conflict areas, justice sector reforms have been the priority of international community. Often, violence not only destroys physical infrastructure but also social links, perceptions and habits. In this section we will show how, despite reconstruction efforts, access to justice remains a challenge.

Box 10.1 Legal frameworks, instruments and mechanisms

National and international legal frameworks prohibiting CRSV in CAR

At the IHRL level, there are numerous international legal instruments mentioned above that, whether binding or not, prohibit CRSV. According to the new adopted CAR Constitution,[33] the Rome Statute, IHRL Conventions and the Additional Protocols to the GCs that were ratified respectively in 2001, 1977 and in 1984, all became binding in the national legal framework. At the national level, sexual violence – whether conflict-related or not – is punished by Criminal Law, which provides for aggravating circumstances for some crimes. The 2010 Criminal Code punished rape with forced labour, and with double forced labour when the crimes are committed against a child.[34] Furthermore, when rape leads to the death of the victim, or is preceded by torture, kidnapping and/or ill treatments, the sanction can amount to the death penalty. Rape committed under threat of a weapon or by many people is to be sanctioned by forced labour for life.

Rape, therefore, is severely punished under Criminal Law, even if its criminalisation has varied during the last decades. Its legal ranking was changed from a crime to a misdemeanour in the 1990s, and then back to a crime in 2015, making it complicated for prosecutors and judges to properly sanction the offence. The reason for downgrading the crime of rape was economic: criminal proceedings are very expensive for the State to organise and are not held once a year as prescribed by the law. Thus, in order to avoid these proceedings – which are mandatory for crimes – it was recommended judges prosecute rape as a misdemeanour. As a consequence, penalties resulting from trials were more lenient.[35] In 2015, rape was again legally ranked as a crime. In addition to rape, Criminal Law punishes other acts of sexual violence, including forced prostitution, torture and other ill treatments, and sexual exploitation and slavery. By integrating the Rome Statute provisions, the CAR criminal code takes into account the particular offence of sexual violence during conflict. The punishment of rape is no longer limited to being an ordinary crime, but can be aggravated by circumstances of conflict. Therefore, sexual violence and other violations of IHL in CAR can be punished as crimes against humanity and war crimes.

National legal instruments protecting women rights

In addition to a very strict Criminal Code, CAR has adopted specific laws protecting women from violence in general and sexual violence in particular, whether in conflicts or not. Above all, the 2015 Constitution prohibits rape, torture and other ill treatments. The law adopted on 27 December 2006 on the protection of women against violence[36] punishes all sexual crimes cited in the criminal code and, moreover, considers and punishes attempted rape as actual rape. This constitutes an evolution from restricting rape to penetration, as stated in the criminal code. In general, among all acts of sexual violence, huge emphasis is placed on rape. The so-called Bangayassi law on reproductive health, adopted on 20 June 2006,[37] emphasises sexual violence against women and children. It punishes the forced prostitution of women and children, and also foresees the right to abortion in cases of pregnancy after rape, therefore prohibiting forced pregnancy.

Post-conflict special mechanisms

Following the recommendations of the Bangui reconciliation forum, a national law was adopted in 2015 creating and organising a special criminal court[38] the focus of which would be judging grave human rights violators at a country level. The court will benefit from the support of international judges working with national ones, therefore enhancing the capacity of national courts to provide justice. Similarly, a 2015 government decree[39] provided for the creation of a rapid intervention unit to help police officers and *gendarmes* in collecting evidence regarding sexual violence against women and child, and facilitating victims' access to justice.

Challenges to accessing justice for victims in CAR

Victims of sexual violence lack access to justice both because the conflict has completely destroyed the penal system, and because structural and cultural barriers impede victims' capacity to claim their rights.

Conflict and generalised violence

The CAR conflict's impact on tribunals, judges, prosecutors etc. has led to the closure of the judiciary. Judgments regarding CRSV are conducted by seven criminal courts across the country, the majority of which were attacked and looted during fighting. Hence all courts have remained closed until 2015 when the first criminal proceedings resumed in Bangui. As a result, the country's 28 ordinary courts and 162 magistrates effectively ceased to function (Amnesty International, 2017:28). In areas where fighting has stopped, magistrates have been redeployed to 23 courts across the country, but the majority of them returned to Bangui due to the situation of insecurity.[40]

The Bangui criminal courts resumed trials in July 2015 after almost ten years without a judgement.[41] In many cases in the East of the country, Seleka fighters have "systematically attacked or threatened judges, prosecutors and auxiliaries of justice. The legal and criminal response remains nascent or non-existent. In addition to the impunity of perpetrators the reiteration of their abuses, victims/survivors cannot initiate and/or complete their remission process" (MISAC, 2015).

It is clear that in countries such as CAR the intensity of conflict and the continuation of fighting even after peace agreements are signed are fundamental obstacles to the resumption of justice. Under such conditions, victims, lawyers, prosecutors and judges are all threatened by armed groups and are not able to take part in the claiming of justice. In parts of the country under the influence of armed groups, including Kaga Bandoro, Bambari, Ndélé, Batangafo and Birao, the local criminal justice system cannot arrest and prosecute those suspected of even minor or more serious crimes. There is no system to protect victims and witnesses from intimidation, making high-profile cases very difficult to prosecute. Magistrates working on high-profile cases have reported serious security threats aimed at themselves and their families.[42]

Weakness of the judicial system

Despite the changes made to the CAR legal system in order to facilitate victims' access to justice, there is still a culture of impunity in the country. In fact, after the 2003 mass violence none of the people accused of grave human rights violations were prosecuted. In a judgment delivered in 2006, the Bangui Court of Cassation noted the limits of national jurisdictions to prosecute international crimes and invited the ICC to investigate in CAR. Unfortunately, in 2007, the ICC only investigated the crimes committed by Jean-Pierre Bemba and was not interested in possible Central African accomplices such as A Patassé, P Miskine, V Barril, M Ndbababe, L Bangue-Tandet and Simon Pierre Koloumba (FIDH, 2006:38). As a result, justice was not granted to victims. On the contrary, amnesty agreements were adopted in 2008 for perpetrators of grave crimes (FIDH, 2013:42). In 2014, the ICC opened a second enquiry on CAR crimes but has not yet issued any indictments.

Socio-economic obstacles

In CAR, linguistic, financial, literacy and geographic barriers also hinder access to justice. The first and main obstacle faced by victims is related to judicial fees. Those with the financial means or political connections can obtain favourable rulings, while the poorest have to pay additional fees (Knoope & Buchanan-Clarke, 2017:11). Research by the World Bank revealed that economic inequality "contributes to the perception that money buys justice. Unfavourable outcomes for poor people are often interpreted in this light, and, indeed, the poor often came out the losers in the cases tracked by this research" (World Bank Group, 2012:49). In general, victims of rape have to pay judicial fees that are equivalent to 150 euro in a country where 68% of the population live on a dollar a day or less. Despite the support of international non-governmental organisations (NGOs) covering these charges, many victims are discouraged by the amount that has to be paid.

Cultural barriers also hinder victims of sexual violence, including CRSV, in accessing justice. When perpetrators are members of the community, victims are often prevented by their own families from reporting abuses to service providers, NGOs or the police. In the rare cases[43] where legal procedures are initiated, many survivors of sexual violence abandon the process in favour of traditional arrangements. It is estimated that 80% of cases reported to NGOs are dropped at the judicial phase.[44] Victims are also often victimized by their community, thereby obliging them to remain silent in order to avoid community rejection. This is why rape in particular is highly under-reported and justice inaccessible. From another standpoint, men are even less likely to report SGBV because of the fear of being judged by their families and communities (Case Matrix Network, 2017:19).

Gender inequality also constitutes an important obstacle for access to justice. In CAR, "women's opinions or problems are not treated with the same respect that those of men" before the formal justice system (World Bank Group, 2012:49). Finally, low levels of education and in some cases extremely long distances between police stations, lawyers, tribunals and the victims' residences are structural obstacles that lead victims of CRSV and their families to opt for informal settlements (Amnesty International, 2017).

The perception that victims have of the judicial system also explains the low access to justice. Courts have a reputation for being politicized, corrupt and insufficiently independent. In Bangui, it appears that about half of people looking for justice, "judged that the system is corrupt (45%), and many think that justice favours the rich (33%) and that payment is required for justice to be done (24%)"; while only "28% said that they had good or very good confidence in the justice system, whereas 29% said that they trusted judges and justice" (Vinck et al., 2017:56).

Conclusions

Despite important improvements registered during recent years, mainly at the level of international criminal law, a lack of clarity when addressing CRSV starts with the definition itself. The existing instruments of international law related to CRSV do not provide a satisfactory answer due to their inapplicability at a domestic level. Recognising the actual obstacles encountered by victims – showcased by the situation in CAR and including cultural stigmas; lack of access to related services such as health; the futility of a process without guarantees; financial barriers – allow for a better understanding of what access to justice should comprise.

The CAR has come a long way in providing improved access to justice for victims of sexual abuses. The legal infrastructure is better equipped to hold perpetrators of grave sexual abuses accountable. Even so, socio-economic factors continue to hinder access to justice. A survey conducted by the American Bar Association on justice and security in CAR reveals that for the respondents "justice consists of establishing the truth (48%) and punishing those responsible (47%)" (Vinck et al., 2017:56). This suggests that for the victims, justice is not only a punitive tool. Transitional justice mechanisms provide additional and complementary approaches of justice, such as truth and reconciliation, reparations and institutional reforms.

Our study shows that ensuring adequate access to justice for victims of CRSV entails multidimensional efforts, including legal, military, judicial, political, psychosocial, economic, education and gender measures. First and foremost, there is the judicial dimension. The system needs to be enabled to bring perpetrators of sexual violence to justice. International jurisdictions, national ordinary courts and Special Criminal Courts should all be used in a complementary approach to facilitating access to justice. However, it has been proven that in conflict-affected areas criminal justice is not the only way to achieve justice. It is therefore essential that non-judicial mechanisms such as a Truth and Reconciliation Commission should be mandated to facilitate disclosure of CRSV cases and encourage reparations are made to victims. Given the importance of conflict-related violence in CAR, it would be worth creating a sub-commission in order to hear victims, document violations, and make recommendations to prosecutors and decision makers. Similarly, reparation mechanisms should target both individual survivors of CRSV and their communities. In general, victims of sexual violence lack recognition of their victimhood and reparations, including psychosocial support.

There is a clear need, in the form of measure and policies, to address conflict sexual-based violence from a gender justice perspective. Other gendered actions – already foreseen in various UN Resolutions and including ensuring that a greater number of women are at the decision-making table – will allow more gendered solutions at the judiciary and legislative stages, facilitating better access to justice for women victims of CRSV.

Last but not least, legal and institutional reforms – including education programmes, affirmative acts, judicial fees waive, sensitisation campaigns, mobile justice – should be victim-based and transformative in design, implementation and impact. This should help in subverting socio-economic and cultural barriers preventing victims from accessing justice.

Notes

1 The Prosecutor v. Jean-Paul Akayesu (Trial Judgement), ICTR-96-4-T (International Criminal Tribunal for Rwanda [ICTR], 2 September 1998).

2 UN General Assembly. Rome Statute of the International Criminal Court. 17 July 1998. Article 7 g).

3 Prosecutor v. Anto Furundzija (Trial Judgement), IT-95-17/1-T (International Criminal Tribunal for the former Yugoslavia [ICTY], 10 December 1998).
4 ICC. Elements of Crimes. 2011. Article 7 (1) (g)-1.
5 UN General Assembly. Convention on the Elimination of All Forms of Discrimination Against Women. United Nations, Treaty Series. 18 December 1979. I. Introduction.
6 Beyond the field of International Law, the UN has adopted definitions bringing together several elements of International Law, see definition at UN Security Council, Report of the Secretary-General on Conflict-related sexual violence. April 2016. S/2015/203.
7 Lieber Code. Instructions for the Government of Armies of the United States in the Field. 24 April 1863.
8 ICRC. Geneva Convention (IV) relative to the Protection of Civilian Persons in Time of War. 12 August 1949. Article 27.
9 ICRC. Additional Protocol I to the Geneva Conventions of 12 August 1949 and relating to the Protection of Victims of International Armed Conflicts. 8 June 1977. Article 75.2.
10 African Union. Protocol to the African Charter on Human and People's Rights on the Rights of Women in Africa. 11 July 2003.
11 Case law consulted at the African Human Rights Case Law Database, Center for Human Rights, University of Pretoria
12 Democratic Republic of the Congo v. Burundi, Rwanda and Uganda, AHRLR 19 (ACHPR 2003).
13 UN General Assembly. Rome Statute of the International Criminal Court. 17 July 1998. Article 7 g).
14 Prosecutor v. Jean-Pierre Bemba Gombo, Decision on Sentence pursuant to Article 76 of the Statute, ICC-01/05-01/08-3399 (Trial Chamber III, International Criminal Court, 21 June 2016).
15 Prosecutor v. Charles Taylor, Judgment, SCSL-03-01-T (Trial Chamber II, The Special Court for Sierra Leone, 18 May 2012).
16 Security Council Resolutions on Women Peace and Security, 1325 (2000); 1820 (2008); 1888 (2009); 1960 (2010); 2106 (2013); and Children in Armed Conflict, 1612 (2005).
17 Actors other than UN have also contributed to improve the quality of data collection. For instance, one of the most remarkable initiatives is the Sexual Violence in Armed Conflict Dataset, available to access at www.sexualviolencedata.org/dataset.
18 UN Security Council. Report of the Secretary-General on Conflict-Related Sexual Violence. April 2016. S/2016/361.
19 UNHCR, Réponse Régionale à la crise des Réfugiés en République centrafricaine, http://data.unhcr.org/car/regional.php, consulted on 3 August 2018.
20 Ibid.
21 UN Security Council. Report of the Secretary-General on Conflict-Related Sexual Violence. 2015. S/2015/203.
22 Ibid. Paragraph 14.
23 The first time in the ICC's history in which rape and sexual violence were ranked as the most prominent charges levelled against a defendant was in the Bemba trial for crimes committed in CAR in 2003.
24 Prosecutor v. Jean-Pierre Bemba Gombo, Decision on Sentence pursuant to Article 76 of the Statute, ICC-01/05-01/08-3399 (Trial Chamber III, International Criminal Court, 21 June 2016).
25 UN Security Council. Report of the Secretary-General on Conflict-Related Sexual Violence. April 2016. S/2016/361. Paragraph 26.

26 Ibid. Paragraph 28.
27 Prosecutor v. Jean-Pierre Bemba Gombo, Judgment on the appeal of Mr Jean-Pierre Bemba Gombo against Trial Chamber III's "Judgment pursuant to Article 74 of the Statute" (Appeals Chamber Decision, International Criminal Court, 8 June 2018).
28 UN Security Council. Report of the Secretary-General on Conflict-Related Sexual Violence. April 2016. S/2016/361. Paragraph 26.
29 Prosecutor v. Jean-Pierre Bemba, Judgment pursuant to Article 74 of the Statute, Case No. ICC-01/05-01/08 (International Criminal Court, 21 March 2016). Paragraph 633.
30 Prosecutor v. Jean-Pierre Bemba Gombo, Decision on Sentence pursuant to Article 76 of the Statute, ICC-01/05-01/08-3399 (Trial Chamber III, International Criminal Court, 21 June 2016). Paragraph 44.
31 UN Security Council. Report of the Secretary-General on Conflict-related sexual violence. April 2016. S/2016/361.
32 See "'Bestiality claims by rights group against peacekeepers in Central African Republic" in *Daily Telegraph*, 31 March 2016. www.telegraph.co.uk/news/2016/03/31/bestiality-claims-by-rights-group-against-peacekeepers-in-centra, accessed 1 September 2016.
33 Constitution of the Central African Republic. Adopted March 2016.
34 Law No. 10.001. Criminal Code. Central African Republic. 6 January 2010.
35 Interview with Daniel Bangui, lawyer and project director of America Bar Association in Bangui. September 2016.
36 Law No. 006.032. On the protection of women against violence. Adopted 27 December 2006.
37 Law No. 06.005. On reproductive health. Adopted 20 June 2006.
38 Law No. 15.003. Creating and organizing a special criminal court. Adopted 2015.
39 Decree No. 15007. Creating a mix unit of rapid intervention and repression of sexual violence against women and child. Adopted January 2015.
40 Interview with the prosecutor of Paoua tribunal and judge of Bambari Criminal Court, September 2016.
41 According to an Amnesty International report, the last criminal session took place 2010. See Amnesty International (2017:24).
42 UN Security Council. Special Report of the Secretary-General on the Strategic Review of the United Nations Multidimensional Integrated Stabilization Mission in the Central African Republic. 22 June 2016. S/2016/565.
43 Only 2% of the 60,000 cases reported to courts in 2015, according to the Gender-Based Violence Information Management System (GBV IMS).
44 Interview with lawyer and project director of America Bar Association in Bangui.

Bibliography

Amnesty International (2016). Amnesty International Report 2015/16 – Central African Republic. 24 February 2016. Available at: https://www.refworld.org/docid/56d05b6911.html.

Amnesty International (2017). République Centrafricaine. Le long chemin vers la justice. L'obligation de rendre des comptes. London, Index number: AFR 19/5425/2017. Available at: https://www.amnesty.org/download/Documents/AFR1954252017ENGLISH.PDF

Case Matrix Network (2017). National Legal Requirements: Sexual and Gender-Based Violence in CAR. February 2017.

FIDH (2006). RCA, Oubliées, Stigmatisées: La double peine des victimes de crimes internationaux. October 2006.

FIDH (2013). République centrafricaine: Un pays aux mains des criminels de guerre de la Séléka. PARIS. Available at: https://www.fidh.org/IMG/pdf/rapport_d_enque_te_rca-ld3.pdf

Human Rights Watch (2015). Central African Republic: Muslims Held Captive, Raped. UN, Government Should Free Ethnic Peuhl Women, Children Held by Anti-Balaka. April 2015.

ICRC (2015). Prevention and Criminal Repression of Rape and Other Forms of Sexual Violence during Armed Conflicts. 11 March 2015. International Committee of the Red Cross Advisory Service on International Humanitarian Law.

Knoope, P., and Buchanan-Clarke, S. (2017). Central African Republic: A Conflict Misunderstood. Institute for Justice and Reconciliation Occasional Paper 22.

MISAC (2015). R.C.A. – Monitoring 2015 des violences basées sur le genre et des violences sexuelles. Bulletin infographique No. 2. December 2015.

Nordas, R. (2011). Sexual Violence in Armed Conflict, Key Findings: Sexual Violence in African Conflicts. CSCW Policy Brief 01.

OCHA (2015). Central African Republic: A Call for Humanitarian Assistance. Responding to the Needs of Those Affected by the Emergency in CAR. Humanitarian Needs Overview (HNO) and Humanitarian Response Plan (HRP). Available from: www.unocha.org/sites/dms/CAR/Flyer%20SRP%20Draft4.pdf (accessed 18 March 2019).

PNUD (2016). Le développement humain pour tous. Rapport sur le développement humain 2016.

Ruiz, L. (2016). Gender Jurisprudence for Gender Crimes? ICD Brief. 20 June.

Seelinger, K. (2014). Domestic Accountability for Sexual Violence: The Potential of Specialized Units in Kenya, Liberia, Sierra Leone and Uganda. *International Review of the Red Cross* 96:539–564.

Vinck, P., Pham, P., Kelly, C., and Meyer, T. (2017). Justice and Security Diagnostic, Bangui, Central African Republic. Harvard Humanitarian Initiative and American Bar Association Rule of Law Initiative. November 2017. Available from: www.dmeforpeace.org/wp-content/uploads/2019/01/aba-roli-car-bangui-diagnostic-report-0917.pdf (accessed 18 March 2019).

Wood, E. (2014). Conflict-Related Sexual Violence and the Policy Implications of Recent Research. *International Review of the Red Cross* 96:457–478.

World Bank Group (2012). Understanding Access to Justice and Conflict Resolution at the Local Level in the Central African Republic (CAR). February 2012.

11 Domestic violence against rural women in Nigeria

Effective access to justice?

Ifeoma Pamela Enemo

Introduction

Women living in the rural areas of Nigeria referred to here as rural women are generally poor and face a number of challenges due to their living in remote areas. They are often lacking in matters of basic need, such as food, clothes, and shelter, and have limited access to health services, portable water, sanitation, and information (Zaid & Popoola, 2010). Amongst the major challenges they face are domestic violence and access to justice.

The problem of domestic violence in Nigeria is very serious and widely prevalent, negatively impacting the victims, their families, and even wider communities. Domestic violence seems even more prevalent in rural areas than in urban areas; thus, there is a need to focus on rural women, who, oppressed by culture and tradition, are often left powerless and poor (Chwarae Teg, 2015). The question whether these women effectively have access to justice arises.

What is domestic violence?

When violence takes place between family members or intimate partners, it is known as Domestic or Family Violence. If within an intimate relationship, it can also be labelled Intimate Partner Violence.

Domestic violence may take a number of forms, including physical aggression or assault, stalking, sexual assault, and rape. The latter, includes a person being forced to have sex with someone with whom they might otherwise engage in consensual sex. This may be called marital rape if it takes place between a married couple, though this is not yet recognised in Nigerian law. Other forms include: emotional/psychological abuse, physical neglect, economic or financial abuse, and verbal abuse. Controlling behaviour is another form of domestic violence, aimed at compelling someone to comply with an abuser's wishes, such as what to wear or who to speak with.

Domestic violence shall in this chapter be viewed from the angle of the wife or partner suffering the abuse. However, it should be borne in mind that much of the abuse taking place in rural areas happens behind closed doors, with no witnesses except family members. It is thus difficult to prove unless the abuser pleads guilty. Victims are often unwilling to report incidents, making it difficult to compile accurate data, and are generally unwilling to take civil action. It is a truism in Nigeria, particularly rural areas that a woman who institutes a legal action against her husband – claiming damages for false imprisonment, for example – has actually decided that the marriage is over. She then has the choice of either not returning to her marital home, or returning to face further, possibly even worse, abuse. She will likely also be ostracised by members of her extended family.

Factors promoting domestic violence

Women in rural areas engage largely in subsistence farming, and for the most part have little or no access to formal education, particularly in northern Nigeria (Ashimolowo & Otufale, 2012). With no access to credit facilities, they are often unable to satisfy even basic needs such as food, clothes or shelter (Zaid & Popoola, 2010). They therefore live in deprivation, despite mostly being married.

It is worth noting that rural women are more likely to suffer domestic violence than those in urban areas, and also face more challenges in responding. These challenges are myriad, and include poverty, lack of education, lack of access to information, as well as cultural values such as kinship ties and a conservative view of the status accorded women. Consequently, the rate of domestic violence in rural areas is high. The data from Nigerian Demographic and Health Survey (NDHS) of 2013 shows that spousal violence is high, with one-in-four women reporting they had experienced physical, sexual, or emotional violence by their husband/partner. Furthermore, 35% of women believed that wife-beating is justified as a response in certain circumstances (NPC Nigeria & ICF International, 2014).

A major factor fuelling domestic violence in rural areas is that men often exhibit a very domineering attitude towards women, who on their part are cowed into becoming subservient and timid. This is particularly the case where there is wide age gap between husband and wife and is exacerbated by poverty, with economic pressure often inducing feelings of frustration and anger in men that are manifested in domestic violence against their partners. It is further worsened by the fact that resources and services for victims of domestic abuse are few to non-existent.

Other factors promoting domestic violence against the rural women include a wife's inability to give birth to a male child, mistaken interpretations of religious teachings, and the unfortunate provisions within Nigerian law allowing wife chastisement.

Effects of and responses to domestic violence

Domestic violence has led to the death of many women in rural and even urban areas of Nigeria. Beyond this, many women have been maimed and disfigured, or mentally and emotionally damaged, while others have been rendered homeless due to domestic violence perpetrated against them. A 2005 Amnesty International Report on Nigeria states that

> on a daily basis, women are beaten and ill-treated for supposed transgressions, raped and even murdered by members of their family. In some cases, vicious attacks leave them with horrific disfigurements. Such violence is too frequently excused and tolerated in communities and not denounced. Husbands, partners and fathers are responsible for most of the violence against women.
>
> (Cited in Abayomi & Olabode, 2013)

Many women in rural areas are, unfortunately, so indoctrinated by sociocultural norms and structures that they have internalised the idea that they are inferior to men. In a group discussion held with women in Igbo land, the view held was that a husband could beat his wife if she had done something wrong – that it is a corrective and training measure. The caveat was that the man should realise that women are weak and, therefore, only beat his wife moderately. To these women, a woman deserved beating if she talked back, disobeyed her husband, refused him sex, presented poorly cooked food, or failed to care for the children. She could also be beaten if she disrespected her husband's parents or relations or openly challenged her husband if she saw him with another woman. They felt, though, that such beatings should be rare: "after all if he hits the wife hard and injures her, he will incur hospital bills (Ilika, 2005)."

This mindset encourages the abused women to keep silent over serious abuses and remain in their relationships. As a result, women find it very difficult to leave abusive marriages, especially when other factors – such as repayment of bride price and the stigma of being a failure in marriage – are considered. Despite this, it is important to mention that there are some rural women who are willing to report their abuser to the police, their church, or elders. Unfortunately, the outcome of such actions often impacts negatively on the women. The woman may be thrown out of her home; the Police may refuse to intervene in what they perceive to be a domestic quarrel, and the woman may be ostracised by family members.

How effective is access to justice by rural women?

Effective access to justice is essential to rural women who are victims of domestic violence. Such access to legal redress would require that they are aware of their rights and have access to institutions that can remedy violations of those rights. The Food and Agriculture Organization of the UN (FAO) has argued that access to justice shouldn't be conceived of as limited to lawyers and courts. Rather, it includes the assurance that rights, and their correlative protections, are recognised through law, both formal and informal. It is also their view that this includes access to institutions, including customary/traditional ones, and to clear, simple, and affordable procedures for remedying abuses. In other words, law and justice mechanisms should be made as simple as possible, and be accessible to all, including the most vulnerable (FAO, 2013).

The question, then, is whether rural women have effective access to justice in Nigeria. The answer, regrettably, is that in most cases of domestic violence they do not.

Formal methods of accessing justice

Rural women have two options for accessing justice through formal means: police intervention and the courts. These options are explained below.

Police intervention

A major problem encountered by rural women in reporting instances of domestic abuse to the police is the levity with which such matters are treated. The police may choose not to enter premises where domestic violence is taking place because they deem it a private matter, and so there are no "reasonable" grounds to suspect that a breach of the law has actually occurred. Police officers routinely underestimate the reality or fear of violence, dismissing women's appeals for help, and often subscribe to the view that the woman probably provoked the violence in some way. In cases where Police officers do not act on a complaint, they compound the lack of response by failing to refer women to other places or organisations where they might get help, such as non-governmental organisations (NGOs) or the Legal Aid Council. A rural woman, using the last of her money to transport herself to the police station in order to report yet another act of domestic violence by her husband, was told by the policeman on duty: "Is that why you came here? What of my wife that I beat every day, has she reported to anyone?" This, unfortunately, is emblematic of the attitude of many within law enforcement, with such abuse considered a private affair between husband and wife. Generally speaking, the courts and police in rural areas simply do not respond to protect women who formally complain of domestic abuse if the violence is considered to be within cultural norms. Even when abusers are arrested or detained, police corruption is such that they are frequently quickly released to return home and commit further acts of violence, deterring the victim from making any future complaint. It is often only in extreme cases where serious disability, or even death, occur that the police finally act.

A key innovation of the South African Domestic Violence Act 1998 is the introduction of statutory monitoring and oversight of police enforcement of the law. Here, failure by the police to assist victims/complainants is viewed as a disciplinable offence, and officers are expected to treat victims with sensitivity and care. This is commendable and worthy of emulation.

The courts

An aggrieved person in any State can apply to the High Court in Nigeria for redress regarding allegations that constitutional provisions against domestic violence have been, are being, or are likely to be contravened against them. The court can respond to such applications by issuing injunctions or giving directions as may be considered appropriate for the purpose of enforcing these economic, social or cultural rights.

Domestic violence is regarded by some Nigerians as a social problem that ought not to be under the jurisdiction of the criminal justice system. This has seriously affected the attitude of the court, with social, cultural, and religious beliefs (especially in rural areas) negatively impacting the enforcement of domestic violence laws in the courts. Harsh punishments for domestic violence often end up penalising the wife or family members, as fines may be paid from a joint bank account, and the imprisonment of the accused may cause financial hardship to the victim, given the accused in most cases is the household breadwinner. Women also have to face the fear of possible revenge by the accused once they have served their sentence, as well as situations where they are isolated from their extended family or the community due to their having taken legal action (Umeobi & Ikpeze, 2012). These represent serious inhibitions to rural women accessing the courts.

All the above is exacerbated by a painfully slow judicial system, with cases adjourned due to technicalities, the inability of police to produce witnesses, corruption, lack of modern management equipment, and many other reasons.

Informal methods of accessing justice

Most rural women do not bother accessing justice through formal means due to the obstacles and challenges they face. They may therefore have to resort to informal methods; in the first place making a complaint to either the family head, other relatives, or family friends. If the matter is not resolved, it may go to the *Umunna* (extended family), or *Igwe* (king). The matter could equally be taken to a priest, a pastor, or an imam. This informal method has the attraction of confidentiality and is also accessible to rural women in that they can make their report without having to spend money.

However, despite this method being geographically and economically accessible to rural women, there is the challenge that the traditional heads or rulers are guided by customs which often do not respect women's human rights, and instead reflect prevailing attitudes regarding violence against women. Those handling these matters are almost all men, and their judgements reflect the bias towards male privilege and rights. Even so, rural women for the most part prefer this method, since they are more familiar with the people presiding over the matters, and understand the processes and potential outcomes. While proceedings in such cases are not usually recorded, it does seem a record system is currently taking root and that would give women some confidence that any decisions reached would not be breached in future (Arnot, 2015).

Obstacles to effective access to justice

Most rural women have not been adequately exposed to human rights education, nor adequate information about the courts. Many are unaware of their legal rights and do not have the financial resources to take a case to court or pay for legal services. Furthermore, Nigeria's Legal Aid Council has failed to help poor rural women access judicial remedies due to chronic underfunding.

Access to justice by rural women is therefore inhibited by factors such as poverty, marginalisation, high court costs and lack of access to legal assistance. Below, some of the major obstacles are discussed further.

Poverty

Poverty among the rural women makes them vulnerable to a variety of human rights abuses, including domestic violence, and this has been exacerbated by the economic recession in Nigeria. Poverty means rural women are usually economically dependent on their husbands, preventing them from pursuing claims against them. The cost of legal representation is unaffordable to rural women, as are transportation costs, which hinder them from accessing legal assistance from the Legal Aid Council or NGOs based in faraway urban areas. The very poor among them would need to trek unbearable long distances to reach police stations, court houses, or even a lawyer's chambers. They can also not afford many other costs associated with the justice system in Nigeria, for example, court fees which can definitely prevent the rural women from pursuing criminal or even civil cases on domestic violence. Again, the fact that they would lose income while away from their subsistence activities is another obstacle.

Discriminatory laws

Rural women can only seek remedy if the law can establish and protect their rights. Customary laws in force in some parts of Nigeria, such as the southeast, do not permit women to own or inherit land or landed property. This makes it difficult for them to leave a marriage due to domestic violence, as being denied these sources of income and livelihood means they often are unable to find means to financially support themselves. With respect to formal laws penalising criminal acts in Nigeria, the Criminal Code Act applies in Southern Nigeria, while the Penal Code Act applies in Northern Nigeria (see Box 11.1).

Box 11.1 The Penal Code (Northern Nigeria) and the Criminal Code (Southern Nigeria)

The Penal Code

The Penal Code gives a husband the right to chastise his wife, provided the chastisement is reasonable. It does not, however, stipulate what might be considered "reasonable", leaving open the interpretation that such chastisement can include physical violence.

According to section 55 (1)(d), of the Penal Code,

> Nothing is an offence which does not amount to infliction of grievous hurt upon any person which is done … by a husband for the purpose of correcting his wife, such husband and wife being subject to any native law and custom under which such correction is lawful.

The Penal Code's definition of "grievous hurt" is set at a very high level – for example, it specifies "any hurt which endangers life or which causes the sufferer to be during the space of twenty days, in severe bodily pains" – meaning lower levels of violence are in effect legally acceptable.

The Criminal Code

The Criminal Code provides for assault, making it possible for a victim of domestic violence to be protected under it. Section 353 states that any person indecently assaulting a man is guilty of a felony and is liable to three years' imprisonment, while section 360 states that any person indecently assaulting a woman or girl is guilty of a misdemeanour and liable to two years' imprisonment. In distinguishing between men and women in this way, the law is clearly discriminatory.

One of the most serious forms of domestic violence is sexual violence, including rape. According to Section 358 of the Criminal Code, the punishment for rape is life imprisonment with or without caning. However, marital rape is not recognised under the Criminal Code (this is also the case under the Penal Code if the wife has attained puberty), as husband and wife are regarded as a legal entity deemed to have granted consent to a lifelong sexual relationship.

Lack of information and knowledge

Rural women lack information regarding the laws protecting them, their rights, and even how to go about claiming their rights. This is attributable to the high level of illiteracy among rural women, with most never having attended school. Given this, when affected by domestic violence, they have no idea on what practical steps they should take to seek legal redress. Even when they do have some idea of their rights, their inability to read and write deters them from making use of the justice system.

Sociocultural issues

Women in rural areas are in a socially subordinate position, and this affects them adversely in every area of their lives. Where a domestic violence dispute occurs, the women are unable to seek justice from the police or courts due to fear of retribution and ostracism by family and community members.

Conclusion

Rural women, like any other Nigerian citizen, have a right to dignity and freedom from discrimination. Effective access to justice would help them realise such rights and reduce the prevalence of domestic violence against them. Poverty, discriminatory laws, lack of information and knowledge, and sociocultural issues are some of the obstacles impeding access to justice by rural women. Unfortunately, rural women often – for understandable reasons – prefer to remain silent rather than reporting incidents of domestic violence. Addressing domestic violence and access to justice for women in the rural areas therefore requires a strenuous joint effort from various parties at all levels of society to ensure victims' needs are met and offenders are held accountable for their actions. With this in mind, the following recommendations serve as a starting point for how such change might be achieved.

NGOs, community-based organisations (CBOs), and civil-society organisations (CSOs), in collaboration with the media, should embark on awareness raising and sensitisation of rural women as to their rights. They should also sensitise men on the need for a change of attitude towards women, particularly regarding domestic violence. In addition, they should organise the training of paralegals and establish legal clinics and branch offices in rural communities, thereby ensuring access to rural women victims of domestic violence.

Police officers need to be trained on how to address issues affecting women, with human rights desks established in every police station for the protection of victims. In addition, Nigeria's lawmakers should familiarise themselves with and consider emulating the provisions of the Domestic Violence Act 1998 of South Africa, in respect of actions to be taken by the police in matters of domestic violence, including sanctions for misconduct. Judges should also be trained on the legal instruments available for protecting the human rights of women, and cite and apply them positively in their judgments. This should also help ensure trials for domestic violence issues are conducted with appropriate speed.

The Federal and State Governments should take positive action to promote women's participation in politics and decision-making bodies. They should also enact appropriate legislation to deal decisively with all forms of discrimination, specifically prohibiting domestic violence against women. Furthermore, poverty reduction is a priority task which the Federal Government must embark on with regard to the economic growth and development of rural areas, thereby enabling effective access to justice by the rural women. The Federal Government should also provide more funds to those judicial institutions promoting access to justice, such as the Legal Aid Council.

It is important to stress that the prevention of domestic violence is a serious task requiring fundamental changes in Nigerian society, and it is not something that can be left to politicians, the police and courts alone. Rather, a coordinated community effort by traditional rulers, community leaders, NGOs, and other stakeholders would help in empowering rural women, realigning rural men's view of women, and increasing the number of abusers arrested and prosecuted.

Bibliography

Abayomi AA and Olabode KT (2013). Domestic Violence and Death: Women as Endangered Gender in Nigeria. *American Journal of Social Research.* 3(3):53–60. doi:10.5923/j.sociology.20130303.01.

Arnot B (2015). How Traditional Justice in Nigeria Is Changing. *Voices Magazine.* 24 February 2015. www.britishcouncil.org/voices-magazine/how-traditional-justice-nigeria-changing (accessed 30 August 2018).

Ashimolowo OR and Otufale GA (2012). Assessment of Domestic Violence among Women in Ogun State, Nigeria. *Greener Journal of Social Sciences.* 2(3):102–114. nigeriahealthwatch.com/wp-content/uploads (accessed 3 August 2016).

Chwarae Teg (2015). A Woman's Place in Lesotho: Tackling the Barriers in Gender Equality. A Report by Chwarae Teg on Behalf of the Welsh Government. pp. 3–7. www.cteg.org.uk/wp-content/uploads/2015/04/chwarae-teg-report-a-womans-place-in-lesotho-DT-en.pdf (accessed 4 August 2018).

FAO (2013). Rural Women and Access to Justice: AO's Contribution to a Committee on the Elimination of Discrimination Against Women (CEDAW) Half-day General Discussion on Access to Justice (Geneva, 18 February 2013). www.ohchr.org/documents/HRBodies/CEDAW/AccesstoJustice/FAO.pdf (accessed 2 August 2016).

Ilika AL (2005). Women's Perception of Partner Violence in a Rural Igbo Community. *African Journal of Reproductive Health.* 9(3):77–88. www.bioline.org.br/pdf?rh05042 (accessed 25 August 2013).

National Population Commission (NPC) [Nigeria] and ICF International (2014). Nigeria Demographic and Health Survey 2013. Abuja, Nigeria and Rockville, MA: NPC and ICF International. https://dhsprogram.com/publications/publication-FR293-DHS-Final-Reports.cfm (accessed 28 August 2018).

Umeobi CA and Ikpeze OV (2012). Domestic Violence against Women; Governments Laissez Faire and Police Lackadaize in Assumption of Jurisdiction: A Mims Government. *Nasarawa State University Law Journal.* 5:56–69.

Zaid YA and Popoola SO (2010). Quality of Life among Rural Nigerian Women: The Role of Information. *Library Philosophy and Practice (e-journal).* http://digitalcommons.unl.edu/libphilprac/513 (accessed 1 June 2016).

12 Strengthening access to justice for women refugees and asylum seekers in South Africa

Fatima Khan and Ncumisa Willie

Introduction

In 2011, the International Migration Annual Review estimated there were a billion migrants in the world (International Organization for Migration, 2011). In 2019, the United Nations High Commissioner for Refugees (UNHCR) reported that the world was witnessing the highest levels of displacement on record and that an unprecedented 70.8 million people around the world had been forced from their homes, among them nearly 25.9.3 million refugees (UNHCR, 2019). South Africa has also experienced an increase in migration, and in 2009 the UNHCR noted that the country had received the highest number of asylum seekers individually processed by a government.[1] All of this places an added responsibility on receiving states to treat victims of forced migration with dignity, compassion and understanding. However, it is common knowledge that refugees and asylum seekers often experience discrimination and exclusion in host countries and that the law is not always protective of their needs. Therefore, access to justice is important, as it is often the only way that refugees and asylum seekers can enjoy the rights they are entitled to in host countries. In this chapter we attempt to analyse what the right to access to justice in South Africa means for refugee and asylum-seeking women. Here, we understand access to justice to mean access to not only the judicial system but also to the state institutions and services which allow an individual to live a dignified life. To this end, access to the asylum process is viewed as an important gateway to access to justice.

This chapter will briefly introduce the refugee situation in South Africa, arguing that although South Africa has a progressive Constitution, with a Bill of Rights which affords comprehensive rights to all who live in the country, access to those rights is subject to one's social position, gender, nationality and sometimes one's sexual orientation. The chapter thus seeks to analyse how refugee women's multiple identities affect their ability to access justice in South Africa.

Conceptualising the notion of access to justice

Access to justice can be defined in numerous ways, both narrowly and more broadly. The narrow conception of access to justice originates from the 18th to 19th centuries: during this time access to justice was narrowly conceptualised as referring to an individual's formal right to litigate and defend themselves. Accordingly, Cappelletti and Garth defined access to justice as the right to "have your day in court" (Cappelletti & Garth, 1978:8). During this period, access to justice was perceived as a natural right which accrued to all men. However, this conception of access to justice did not impose a positive duty on the State to protect this right. Consequently, the narrow conception of access to justice focuses on access to the legal or justice system. A broader definition of access to justice expands this notion to include social institutions and variables (Currie & De Waal, 2013:704). It takes cognisance of the fact that access to justice includes social justice, which is mitigated by many factors such as poverty, gender, nationality and age. The broader conception of access to justice also seeks to reform and streamline many areas of the legal system and social institutions. In the broader sense, access to justice is viewed in light of social variables that negatively impact the ability of certain groups to access the justice system. Given this broad and context-sensitive conception of access to justice, it is clear that the concept is highly nuanced and subjective, making a universal definition impossible (Good, 2009:47).

In South Africa, access to justice is often framed within the context of the legal system and administrative justice. This framing highlights two crucial objectives of the legal system: the legal system must be equally accessible to all, and it must lead to results that are individually and socially just. In 2000, the Constitutional Court stated that "... access to justice advocates for greater responsiveness in the administration of law".[2]

Access to justice therefore involves preventing the violation of one's rights and attaining an effective remedy whenever those rights are breached. It can also be conceived as removing barriers to the attainment of justice. It is clear that the concept of access to justice has evolved over the years from a narrow definition referring to access to legal services and other state services (access to courts or tribunals), to a broader one that includes social justice, economic justice and environmental justice. Recently, the South African Commissioner for Human Rights noted,

> [j]ustice is not the exclusive preserve of the courts. The Constitution ... is designed to achieve justice in the broader sense including social justice and various functionaries including government, independent institutions, the private sector and indeed civil society take on a special responsibility for the achievement of justice and thus access to justice is more, much more tha[n] simply access to courts
>
> (Kollapen, 2003)

In this chapter, we analyse the barriers to attaining the rights and the remedies that should be available to refugee women in South Africa. In doing so, we look at the obstacles present in the asylum-seeking process and in government institutions that refugee women interact with on a daily basis. These barriers substantially influence access to social, economic and legal rights for refugee women in South Africa. This is because for refugees, and particularly refugee women, access to justice in South Africa is highly dependent on the acquisition of legal documentation. We therefore take the approach that access to justice can be seen in an individual's everyday experiences. The chapter will begin by tracing the origins of the access to justice concept from an international law and regional perspective, as well as examining how South Africa translates the international right into its domestic laws. It will then look at the barriers to access to justice faced by refugees and refugee women in South Africa.

Access to justice in International Law

The right to access to justice is set out in a number of international legal instruments and protocols. Spigelman states that access to justice emerged as a human right when provisions related to it were included in the International Human Rights instruments adopted after World War Two (Spigelman, 2000:141). The Universal Declaration of Human Rights of 1948 (UDHR)[3] makes direct reference to the right to access justice in articles 8, 10 and 11. These provisions recognise the right to procedural and substantive access to justice. Following its establishment, the UDHR set out to establish ways in which the rights contained in its provisions could become legally binding on States. International Covenant on Civil and Political Rights (ICCPR)[4]and its protocols were established to achieve this goal. The ICCPR and its protocols, together with the International Covenant on Economic Social and Cultural Rights (ICESCR), [5] are thus the main binding sources of the right to access to justice in international law. The International Bill of Rights[6] also contains crucial principles pertaining to the right to access to justice.

The rights and responsibilities of refugees are contained in the 1951 United Nations Convention Relating to the Status of Refugees.[7] This Convention makes direct reference to the right to access to justice for refugees via the courts. Article 16 of the Convention states that a refugee has the right to free access to the courts in the territory of every State party to the Convention. Moreover, refugees have the right to be granted the same access as nationals in the State in which they reside. This non-discrimination clause requires States to grant the same rights to refugees as they would to their own citizens, including the right to free legal assistance. This means that refugees have the right to access courts not only in the country in which they are seeking asylum and are habitual residents but, by virtue of the fact that they are refugees, in all States party to the Convention.

African Charter (Banjul) on human and peoples' rights

From an African regional perspective, the 1981 African Charter (Banjul) on Human and Peoples' Rights (ACHPR)[8] makes provisions for the right to access justice. Article 6 states that every individual shall have the right to liberty and to the security of his person, and in particular that no one may be arbitrarily arrested or detained. Furthermore, Article 7 states that "every individual shall have the right to have his cause heard."

These articles lay the foundation for the conception of the right to access justice in African international law. However, many scholars argue that these provisions are not sufficient in addressing this right. It is therefore argued that articles 60 and 61 of the ACHPR address these inadequacies by enabling it to draw inspiration from international law on human rights and to take into consideration as subsidiary measures other general or special international conventions, customs generally accepted as law, principles of law recognised by African States, as well as legal precedents and doctrines. These recommendations and standards are not law, though they assist in the interpretation of the ACHPR. It is thus clear that access to justice in these international instruments establishes two distinct rights: the procedural right of effective access to a fair hearing and a substantive right to a remedy. What follows is an assessment of the right to recourse should the right to access be breached.

Access to remedies

It is commonly accepted that with every legal right comes a corresponding duty to establish procedural mechanisms to give effect to that right. Human rights law has emphasised the point that a legal right without access to any mechanism to effectively enforce it is meaningless. This is why the ICCPR in Article 2(3) places on States the obligation to ensure that everyone has access to remedies for violation of any of the rights recognised in the Convention. This article expands on Article 8 of the UDHR, which states that "Everyone has the right to an effective remedy by the competent national tribunals for acts violating the fundamental rights granted to him by the constitution or by law."

Thus, these provisions demonstrate that the existence of a right is not adequate in itself; there needs to be a corresponding, effective remedy for enforcing that right. Moreover, the ICCPR also states that, in order for the rights contained in its provisions to be enjoyed, States need to take appropriate steps and adopt available remedies in order to take account of the special vulnerabilities of certain groups of people. This chapter posits that refugees and asylum seekers fall under this category of vulnerable persons.

A brief history of refugee law in South Africa

The history of refugee law and policy in South Africa spans the colonial, Apartheid and post-Apartheid eras. It shows that South African refugee law and policy have evolved from a preoccupation with race as its organising framework under colonialism and the Apartheid regime, to a framework that places human rights at its centre under the new Constitution.

By 1994, South Africa had decided to move away from a policy of exclusion to one of inclusion on the basis of its new constitutional values. South Africa not only ratified the international refugee law instruments but also enacted refugee-specific legislation, ratifying the OAU Refugee Convention in 1995 and acceding to the UN Refugee Convention and its Protocol in 1996. It is thus only in post-Apartheid South Africa that refugees were accepted on the basis of human rights and international refugee law. These constitutional developments and ratifications significantly altered the basis of South African refugee law and policy.

The Refugees Act

In 1998, South Africa enacted the Refugees Act. While the implementation of the Refugees Act leaves much to be desired, substantively it is compatible with international refugee and human rights law. Among other things, the Refugees Act sets out structures and mechanisms for administering status determination. These structures include Refugee Reception Offices (RROs), which are staffed by reception officers and status determinations officers, as well as two oversight bodies – the Refugee Appeal Board and the Standing Committee of Refugee Affairs – to review and hear appeals against decisions taken by the status determination officers.

The Refugees Act also offers a generous range of rights and entitlements to refugees, defining them in terms similar to the UN Refugee Convention as well as the OAU Refugee Convention. It provides for a person to qualify for refugee status if the person has a well-founded fear of persecution as a result of his or her race, religion, nationality, membership of a particular social group, or as a result of a political opinion, and if they can prove that the State is unwilling or unable to provide protection. This definition has been extended in South Africa to include persons at risk as a result of war or a serious disturbance in their country of origin. In addition, it expressly states that all rights in the Bill of Rights of the South African Constitution apply to refugees. Like the UN Refugee Convention and the OAU Refugee Convention, the Refugees Act has provisions on cessation of refugee status and recognises the principle of non-refoulement.

Refugee law and policy has shifted considerably over the period of change from Apartheid to democracy, with South Africa moving away from the ad hoc approach taken during Apartheid, which allowed abuse by the executive and administrative officials and excluded black refugees. The previous policy used the doctrine of sovereignty to define citizenship as a prerogative of the State, such that the State could choose without censure who it granted refugee status and citizenship to. Now, this right is counterbalanced by the country's commitment to human rights.

Textual context of the right of access to justice in South Africa

The right of access to justice is included in the Bill of Rights (Chapter 2 of the South African Constitution), together with all other rights. Any interpretation must therefore have regard to all the other rights in the Bill of Rights. As the Constitutional Court has affirmed, all the rights contained in the Bill of Rights are interrelated and mutually supportive (Currie & De Waal, 2013). Together, these rights have a significant impact on the dignity of people and their quality of life. The interrelatedness requires that access to justice must be in place in order that all the other rights contained therein, especially socio-economic rights, can be realised (Nyeti, 2013:901). Whilst the right of access to justice is necessary for the realisation of all other rights in the Constitution, the contrary is also true. In order that refugee women be able to access justice, other rights (especially social and economic rights) must be realised. In the opinion of the Constitutional Court,

> [t]here can be no doubt that human dignity, freedom and equality, the foundational values of our society, are denied those who have no food, clothing or shelter. Affording socio-economic rights to all people therefore enables them to enjoy the other rights enshrined in Chapter 2. The realisation of these rights is also key to the advancement of race and gender equality and the evolution of a society in which men and women are equally able to achieve their full potential.
>
> (Nyeti, 2013)

Therefore, the right of access to justice and access to asylum cannot be seen in isolation, as they have a close relationship with other socio-economic rights. These rights must all be read together in the setting of the Constitution as a whole. The concept of access to justice must therefore be interpreted as including elements of other rights necessary for its attainment.

Access to justice and the South African Constitution

South African legislation gives the right to access to justice through its Constitution. The South African Constitution is the supreme law of the land and contains a chapter on the Bill of Rights, which has been hailed as one of the most progressive in the world. It envisages an egalitarian society based on democratic values, social justice and fundamental human rights, with the rights contained in the Bill of Rights applicable to everyone in South Africa irrespective of creed, gender or nationality. The South African Constitution also makes provision for the incorporation of customary international law into the legal system. Therefore, when making judgements, national courts must consider international law, with Section 231 of the South African Constitution stating that "customary international law is law in the Republic unless it is inconsistent with the constitution of an Act of Parliament", while Section 39(1) of the Constitution obliges courts to consider international law when interpreting the Bill of Rights. While not necessarily binding, these provisions mean that international law is, at the very least, highly influential. Moreover, the Constitution states that courts may also consider foreign law in the interpretation of the Bill of Rights. Thus, when interpreting South African laws and the right to access justice, there is a need to consider international and foreign law. Accordingly, South Africa's access to justice obligations are referenced from the ICCPR and the African Charter.

Section 34 of the South African Constitution

The right of access to justice is contained in Section 34 of the Constitution, which and holds that: "Everyone has the right to have any dispute that can be resolved by the application of law decided in a fair public hearing before a court or, where appropriate, another independent and impartial tribunal or forum."

This provision is similar to Article 14(1) of the ICCPR. The right contained in Section 34 imposes both a negative and a positive duty on the State. The negative duty is that the State should not impede access to the court, nor should it pass any legislation which prohibits recourse to courts or prevents courts performing their constitutional functions. Scholars have argued that this obligation extends beyond taking active measures to curtail the powers of the courts and includes failure to take action to remove existing impediments. Where it is refugees who are prejudiced by such inaction, then the State is also in violation of its obligations under Article 16 of the UN Refugees Convention. This not only guarantees access to courts but also addresses the requirement of *cautio judicatum solvi* and the non-availability of legal aid, which may in practice jeopardise refugees pursuing their legal rights.

The right contained in Section 34 consists of three components (Currie & De Waal, 2013:715). First, there is the right to access courts. Anyone who has a legal dispute must be able to bring it to a court of law or a legally constituted tribunal to seek a remedy. In this regard, the socio-economic conditions of the individual, including barriers that might hinder them from utilising the justice system, must be considered.[9] The second component places a positive duty on the State to establish effective dispute-resolution institutions and mechanisms. These include courts, traditional courts, tribunals or forums. Third, Section 34 guarantees that disputes be resolved in a fair and public hearing (Currie & De Waal, 2013:715).

Interpretation of Section 34

South African courts have interpreted the right to access courts as going beyond merely gaining access, to include also meaningful and effective access as well as remedies. In *President of the Republic of South Africa and Another v*

Modderkip Boerdery (Pty) Ltd, the Constitutional court saw in Section 34 not only the right of access to courts but also the right to an effective remedy.[10]

Access to justice for refugees in South Africa

Refugees are commonly referred to as a vulnerable group in human rights law, and the South African Constitutional Court has recognised refugees as vulnerable on many occasions.[11]This is because unlike regular migrants, refugees have fled their home countries due to a well-founded fear of persecution or events seriously disturbing the peace. They thus cannot be reasonably expected to return to their country of origin, as doing so would endanger their lives, and thus cannot call on their countries of origin to resolve their disputes or grievances. Refugees are thus forced to rely on the country of asylum to access justice, and because they are not citizens, they often face numerous obstacles. South African law addresses the refugees' rights to access to justice through two legal instruments: the Constitution and the Refugees Act, the latter of which affirms the rights contained in the Constitution.

The principle of equality is applicable to all rights contained in the Constitution. This is an important right for refugees, especially refugee women because of their vulnerability and susceptibility to being discriminated against. This is particularly relevant in a country such as South Africa, which has an urban refugee policy that provides no refugee-specific framework for service delivery. In this context, the right to equality is crucial in ensuring that legal status is not used as a reason to deny refugees access to justice. Refugees and asylum seekers have the same access to services, including legal assistance, as South African nationals. Furthermore, this clause requires substantive, rather than formal, equality. This means that the state has to take active steps to ensure equality is achieved, entitling refugees to equal access to courts and equal, discrimination-free treatment during the court process. Section 27 (b) of the Refugees Act states that, "[a refugee] Enjoys full legal protection, which includes the rights set out in Chapter 2 of the Constitution and the right to remain in the Republic in accordance with the provisions of this Act".

The Refugees Act, therefore, confirms that the rights contained in the Bill of Rights are applicable to refugees and asylum seekers. However, such Constitutional guarantees regarding access to justice do not always translate into reality, and refugees face various obstacles in accessing the rights they are entitled to.

Examining the obstacles faced by refugee women: an intersectional feminist framework

In order to capture the complexities of refugee women's access to justice in South Africa we will make use of an intersectional feminist framework (IFF), which seeks to analyse how multiple forces work interact to reinforce conditions of inequality and exclusion. We avoid favouring one relation of power to the exclusion of others as it risks misrepresenting the full diversity of women's experiences. We thus seek to examine how multiple factors simultaneously determine access to justice and service among refugee women, including socio-economic status, race, class, gender, sexualities, geographic location, refugee and immigration status, as well as broader historical and current systems of discrimination.

We refrain from utilising a gender-only lens, as it fails to take into account the inequalities that permit women from more affluent social classes to gain easier access to certain institutions, and to use such access to oppress refugee women. We also avoid a gender-based analysis, as it is unable to account for the racialised and ethicised stereotypes and discourses that prevent certain women gaining access to institutions of justice. IFFs analyse the interconnections between legal status, nationality, gender, sexuality and class to show how different identity entry points operate as a hurdle to refugee women accessing justice.

Obstacles to accessing justice

South Africa is one of few African countries which has implemented an urban refugee policy. The Refugees Act makes no provision for refugee camps, and it is argued that a refugee camp structure could face constitutional challenges given the Constitution provides for freedom of movement. Whilst South African law provides very progressive rights to refugees and asylum seekers in its legal frameworks, the difficulty is translating these rights – including the right to access to justice – into meaningful entitlements. It is therefore helpful to analyse the obstacles faced by refugees in accessing justice in South Africa.

Even though rights to access justice exist in South African legislation and the Constitution, the poor and other marginalised communities remain on the side-lines. Those most vulnerable to restricted access to justice in South Africa are usually women, children, refugees and stateless persons. The reasons for this marginalisation are interconnected and include poverty, illiteracy and lack of knowledge of existing access to justice.

In the urban setting the enjoyment of all rights is contingent on access to valid documentation, meaning access to justice for refugees is dependent on the possession of such documents. In this way, the refugee document becomes the gateway to all rights, including the right to access justice.

Unlike refugee camps where refugees interact with the UNHCR, the first institution that refugees interact with in South Africa is the Department of Home Affairs ("The Department") which is responsible for all forms of legal documentation, the filing of asylum claims, adjudication of these claims and the granting of status (Landau, 2006). Consequently, any analysis of refugee women's access to justice has to begin with the asylum application process itself. Does the asylum process in South Africa reflect the notion of access to justice as enshrined in the constitution? Understanding how South Africa effects the right to access justice via the asylum process is crucial, as it sets the stage for how refugees and asylum seekers are treated in the state generally. In analysing access to justice via the asylum process, we will explore the various obstacles that refugee women face, and how this influences their access to other forms of justice, such as the courts, police protection and access to social justice.

Inaccessibility of RROs

Refugees and asylum seekers in South Africa have been denied physical access to RROs, and even where they are able to access the offices, they are often confronted by long queues which result in many people having to wait outside for days unattended (Landau, 2006). The barriers faced by refugees in accessing RROs have been highlighted in a number of cases where NGOs have resorted to taking the Department of Home Affairs to court in order to resolve access problems. In the *Kiliko and others v The Minister of Home Affairs and Others* case, [12] the applicants narrated how they were denied access to the RROs and were often forced to sleep outside the office, where they were victimised by local criminals who robbed them of the little money they had. They argued that the Department, by restricting access to the RROs, had unreasonably and unlawfully failed to provide them with the necessary facilities and proper opportunities to submit their asylum applications. The court found that the Department was in breach of its obligations towards refugees as enshrined in the Refugees Act and the South African Constitution. The court further stated that the Department's failure to meet its obligations violated the fundamental rights of the applicants. The Department was thus ordered to put in place measures to ensure access to the Cape Town refugee office. In 2013, Adonis Musati, an asylum seeker, died of hunger after sleeping outside the Cape Town Refugee Office without water or food for a month.[13] Problems of access are not only present in the Cape Town Office but are a common trend in all RROs. Following the Cape Town case was the *Tafira and Other v Ngozwane and Others* case, [14] brought in the Transvaal Provincial Division, which also dealt with access issues.

Moreover, refugees and asylum seekers face access barriers related to corrupt state officials, who prevent asylum seekers and refugees from accessing services if they do not pay bribes (Landau, 2006). In his research on refugees and asylum seekers in South Africa, Landau found that even asylum seekers with a prima facie refugee claim are expected to pay a series of unofficial fees in order to lodge an application for asylum. The first payment was usually paid to the private security guards employed by the Department to guard the entrance of the building. Refugees would then have to pay a "translator" irrespective of whether they required translation services or not. Next, they would have to offer a fee to the RROs in order to file their asylum claim, a process which is meant to be free. Those unable to pay are usually denied entry by the security guards (Landau, 2006).

Even after submitting a claim, refugees face further obstacles while their applications are being adjudicated, with some waiting for up to five years for their asylum claims to be finalised. This is despite the Refugees Act stating that the asylum process should only take up to 180 days (Belvedere, 2007). During this period, asylum seekers remain in a state of limbo; they are legally entitled to remain in the country but have limited rights as they are not recognised refugees.

Those who are granted refugee status face further difficulties in acquiring suitable identity documents. This is due to a prevalence of bias, xenophobia, ignorance of refugee rights and nationalism. In South Africa, most non-nationals are perceived as illegal migrants who are not entitled to be in the country, let alone enjoy rights such as access to justice. This erroneous view has permeated government institutions, who often refuse to assist recognised refugees because they are non-nationals (Landau, 2006). This is exacerbated by ignorance of refugee law among public servants. The lethal combination outlined above has resulted in the exclusion of refugees from accessing key rights, such as access to justice. In some instances, the legal aid board has refused to assist asylum seekers and refugees because they are non-nationals. In other instances, Judges and presiding officers have displayed a lack of knowledge of the laws pertaining to non-nationals, as well as crass methodological nationalism. An example is the *Centre for Child Law and Another v Minister of Home Affairs and Others*, a 2005 case where the presiding judge refused to hear a matter pertaining to the arrest, detention and deportation of foreign children because he was of the view that he did not have the jurisdiction to adjudicate matters pertaining to foreign minors. This was despite the Children's Act, which governs the treatment of children, making no distinction between national children and foreign children.

Social and financial Services

Additionally, access to social and financial services for refugees is hindered by a blend of insufficient documentation, ignorance and outright discrimination (Amit, 2011). In a national study of refugees in South Africa, Belvedere found that 17% of refugees had been denied emergency medical assistance because of expired documentation or ignorance on the part of hospital staff (Belvedere, 2007). In some hospitals, refugees were allegedly charged international rates even though the Refugees Act guarantees refugees access to the same basic health-care services as South Africa nationals.

Poverty

Poverty affects access to justice for refugee women because of the costs associated with accessing courts and other legal tribunals. In some instances, the courts have even used poverty to deny justice to poor non-citizens. In the *Mustafa Aman Arse v Minister of Home Affairs and 2 Others* case, an asylum seeker was deemed too poor to be considered trustworthy and therefore was not released from detention by the court.[15] In *J. Alam v Minister of Home Affairs*, the state relied on the applicant's financial means, domicile and asylum seeker status to ask the court to deny him access, as he could not afford to pay security. However, this time the court recognised the vulnerability of asylum seekers and held that it would not be "fair and just" if they were not excused from providing security for costs, in line with international law.

Thus, in some instances, refugees are denied access to justice because of the intersecting identities of being refugees and being poor. The State has a duty to provide free legal assistance within its means to those who are unable to afford legal service, but poor refugees and asylum seekers are sometimes denied these services because of their status and nationality, irrespective of the fact that they are legally entitled to the same legal services as South African nationals. In the case of *S v Manuel*, [16] an Angolan refugee was refused legal assistance by the Legal Aid Board because it erroneously believed he was unlawfully residing in the country. The Legal Aid Board stated that it could not represent him, as he was an illegal migrant and not South African. The Magistrate affirmed this position and Mr Manuel was forced to represent himself in the criminal matter. He was subsequently found guilty and the matter taken on appeal to the High Court, which found that the Legal Aid Board and the magistrate had failed to explain to Mr Manuel his Constitutional right to free legal assistance. The court found that not only was Mr Manuel not an illegal foreigner, but he was entitled to legal assistance at the expense of the state if he could not afford it himself. This case clarified the legal position pertaining to refugees who cannot afford legal assistance while also illustrating the lack of knowledge regarding refugees' rights in the judicial system and the methodological nationalism employed by judicial officers.

Implications for refugee women's access to justice

The barriers listed above affect refugee women in particular ways. First, gender roles mean that women are often saddled with the duty of child care, meaning they not only have to obtain documentation for themselves but also their children. This means that unlike their male counterparts, refugee women cannot spend the night outside RROs queuing with their children. The Department reinforces this situation when dealing with children's asylum claims, as children are generally documented with their mothers instead of their fathers. The children's records are thus placed in their mother's files, placing the responsibility for the regularisation of their papers squarely in the mother's hands. Women with asylum documents are then expected to bring their children with them to the RROs in order to renew their permits. This places a great financial burden on mothers as they are legally required to extend their permits every three months. Failure to extend an asylum permit constitutes a statutory offence, punishable by a fine of up to R5000 or imprisonment of up to five years. This financial burden is exacerbated by the fact that the Department recently instituted a new policy of closing RROs in urban areas such as Cape Town, Port Elizabeth and Johannesburg, requiring refugees in these areas to travel to RROs near the border, in places such as Durban, Pretoria and Musina.[17] These RROs are over 1,000 kilometres away from the urban areas where most refugees reside. Moreover, given the access problems highlighted above which require refugees to spend a number of days outside RROs, additional costs are incurred by the need for accommodation, as it is not safe for women and children to sleep outside. Likewise, given the high rate of crime and xenophobia-related crimes, refugee women are often the first to be attacked or robbed of their belongings by criminals who prey on refugees near RROs.[18]

Second, even if women overcome these obstacles and are able to present themselves and their children at the RROs, they are often unable to pay the bribe required of them because they are unemployed. Where women are employed, it is as nannies, cooks or cleaners. In South Africa, refugee women are often preferred for these positions as their precarious legal status makes them easier to exploit, and they can be paid less than local women for the same jobs (Amit, 2011). This is because refugee women find it harder to seek recourse through legal structures, either because they are too poor and are forced to accept exploitative wages; they do not know how to enforce their labour rights; or enforcement institutions refuse to assist them because of their legal status. There are cases where employers refuse to allow domestic workers time off in order to extend their refugee status, then threaten to expose that they do not have valid legal documents if they complain about exploitative labour practices. We can therefore see that refugee women's multiple identity entry points are used to prevent them from accessing justice in South Africa. The combination of their gender, class, nationality, ethnicity and sometimes religious affiliation is used to exploit them and deny them legal recourse. In addition, refugee women are often denied access to institutions of justice because they are refugees, are poor and do not speak any South African languages.

Most employers in the formal sector prefer to hire locals. This is due to the erroneous belief that refugees are not allowed to work, or because of the xenophobic tendencies prevalent in South Africa. It is for this reason that many refugees and asylum seekers work in the informal sector: women often work as hawkers selling perishable goods or clothing, or as hairstylists. They are often vulnerable to robbery and have reported that when they approach the police for assistance, officers are often reluctant or unwilling to investigate the crime. Instead, the women are often asked to produce their status documents. This methodological nationalism compounded with xenophobia and sexism makes it difficult for women to enforce their rights through the legal system (Belevedere, 2007). Their class position also makes it harder for them; unlike their wealthy counterparts, they cannot hire private attorneys. Therefore, the location of refugee women at the intersection of gender, nationality, class and race ensures that their access to justice is different from the situation faced by refugee men. Also, refugee women are sometimes unable to report cases of sexual abuse or domestic violence because police stations are predominately staffed by male officers.

Conclusion

As in many countries, South African society remains largely gendered, with traditional gender roles remaining intact. Women are perceived as the primary caregivers, meaning it is often the duty of refugee women to ensure that children are documented. This places an additional burden on women who have children, as they have to balance their child-care duties with their struggles to gain access to RROs. Unlike their male counterparts, refugee women cannot spend the night queuing outside RROs, and when they are required to pay bribes, they not only pay for themselves but also for their children. They are often unable to meet the financial burden, as they are either unemployed or work in domestic settings which bring in little to no financial income.

What we see is how prevailing social norms in the society permeate through the law and State institutions, and how the law is used to maintain these social norms. We therefore argue that the law does not operate in a vacuum, and in South Africa its application is influenced by xenophobia, class, methodological nationalism and sexism. It is the intersection of these forces that make it hard for refugee women, in particular, to access the rights they are entitled to.

Notes

1 see *The Citizen*. South Africa has the highest number of asylum seekers. 21 June 2016. https://citizen.co.za/news/south-africa/1170265/more-asylum-seekers-in-sa-report (Accessed 7 September 2018).
2 *Lesapo v North West Agricultural Bank and Another* 2000 (1) SA 409 (CC).
3 UN General Assembly, *Universal Declaration of Human Rights*, 10 December 1948, A/RES/217 (III).
4 UN General Assembly, *International Covenant on Civil and Political Rights*, 19 December 1966, 999 U.N.T.S. 171.
5 UN General Assembly, International Covenant on Economic, Social and Cultural Rights, 16 December 1966, 999 U.N.T.S. 171.
6 UN General Assembly, Preparation of two Draft International Covenants on Human Rights, 5 February 1952, A/RES/543 (VI).
7 United Nations Convention Relating to the Status of Refugees, 189 UNTS 150, adopted on 25 July 1951 in Geneva and entered into force on 22 April 1954.
8 African Charter on Human and Peoples' Rights (Banjul Charter) adopted 27 June 1981, OAU Doc. CAB/LEG/67/3 rev. 5, 21 I.L.M. 58 (1982), entered into force 21 October 1986.
9 *Nyathi v MEC for the Department of Health, Guateng and Another* 2008(5) SA 94 CC.
10 *President of the Republic of South Africa and Another v Modderklip Boerdery (Pty) Ltd* 2005 (5) SA 3 (CC).

11 *Minister of Home Affairs and other v Watchenuka and another* [2004] 1 All SA 21 (SCA).
12 *Kiliko and others v Minister of Home Affairs and others* [2007] 1 All SA 97 (C).
13 See *The Yale Globalist*. Awaiting Asylum: The shifting policies towards asylum seekers in South Africa. 23 December 2013. http://tyglobalist.org/in-the-magazine/features/awaiting-asylum-the-shifting-policies-towards-asylum-seekers-in-south-africa (accessed 6 March 2019).
14 *Tafira and others v Ngozwane and others* (12960/06) [2006] ZAGPHC 136 (12 December 2006).
15 *Arse v Minister of Home Affairs and others* 2012 (4) SA 544 (SCA).
16 *S v Manuel* 2001 (4) SA 1351 (W).
17 *Abdulaahi and Others v The Director General of Home Affairs and* Others Case 7705/2013.
18 see *openDemocracy*. Women and the xenophobia narrative in South Africa. 20 August 2015. www.opendemocracy.net/gavaza-maluleke/women-and-xenophobia-narrative-in-south-africa (accessed 6 March 2019).

Bibliography

Amit, R. (2011). No refuge: Flawed status determination and the failures of South Africa's refugee system to provide protection. *International Journal of Refugee Law* 23(3):458–488.

Belvedere, F. (2007). Insiders but outsiders: The struggle for the inclusion of refugees and asylum seekers in South Africa. *Refuge* 24(1):57–70.

Cappelletti, M. and B. Garth (1978) Access to justice: The worldwide movement to make rights effective. In: *Access to Justice Vol 1: A World Survey*. Cappelletti, M., B. Garth, K. Koch and J. Weisner (eds). Milan: Sijthoff and Noordhoff.

Currie, I. and J. De Waal (2013). *The bill of rights handbook*. 6th edition. Cape Town: Juta.

Good, M. (2009). Access to justice, judicial economy and behaviour modification: Exploring the goals of Canadian class action. *Alberta Law Review* 47:185.

International Organization for Migration (2011). *World Migration Report 2011: Communicating Effectively About Migration*. Available: https://publications.iom.int/system/files/pdf/wmr2011_english.pdf (accessed 6 March 2019).

Kollapen, Jody (2003). Access to Justice within the South African context. Keynote Address to Access to Justice Round-Table Discussion 5. Open Society Foundation for South Africa. (Parktonian Hotel, Johannesburg 2003).

Landau, L. (2006). Protection and dignity in Johannesburg: Shortcomings of South Africa's Urban Refugee Policy. *Journal of Refugee Studies* 19(3):308–327. Oxford University Press.

Nyeti, M. (2013). Access to justice in the South African social security system: Towards a conceptual approach. *De Jure* 46(4):901–916.

Spigelman, J. (2000). Access to justice and human rights treaties. *Sydney Law Review* 22:141.

UNHCR (2019) *Global Report 2019: South Africa*. Available: www.unhcr.org (accessed 26 March 2020)

13 Conclusion

Gendered justice policies on reaching the most vulnerable and extreme poor in SSA

Lea Mwambene, Adam Dubin and David Lawson

This book focuses on the challenges, obstacles and successes of developing and implementing gender-focused access to justice policies, laws and programming in the Sub-Saharan African (SSA) region. Reports show that about half the region's population live below the poverty line, a significant proportion of whom are women (Wadhwa, 2018). Despite a broad framework of treaties obligating states to fulfil socio-economic and women's rights, without access to justice, the fulfilment of such rights remain elusive (International Covenant on Civil and Political Rights [ICCPR], International Covenant on Economic, Social and Cultural Rights [ICESCR]). The reasons behind access to justice being denied arise from a variety of factors, highlighted in the chart below. These frequently occur in concert, creating a complex dynamic that reinforces cycles of poverty (Figure 13.1).

Indeed, while Chapters 2, 3 and 4 indicate that some policies and programmes may be responsive to the needs of women and girls in SSA when attempting to access justice, they also point to the need for new approaches and solutions. Gender responsive budgeting, for example, is one such policy that embeds human rights within government frameworks in order to realise equal access to justice for both men and women (Lawson et al., 2019). Combined with appropriate fiscal space considerations, gender responsive budgeting can be adopted as an approach to use a country's national and/or local budget(s) as a tool to address gender inequalities and promote inclusive development. Three primary motivations are proffered for gender budgeting: (1) gender inequality and economic growth, (2) gender inequality and equitable development and (3) gender inequality and human rights. The third motivation is – in our opinion – supportive of equal access to justice, representing the use of gender budgeting to help governments fulfil their international legal obligations regarding gender equality and the realisation of relevant human rights. We therefore propose that human rights be made an integral part of gender budgeting's investment process, whilst also considering fiscal space components.

The gender inequality and human rights approach addresses a number of specific challenges relevant to the relationship between gender inequality, human rights and gender budgeting in SSA. Moreover, it supports our recommendations regarding how to improve women's access to justice on the continent. Chapters in Parts 2 and 3 of this volume have shown how countries have failed

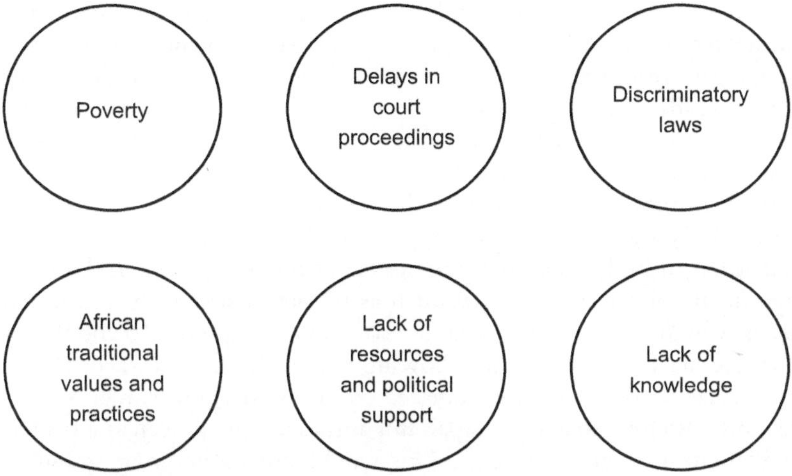

Figure 13.1 Reasons for access to justice being denied.

to harmonise their laws and policies with international and regional human rights standards regarding the Right to Access Justice, with a lack of political will in allocating resources highlighted. Linked to the above point, Chapters 3, 6 and 7 demonstrate that international human rights standards addressing women's rights to access justice have not been interpreted in a way that is responsive to African women's experiences. Such experiences are affected by a number of interconnected socio-economic challenges, including a lack of access to basic (e.g. health-related) services, high illiteracy levels, the futility of court processes absent of guarantees, and financial barriers. Shocks such as the COVID-19 pandemic, in 2020, interlink all the aforementioned factors, and further highlight the complexity faced by the myriad government ministries and departments mandated to champion specific socio-economic rights (Chapter 3). We therefore ask, *How can different ministries work together in order to realise access to justice by women in SSA?* This, perhaps, is a question for another day, but within the context of the present discussion, the answer lies in improving collaboration between different ministries and ensuring gender frameworks can both reduce inequalities whilst also being adequately flexible to respond to economic and political shocks.

Sadly, while many governments assess *whether* they are following the steps of engendering frameworks, they do not necessarily quantify its impact. To put it another way, for example, the focus has typically been on quantifying human rights into a gender budgeting space rather than considering which component of gender budgeting optimises gender equality outputs. Looking at the impact of gender budgeting on gender inequality and fiscal spending is vital to assessing gendered access to justice and developing appropriate gender frameworks for mainstreaming and implementing gender equality.

Chapters 4, 6, 7 and 11 highlight one of the major challenges experienced in SSA – that most proceedings in the formal court system are subject to considerable delays at every stage. Reasons for this include a large number of cases relative to a limited number of courts, and geographical distance to the nearest court. These examples are directly relevant to how governments allocate resources to different ministries and, in this context, the judiciary. In addition, as a response to challenges within the formal justice system, certain governments have introduced "diversion programmes" for children in conflict with the law or first-time adult offenders. Unfortunately, these programmes have been met with a severe lack of funding, meaning in most cases they are simply "paper programmes". Furthermore, it can be seen that African cultural values and practices continue to systematically exclude women in important areas of law, such as property/land rights, inheritance rights, as well as within the marriage institution (Chapters 4, 6 and 9).

We therefore put forward the following recommendations. In order to reduce the delays associated with congested court systems, governments must allocate more resources to courts, expanding infrastructure as well as introducing the digitalisation of court systems. This would streamline court systems and further enable the tracking of justice through each stage of the legal system. Any policies and programmes developed must be attached to adequate funding, and should take into account the specific needs of women within the broader justice system. In addition, there should be a greater focus on quantifying the impact of budget allocations on access to justice and other human rights programmes, as well as better and increased use made of data in attempting to understand the complexities faced when making policy decisions about access to justice. Finally, greater investment in relevant technology should be made, for example the development of mobile apps facilitating greater access to justice. Such apps could provide access to a range of services, from information about laws to filing a complaint in court. At the heart of all this must be a commitment to invest in the advancement of the rights of women and girls (Figure 13.2).

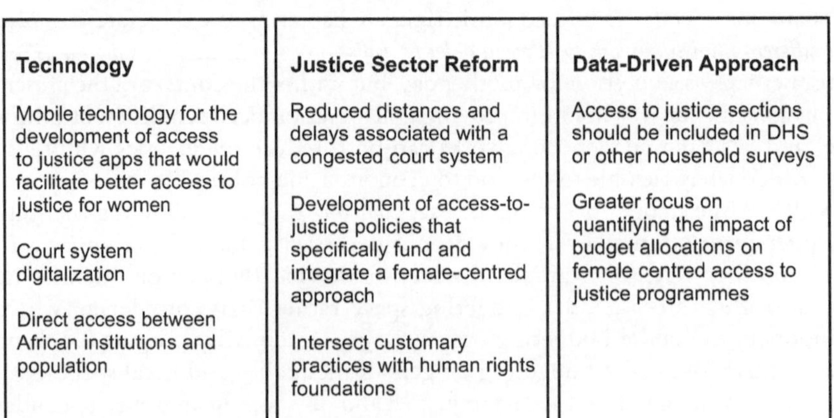

Figure 13.2 Recommendations for reform.

To sum up, many of the countries discussed in this book have responded to the challenge of providing access to justice for women by enacting or reforming laws and policies. However, as has been observed, rights-based strategies mean little if gender budgeting is not taken into account (Wester, 2019). Given women's inadequate position in accessing resources and information, and their lack of power when it comes to effecting change, one cannot assume that gender-neutral policies and programmes will equitably benefit women (UNDP, 2006). Thus, considerably more needs to be done in terms of focusing attention and resource allocation in order to alleviate current gender disparities in access to justice in SSA.

References

Lawson, D., A. Dubin and L. Mwambene with B. Woldemichael (2019), "Ensuring African Women's Access to Justice Engendering Rights for Poverty Reduction in Sub-Saharan Africa", Nordic Africa Institute, Policy Note 2, accessed 20 March 2019, available at http://nai.diva-portal.org/smash/get/diva2:1298068/FULLTEXT01.pdf.

UNDP (2006) "Gender Equality and Justice Programming: Equitable Access to Justice for Women", Primers in Gender and Democratic Governance 2, accessed 1 April 2019, available at www.undp.org/content/dam/aplaws/publication/en/publications/democratic-governance/dg-publications-for-website/gender-equality-and-justice-programming-equitable-access-to-justice-for-women/GenderGovPr_Justice_2.pdf.

Wadhwa, D. (2018), "The Number of Extremely Poor People Continues to Rise in Sub-Saharan Africa", World Bank Blogs, 19 September 2018, accessed 17 February 2019, available at https://blogs.worldbank.org/opendata/number-extremely-poor-people-continues-rise-sub-saharan-africa.

Wester, K. B. (2019), "Violated: Women's Human Rights in Sub-Saharan Africa", *Topical Review Digest: Human Rights in Sub-Saharan Africa*, accessed 1 April 2019, available at https://afworo.org/2013/01/20/violated-womens-human-rights-in-sub-saharan-africa/.

Index

Note: **Bold** page numbers refer to tables; *italic* page numbers refer to figures and page numbers followed by "n" denote endnotes.